C000094009

# The Teachings and Practices of the Early Quanzhen Taoist Masters

SUNY series in Chinese Philosophy and Culture

Roger T. Ames, editor

# The Teachings and Practices of the Early Quanzhen Taoist Masters

Stephen Eskildsen

State University of New York Press

Published by
State University of New York Press, Albany



Printed in the United States of America



For information, contact State University of New York Press, Albany, NY
www.sunypress.edu

Production by Michael Haggett
Marketing by Michael Campochiaro

**Library of Congress Cataloging-in-Publication Data**

Eskildsen, Stephen, 1963–
The teachings and practices of the early Quanzhen Taoist masters / Stephen Eskildsen.
p. cm—(SUNY series in Chinese philosophy and culture)
Includes bibliographical references and index.
ISBN 0-7914-6045-2 (alk. paper)—ISBN 0-7914-6046-0 (pbk. : alk. paper)
1. Taoism–China–Quanzhou Shi–History. 2. Taoist priests–China–Quanzhou Shi–History. I. Title. II. Series.

BL1910.E75 2004
299.5′149—dc22

2004044246

10 9 8 7 6 5 4 3 2

# Contents

# Acknowledgments

My interest in Quanzhen Taoism began in the spring of 1985, when Professor Joseph McDermott (then of International Christian University, Tokyo) recommended it to me as a topic for my undergraduate thesis. I was soon addicted, and by the fall of 1987, I found myself at the University of British Columbia, working on a master's thesis on Quanzhen Taoism under the inspirational guidance of Professor Daniel Overmyer. Although my subsequent research in the Ph.D. program at the same university led me off in another direction (Six Dynasties period Taoist asceticism), my fascination with the early Quanzhen movement was rekindled during my stay at the Chinese University of Hong Kong as a postdoctoral fellow (1997–1998). Chapters 3, 4, 6, 8, and 9 of this book are heavily revised versions of chapters from my 1989 master's thesis, "The Beliefs and Practices of Early Ch'üan-chen Taoism". The rest of the book is based on research conducted during and since my sojourn in Hong Kong. (A slightly different version of chapter 5 has appeared in the *Journal of Chinese Religions* 29 [2001] under the title "Seeking Signs of Proof: Visions and Other Trance Phenomena in Early Quanzhen Taoism.")

My gratitude first goes out to my mentors, Professors Overmyer and McDermott. I also would like to thank the Chinese University of Hong Kong Postgraduate Fellowship Scheme and the National Endowment for the Humanities Summer Stipend Program for financial support of my research for this book. I am deeply grateful as well to the University of Tennessee at Chattanooga, particularly to my friends and colleagues in the Department of Philosophy and Religion, for providing a congenial and supportive environment in which to finish this book.

I dedicate this book to my parents, Edward and Marion Eskildsen, and to all my family and friends that give my life true meaning.

# Chapter 1

## Introduction

### Opening Comments

This book explores the beliefs and practices of the Quanzhen (Complete Realization) School of the Taoist religion during its founding phases in the late twelfth and early thirteenth centuries. The Quanzhen School is a living tradition. It is the dominant school of monastic Taoism in the People's Republic of China, and numerous non-monastic Taoist temples and organizations in southern China, Taiwan, and other countries claim an affiliation with the Quanzhen tradition as well.[1] The emergence and rapid growth of the Quanzhen School during the twelfth and thirteenth centuries has frequently been cited as a pivotal event in the history of Taoism. Quanzhen Taoism in its doctrinal content has been described as the foremost representative of a "new Taoist religion" (*xin daojiao*) that in very fundamental ways differed from the "old Taoist religion" (*jiu daojiao*).

The monks and nuns in Quanzhen monasteries today pursue an austere lifestyle. To my knowledge, most or all of them practice celibacy and vegetarianism.[2] Although part of their regimen consists of reciting liturgies and learning ritual procedures, their most important pursuit is a form of meditation known as *neidan* (internal alchemy),[3] or *jinggong* (motionless exercise). The ultimate goal of this is to gain immortality through the recovery of the Radiant Spirit (*yangshen*) or Real Nature (*zhenxing*) that exists without beginning and without end. One who progresses in this endeavor is thought to gain health, longevity, and inner tranquility. Although physical death eventually occurs, the Radiant Spirit is thought to survive to enjoy an eternal life unbound by the strife of *samsara*.[4]

As we shall see, the early Quanzhen masters lived very austere lives, while teaching and practicing the methods for recovering the Radiant Spirit/Real Nature. Since they were renowned adepts of these methods, the early Quanzhen masters are said to be immortal beings who can be prayed to for aid and guidance, or even encountered in meditative trances and dreams.[5] Images of them are enshrined and worshipped in temples. Non-monastic Quanzhen organizations in Hong Kong, Taiwan, and overseas sometimes communicate with them through spirit writing (*fuji*)—especially with Lü Yan, one of the semi-legendary Quanzhen "patriarchs" (*zu*).[6] While there is no evidence that the early Quanzhen masters themselves practiced spirit writing—or even knew of it—we shall see that they undoubtedly believed in immortal beings who could answer prayers and appear before diligent practitioners worthy of their sympathy. Furthermore, their own claims and doings contributed to bringing about their own deification shortly after their deaths, or even during their lifetimes.

Was the early Quanzhen School aptly describable as "new Taoist religion"? This depends on what one means by such a description. Some modern scholars have characterized the early Quanzhen School as a reform movement that set out to purge Taoism of its magico-religious elements (e.g., alchemy, belief in immortal beings, wonder-working rituals) and restore it to something reminiscent of the simple doctrine of serenity and non-action expounded in the *Daode jing*. These scholars also have laid great emphasis on the fact that the early Quanzhen School borrowed heavily from Buddhism and extolled the simultaneous adherence to the "Three Teachings" (*sanjiao*; Taoism, Buddhism, and Confucianism). Some have even suggested that the early Quanzhen movement should not be labeled "Taoist religion," since it did not set out to propagate the "traditional Taoist religion."[7]

Based on this perspective—the main proponents of which wrote during the 1950s and 1960s—any aspect of Quanzhen belief and practice pertaining to the supernatural seems like a corruption and deviation from the intentions of the movement's founders. However, such a view is misleading. Although the early Quanzhen masters strongly remonstrated against charlatans, they certainly did not deny the existence of immortals, the possibility of miracles, or the efficacy of Taoist rituals. More recent scholarship is beginning to give us a much fuller view of the beliefs and practices of the early Quanzhen masters. However, there is still a strong tendency not to acknowledge or pay much attention to their lively mysticism or their enthusiastic belief in the realm of the transcendent and supernatural.

The syncretism of the Quanzhen School was hardly unique or new. The blending of Confucian and—especially—Buddhist elements into the Taoist religion had by and large already taken place during the Six Dynasties and Tang periods. Confucian social mores (e.g., filial piety, loyalty) had already been well incorporated into Taoist doctrine, as had basic Buddhist notions such as *karma*,[8] *samsara*, and liberation (which was equated to divine, celestial immortality). Secondly, while the early Quanzhen masters sincerely esteemed Confucianism and Buddhism for their capacity to bring about inner peace and moral growth, they clearly saw themselves as successors to legendary Taoist *neidan* master-immortals of the past. As *neidan* masters, their teachings delve into psycho-physiological theories foreign to the Confucian and Buddhist traditions. Recent scholarship has already shed a great deal of light on this fact.[9]

However, the Taoism of the second millennium was certainly very different from that of the first millennium. Perhaps the most striking difference lies in the predominance of *neidan*, which came to overshadow and replace other meditation methods.[10] Significantly, various *neidan* texts articulate theories in which the highest immortality is gained by the Radiant Spirit/Real Nature and not by the physical body, thus they relinquish the much maligned view of earlier Taoists who claimed that the entire body of flesh could evade death and ascend to the heavens.[11] If the so-called "new Taoist religion" is defined in terms of adherence to *neidan* practice and theory, then the early Quanzhen School was certainly one of its most prominent representatives. Although the Quanzhen masters cannot claim credit for inventing the theory and praxis of *neidan* (which had already been developing and evolving for centuries), their approach to self-cultivation can perhaps be deemed distinctive for its straightforward emphasis on inner tranquility and the complementary performance of altruistic deeds. The Quanzhen masters were the most austere and unworldly of ascetics, yet they energetically saw to the spiritual and physical needs of the world. This is their most impressive characteristic, which goes a considerable way toward explaining why they have been revered by so many.

## Historical Summary

At this point it is appropriate to introduce the reader to the Quanzhen masters and provide a brief historical summary on the early Quanzhen movement. This book will focus on the teachings and practices of Quanzhen founder Wang Zhe (sobriquet, Chongyang,[12] 1113–1170) and his direct disciples. His most famous disciples were Ma Yu (sobriquet, Danyang, 1123–1184), Tan Chuduan (sobriquet, Changzhen, 1123–1185), Liu Chuxuan (sobriquet, Changsheng, 1147–1203), Qiu Chuji (sobriquet, Changchun, 1143–1227), Wang Chuyi (sobriquet, Yuyang, 1142–1217), Hao Datong (sobriquet, Guangning, 1140–1212), and Sun Bu'er (sobriquet, Qingjing, ex-wife of Ma Yu, 1119–1183). These seven disciples are commonly referred to collectively as the "Seven Realized Ones" (*qizhen*). Among these eminent disciples, particular attention will be paid to Ma Yu and Qiu Chuji, since these two appear to have left the greatest impact on the movement after the passing of the founder. Unfortunately, much less attention can be given to Sun Bu'er, since no reliably authentic writings of hers have survived.[13] This book also will refer frequently to the teachings of second-generation disciples Yin Zhiping (sobriquet, Qinghe, 1169–1251) and Wang Zhijin (sobriquet, Xiyun, 1178–1263). The works of both men contain frequent reminiscences on the sayings and deeds of their predecessors and confer deeper insight into their teachings.

Wang Zhe was born as the third son of a wealthy family in Dawei Village, Xianyang, west of present-day Xi'an (Shaanxi Province) on 12/22/Zhenghe 2[14] (January 11, 1113). Not much is known about the early part of his life, although the various Quanzhen hagiographies give a miraculous account of his birth and speak admiringly of his striking appearance, keen intelligence, and generous character as a child and young man.[15] He received a good education, and in his adolescence and early adulthood, he aspired to take the civil service examinations. Later he shifted his attention to mastering the military arts and took the military recruitment examinations. The hagiographies do not agree as to whether or not he passed these examinations, and they give no information concerning his eventual employment. One local gazetteer, however, does indicate that he served as a low-ranking official in charge of collecting the wine and liquor tax.[16] Whatever the case, it appears that by middle age he had become disillusioned and had taken to drinking heavily. In the process, he neglected his responsibilities as a husband and father.[17] His eccentric, disorderly behavior earned him the nickname "Lunatic" (Haifeng). It was during this period that he underwent a remarkable conversion that would completely change his life.[18]

The conversion took place in the sixth month of Zhenglong 4 (June 18–July 16, 1159), and the hagiographies claim that it occurred through direct personal encounters with immortals. Wang Zhe, we are told, was sitting in a butcher shop in Ganhe Township drinking wine and eating meat in large quantities when he was encountered by an immortal (who, strangely, appeared as *two* identical-looking young men clad in white woolen garments)[19] and conferred secret lessons. From this time on, Wang Zhe started to act even more strangely. On 8/15 (September 16) of the following year, he met the same immortal(s) at Liquan. They then drank together at a saloon where Wang Zhe had more secret lessons transmitted to him. The hagiographies do not agree on the identity of the immortal(s) encountered on these occasions. Some do not specify who it was,[20] but most say that it was Lü Yan.[21] One source claims that it was indeed two men—Lü Yan and his teacher, Zhongli Quan.[22] Both of these figures were legendary *neidan* master-immortals who allegedly flourished around 800 C.E. and 200 C.E., respectively, and they are revered to this day among the "patriarchs" of the Quanzhen School.[23]

Whatever actually took place, Wang Zhe at this time found the resolve to abandon his home and live as a mendicant. The next year (Dading 1 [1161]), he moved to Nanshi Village, where he made a mound of dirt several feet high and under it dug a vault over ten feet deep. On top of the mound he placed a sign that read, "Here rests Lunatic Wang." Wang Zhe lived inside of this tomb, which he referred to as the "Grave of the Living Dead Man." At four corners surrounding this peculiar dwelling, he planted four cherry apple (*haitang*) trees. When a fellow hermit, Mr. He, asked him what the meaning of this was, Wang Zhe proclaimed, "Some day I wish to make the teachings of the four directions into one!"[24] If Wang Zhe indeed uttered this statement, then it would mean that he already harbored the intention to start a large new religious movement, even while still in the process of working out his own salvation. His living inside of the burial mound most likely symbolized his resolution to put to death his old, worldly self.

In the autumn of Dading 3 (1163), Wang Zhe moved to Liujiang Village, where he trained together with two hermits, He Dejin (sobriquet, Yuchan; probably the same Mr. He who had asked about the cherry apple trees) and Li Lingyang.[25] The three men lived in three little grass huts, located together on a small island in a river. Wang Zhe, we are told, frequently made subtle and profound utterances that ordinary villagers simply disregarded as the ravings of a lunatic. Sometimes he would walk around with a pot of liquor, drinking and singing. Often, somebody would ask him for a drink, whereupon he would cheerfully share his liquor. Hagiographies tell us that on one such occasion, Wang Zhe had yet another momentous encounter with a legendary immortal. One day in Dading 4 (1164) when he was walking home from an outing to Ganhe, a man asked him for a drink. When Wang Zhe handed him the liquor pot, the man consumed its contents in one gulp and then made Wang Zhe refill the pot with water from the Ganhe River and drink it. This water had in fact been miraculously transformed into the "brew of the immortals." The man then asked, "Do you know about Liu Haichan?" (Liu Haichan [or Liu Cao] was a famous *neidan* master-immortal of the early eleventh century—he also is revered as one of the Quanzhen "patriarchs").[26] Wang Zhe responded, "I have only seen pictures of him." The man went off laughing (he *was* Liu Haichan).[27] From this time on, Wang Zhe never drank alcohol. However, he frequently appeared to be drunk. His breath would smell so strongly of liquor that other people could get drunk just by smelling him.[28]

This baffling story—most probably made up for the purpose of linking Wang Zhe to yet another famous figure in *neidan* lore—can perhaps be at least taken as an indication that at around this time, Wang Zhe found the inner strength to overcome alcohol addiction.

On 4/26/Dading 7 (May 16, 1167), Wang Zhe set fire to his hut at Liujiang Village. Some of the villagers, thinking he was in danger, came rushing to his rescue, only to find him dancing ecstatically by the fire. When asked why he was doing this, he explained that in three years somebody would come to rebuild the hut (a prophecy that is said to have been fulfilled three years later, when his disciples erected a Taoist temple and buried his body there). The next morning, Wang Zhe set off by himself on a journey eastward to the Shandong Peninsula (roughly 1,000 miles away). When departing, he declared to his followers, "I am going to the eastern sea to capture a horse (*ma*; a prophetic pun on the name of Ma Yu, his favorite disciple whom he would meet in Shandong)."[29] His following at this time in Shaanxi was probably very small. It may have included only He Dejin, Li Lingyang (these two men were perhaps more his companions than his disciples), and two disciples, Shi Chuhou and Yan Chuchang, whom he had taken on while living in Liujiang.

Although the hagiographies depict Wang Zhe's conversion and training in vivid detail, they nonetheless leave us with some puzzling questions. Who actually was his teacher? Could he have been self-taught? Did he have any connections to organized Taoist religion, and did he receive any formal Taoist ordination? Pierre Marsone has pointed out that Wang Zhe's own writings refer to two men—one Taoist and one Buddhist—who appear to have provided him some guidance.[30] Two of Wang Zhe's poems mention a certain Ritual Master Chi (Chi Fashi) who had written a commentary to the ancient Taoist philosophical classic, the *Daode jing* (a.k.a. the *Laozi*).[31] It appears that Wang Zhe had studied this commentary and perhaps received some personal instruction from Chi Fashi. Two other poems bear clear testimony to the fact that Wang Zhe once considered himself the disciple of Buddhist Dharma master Ren (Ren Fashi), who had taught him methods of confession and the "Eighteen Precepts."[32] It is unclear as to when or for how long Wang Zhe studied under either teacher, and to what extent their teachings influenced the teachings that he would pass on to his own disciples.

Wang Zhe appears to have been particularly familiar with two major Mahayana Buddhist scriptures—the *Diamond Sutra* (*Jin'gang jing*) and the *Heart Sutra* (*Xin jing*).[33] He was probably also familiar with some Chan (Zen) literature, and Hachiya Kunio has pointed out a passage in Wang Zhe's writings that was perhaps inspired by a similar passage in the recorded sayings of Chan master Dazhu Huihai (fl. Ca. 780).[34] More recently, Hu Qide has argued that Wang Zhe's writings and preaching methods bear the influence of Linji Sect Chan master Yuanwu Keqin (1063–1135).[35] However, as Hachiya has astutely observed, Wang Zhe did not abide by the thoroughgoing negation and non-assertion of Mahayana Buddhist philosophy. Fond as he was of borrowing Buddhist language to preach detachment from this provisional, fleeting world of *samsara*, Wang Zhe ardently believed in the eternal, universal Real Nature/Radiant Spirit that is the ground and wellspring of consciousness (spirit [*shen*], Nature [*xing*]), and vitality (*qi*,[36] Life [*ming*]) within all living beings. This to him was not "empty" (lacking inherent existence); it was fully Real (*zhen*).[37]

Wang Zhe's teachings bear considerable affinity to the *neidan* theories and methods of the so-called Zhong-Lü tradition (which claims to be handed down from immortals Zhongli Quan and Lü Yan; representative texts of this tradition that we have at our disposal include *Zhong-Lü chuandao ji*,[38] *Lingbao bifa* [DT1181/TT874],[39] and *Xishan qunxian huizhen ji* [DT245/TT116][40]). In this sense, the stories of his alleged encounters with Lü Yan and Zhongli Quan at least seem indicative of his spiritual heritage. Wang Zhe also appears to have been familiar with the *Daode jing*, *Yinfu jing* (DT31/TT27), *Qingjing jing* (DT615/TT341), and *Huangting neijing jing* (DT330/TT167),[41] all standard reading materials for *neidan* practitioners of the time.[42] Another lesser known text that provided Wang Zhe with considerable inspiration was *Jin zhenren yulu* (DT1046/TT728), the recorded sayings of a certain Realized Man Jin. Although little can be known about this figure, it appears that his full name was Jin Daocheng (sobriquet, Chongzhen), and that he flourished during the eleventh or early twelfth century.[43] In studying all these doctrines and texts, did Wang Zhe have a teacher? Would it have been possible for a devout layman to gather the relevant books and practice *neidan* all by himself? Perhaps not. While it certainly was not unusual for laypeople to learn and practice *neidan* (some of the most famous *neidan* masters were neither monks nor priests),[44] texts do not seem to adequately disclose the actual procedures of cultivating meditative trance.

Marsone has suggested the intriguing possibility that He Dejin and Li Lingyang may in fact have been Wang Zhe's teachers, since both men had roughly ten more years of experience as religious mendicants than did Wang Zhe.[45] While this hypothesis is difficult to verify, the life stories of these two men hint at the existence of a culture of solitary Taoist ascetics who at times could cooperate and learn from each other. Interestingly, both men also are said to have undergone mysterious conversion experiences.

He Dejin's conversion is said to have taken place as the result of a very strange episode involving a fatally ill "person of the Tao" (*daozhe*) whom he had kindly housed and cared for. According to the hagiographic account, the ailing Taoist died after a year in He Dejin's home. Not long thereafter, He Dejin, at the imploring of the deceased's elderly grieving mother, opened the coffin and found it empty. The grieving mother thereupon disappeared as well. The ailing Taoist had thus allegedly feigned his death and attained immortality through the ancient procedure of "corpse liberation" (*shijie*).[46] He Dejin thereupon "abandoned his wife and children to enter the Tao." Some time later he heard that Wang Zhe had similarly undergone unusual experiences and was training in Zhongnan (the county where Ganhe Township and Nanshi Village were located). He thus decided to join him.[47]

Li Lingyang had been a vagrant Taoist ever since encountering and being converted by an "extraordinary person" during the Tiande reign era (1149–1153). He wandered the wilderness "enjoying himself in the Tao," "covering his radiance and obscuring his traces." He would not reveal his personal name to people, so villagers would refer to him as "Realized Man Li."[48]

He Dejin and Li Lingyang were thus both solitary Taoist monks prior to meeting Wang Zhe, and there were perhaps others like them in the local area. The Zhongnan mountains, located in the vicinity of where they lived and trained, are historically—and presently—one of the most important centers of monastic Taoism in northern China.[49] There were perhaps many other solitary monks in the area connected somehow to the local temples and monasteries. (Significantly, it is known that He Dejin and Li Lingyang took up residence at the Zhongnan Taiping Gong monastery some time after Wang Zhe departed eastward.)[50]

Concerning the eastward journey and subsequent ministry of Wang Zhe, the hagiographies provide a great deal of information. Throughout his long journey eastward, Wang Zhe carried an iron jug and begged for his sustenance. In Ye County (Shandong), he bestowed "secret instructions on the cultivation of Reality" upon a certain Liu Tongwei.[51] In Weizhou, he visited the Realized Man Xiao, the leader of the Taiyi School of Taoism. Wang Zhe had hoped to form a cooperative relationship with the "Realized Man," but ultimately he found him incompatible. Upon taking leave of the "Realized Man," Wang Zhe presented him with a poem, the subtleties of which he could not fathom.[52] (This episode involving Realized Man Xiao sounds suspiciously like a polemical embellishment. However, there is some reason to think that Wang Zhe did have some contact with the Taiyi School and received some influence from it in the area of ritual.)[53]

On 7*/18/Dading 7[54] (September 3, 1167), about three and a half months after his departure from Liujiang Village, Wang Zhe arrived in the town of Ninghai, located near the eastern tip of the Shandong Peninsula. There he visited the estate of a local official, Fan Mingshi, who was entertaining a group of guests. Wang Zhe, with his strange attire (dressed heavily in the blazing summer heat), eccentric behavior, and profound utterances, captured the fancy of host and guests alike. Among the guests was a local tycoon, Ma Congyi (later to be renamed Ma Yu), who agreed to allow Wang Zhe to set up a hut in the garden of his estate.[55] Wang Zhe named his new hut "the Hut of Complete Realization" (Quanzhen An). Wang Zhe lived there until the following spring, and in the meantime he succeeded in making disciples out of Qiu Chuji,[56] Tan Chuduan, Wang Chuyi, and eventually Ma Yu. The conversion of Ma Yu was a particularly difficult endeavor, since Wang Zhe had to convince him to abandon his great wealth and divorce Sun Bu'er, his wife of many years. The hagiographies give detailed and frequently incredible accounts of how he accomplished this. We are told that Wang Zhe had himself locked inside the Hut of Complete Realization for 100 days, from 10/1/Dading 7 (November 14, 1167) to 1/10 Dading 8 (February 20, 1168). During this period, he employed various means to convince Ma Yu and Sun Bu'er to end their marriage and become his disciples. He regularly presented them with didactic poems, to which Ma Yu would compose responses. He also gave them sliced pears, taros, and chestnuts to eat, which symbolized the need for husband and wife to separate.[57] (He himself is said to have eaten infrequently during his self-confinement, although sources disagree as to how infrequently.)[58] Furthermore, we are told that he exhorted and instructed Ma Yu by sending his Radiant Spirit out to communicate with him in both his waking experience and his dreams.[59] On 2/8/Dading 8 (March 19, 1168), a month after Wang Zhe ended his self-confinement, Ma Yu became his disciple. Sun Bu'er would hold out for a while longer.

On 2/29/Dading 8 (April 9, 1168), Wang Zhe took his disciples, Qiu Chuji, Tan Chuduan, Ma Yu, and Wang Chuyi, with him to live in a grotto on Mt. Kunyu, which he named the "Smoky Mist Grotto" (Yanxia Dong). Wang Zhe was a stern teacher who often inflicted insults and beatings upon his disciples. This he did to test their resolve and strengthen their character.[60] In order to vanquish their pride, he demanded that they all go out begging in the streets, a requirement that the highly bred Ma Yu found particularly difficult (see chapter 3). Although in fact many people came to train under Wang Zhe, most of them fled. Nonetheless, he did take on some more disciples during this period, the most important among these being the fortune teller, Hao Sheng (who later took on the personal name, Datong), whose mother had just passed away.[61] Interestingly, Wang Chuyi's mother (nee Zhou) also came and became a disciple, assuming the personal name, Deqing, and the sobriquet, Xuanjing.[62]

In 8/Dading 8 (September 4–October 2, 1168), Wang Zhe and his disciples left Mt. Kunyu and began to travel and preach throughout Shandong for over a year. During that span, Wang Zhe succeeded in forming five congregations (*hui*). These were the Seven Treasures Congregation (Qibao Hui) in Wendeng, the Golden Lotus Congregation (Jinlian Hui) in Ninghai, the Three Lights Congregation (Sanguang Hui) in Fushan, the Jade Flower Congregation (Yuhua Hui) in Dengzhou, and the Equality Congregation (Pingdeng Hui) in Laizhou. During this period, Ma Yu's ex-wife, Sun Bu'er, became a disciple (in Ninghai on 5/5/Dading 9 [June 1, 1169]), as did young Liu Chuxuan (in Laizhou in 9/Dading 9 [September 23–October 21, 1169]).[63]

In 10/Dading 9 (October 22–November 20, 1169), Wang Zhe departed from Shandong, taking with him Ma Yu, Tan Chuduan, Liu Chuxuan, and Qiu Chuji. While his intention seems to have been to return to his home region of Shaanxi to re-establish his ministry there, he and his party ended up taking extended lodging at an inn in Bianjing (present-day Kaifeng, Henan Province). Wang Zhe's treatment of his disciples then became harsher than ever before. He resorted to scolding and beatings even more readily, and he subjected his disciples to strange, harrowing ordeals. (These will be discussed in chapter 3.) Roughly two months later, on 1/4/Dading 10 (January 22, 1170), Wang Zhe died, after designating Ma Yu as his successor.

There are numerous questions that need to be asked about Wang Zhe's ministry in Shandong during the last three years of his life. How large did his following become during his lifetime, and what sorts of people were attracted to him? What was the nature of the five congregations?

Judging from the short duration of his ministry and the fact that he relocated so frequently, it seems doubtful that his following could have been too large. Nonetheless, to initiate five congregations seems like a pretty significant achievement. In fact, one source indicates that the Equality Congregation in Laizhou had over 1,000 members.[64] This success was perhaps due to a prevailing religious climate in which the belief in immortals and interest in *neidan* were already fairly widespread among people of various social strata. Wang Zhe was a charismatic personality who embodied and articulated this religiosity in a compelling way.

Wang Zhe's seven top disciples came from various backgrounds. Hagiographic sources all indicate that Ma Yu was a man of great wealth who had received a high level of education. Sun Bu'er, his wife, also had been born into a prominent family and was well educated. Interestingly, even prior to his encounter with Wang Zhe, Ma Yu apparently had a considerable interest in Taoism and had practiced meditation. Yin Zhiping, in his "record of sayings," states: "Master-Father Danyang (Ma Yu) before leaving his family (*chujia*)[65] [to become a Taoist monk] was of robust personality and fond of drinking. However, he had already been practicing methods of exercise (presumably *neidan*) and knew that the root of the Tao naturally exists within ones [Real] Nature."[66] It also appears that Ma Yu had been a generous patron of the Taoist religion. One source states that one night he dreamt of two cranes alighting in his vegetable garden; this inspired him to build a Taoist monastery (*daoguan*) and to invite a certain Taoist Lu (Lu Daoren) to live there.[67] It appears that Wang Zhe also became acquainted with this Taoist Lu and admired his expertise in medicinal healing (see chapter 4).[68]

Tan Chuduan, who was the son of an artisan (goldsmith and silversmith), eagerly pursued an education in his adolescence and became precociously skilled at writing poetry. Interestingly, we are told that a severe illness was what caused him to turn to the Taoist religion in his middle age, and ultimately to assume discipleship under Wang Zhe. One day he contracted a chronic rheumatic illness from lying down drunk in the snow (why he did this is unclear). Convinced that medicines could not cure his illness, he took to constantly reciting a Taoist scripture, the *Beidou jing* (Northern Bushel [the constellation Ursa Major] Scripture).[69] One night in a dream he encountered the Great Emperor and Astral Lords of the Ursa Major and upon waking made the resolution to dedicate himself to the Tao.[70] Some time after this he sought out Wang Zhe, who, we are told, miraculously cured his chronic illness (see chapter 4).

Accounts of Wang Chuyi's life prior to joining the Quanzhen movement are perhaps the most interesting. At age seven *sui*,[71] he is said to have abruptly fallen dead and come back to life. Through this experience he allegedly gained a special insight into life and death. Also at age seven *sui*, he is said to have encountered the immortal Donghua Dijun (a legendary figure who came to be ascribed the status of first Quanzhen Patriarch by ca. 1240),[72] an incident that he himself confirms in his poetry collection *Yunguangji* (4/1a) (see chapter 5). Hagiographies also mention two more such strange encounters that occurred later in his youth. At fourteen *sui*, he allegedly encountered an old man seated on a large boulder who rubbed him on the head and proclaimed to him that he would one day become a great leader of the Taoist religion. On another occasion, he allegedly heard from midair the voice of "the master of the Palace of the Mysterious Court" (Xuanting Gongzhu).[73] After these experiences, he took to going about barefoot dressed in rags, singing and dancing crazily in public. Some people thought he was mad. There were others who, knowing his insanity was feigned, tried to pressure him into getting married. Wang Chuyi scorned all such suggestions. Along with his mother, he practiced the Taoist "methods" (his father had died when he was very young). By the time he was twenty-seven *sui*, he was dwelling in a hermitage on Mt. Niuxian, when he heard about Wang Zhe, sought him out, and became a disciple.[74] As mentioned before, his mother also became a disciple; indeed, one wonders whether Wang Chuyi's intense religiosity, manifested from such an early age, was largely the result of being raised by a devout Taoist mother.

Liu Chuxuan and Hao Datong, it perhaps should be noted, also lost their fathers early, and they are noted in the hagiographies for their faithful devotion to their mothers. Hao Datong was born to a wealthy family of scholar-officials.[75] However, he developed a fondness for more arcane studies (Taoist philosophy[76] and *Yi jing* [Book of Changes]), and he chose divination as his occupation. One source states that he once had a dream in which a "divine man" (*shenren*) revealed to him the secret meanings of the *Yi jing*, and thus he acquired his great divinatory skills.[77] Thus prior to his eventual conversion by Wang Zhe, he had studied some Taoist literature and may have had some propensity for mystical experience. He seems to have been the only Quanzhen master trained in the arts of divination (although all the Quanzhen masters had a great reputation for their alleged clairvoyant powers).

Qiu Chuji was orphaned as a young child. At the tender age of nineteen *sui*, he abandoned the secular world to study the Tao on Mt. Kunyu. He met Wang Zhe and became his disciple a year later. Thus like Wang Chuyi, he had been a Taoist monk prior to joining the Quanzhen fold. Some sources indicate that he was from a prominent family and was well educated.[78] However, one source indicates quite the opposite, stating in fact that he was illiterate and was first taught to read and write by Wang Zhe. The same source goes on to say that he then made amazing progress; he memorized over 1,000 Chinese characters a day, and eventually he became a very adept poet.[79] The reminiscences of Yin Zhiping seem to indicate something similar in regard to Liu Chuxuan and Wang Chuyi:

> Master-Father Changsheng (Liu Chuxuan); even though he did not read books, his writings and statements came flowing out from his insides (lit., "his lungs and belly"). [Works] such as his hundred and twenty "Rui zhegu" (Auspicious Pheasant) poems and his sixty "Feng ru song" (Wind Enters the Pines) poems were all brought about through oral dictation. He also wrote commentaries to the scriptures of the Three Teachings (Taoism, Confucianism, and Buddhism), his brush never stopping. Although deficient stylistically, their principles are more than sufficient. People who understand regard them as surpassing even the standard set by divine immortals.[80]
>
> Grand Master Yuyang (Wang Chuyi) read the *Daode jing* only after having already acquired the Tao.[81]

The attitude conveyed by Yin Zhiping is that the extent of one's literacy and book learning does not determine one's capacity for true spiritual insight. This is indeed consistent with the attitudes of Wang Zhe and Ma Yu, who both harbored reservations regarding the value of studying books.[82] Nonetheless, it appears that Wang Zhe taught reading and writing to Qiu Chuji—as well as perhaps to his other illiterate (or semi-literate) disciples. The Quanzhen masters, in all sorts of circumstances, depended on poetry to express themselves. When coaxing secular people to abandon their sinful, worldly ways, they wrote poems. When relating their meditative experiences, or conveying *neidan* procedures to their disciples, they wrote poems. When they were about to die, they made their final testament through poems (see chapter 7). This emphasis on poetic expression is probably what motivated Wang Zhe to teach reading and writing.

Wang Zhe, as we have seen, had two female disciples (at least), namely, Sun Bu'er (Ma Yu's wife) and Zhou Deqing (Wang Chuyi's mother). Female monasticism would thrive under the subsequent leadership of Wang Zhe's disciples,[83] and it continues to be a prominent feature of Quanzhen Taoism to this day. While it appears that Wang Zhe was reluctant to allow nuns to participate intimately in his inner circle, he did instruct them with strictness resembling that which he employed on monks. One source tells us that when Sun Bu'er came asking to be made a disciple, Wang Zhe told Ma Yu to momentarily leave the premises while he ritually ordained her.[84] He then led her out onto the streets and made her beg for food. He also made her set up and live in a separate hut of her own. Her subsequent lifestyle appears to have been very austere—perhaps no less so than her male colleagues (see chapter 3). She did not accompany Wang Zhe to Bianjing, but she did travel to Shaanxi to pay her respects at his grave after hearing of his death. From there she eventually proceeded to Luoyang to train under the tutelage of an eccentric nun, Feng Xiangu (Immortal Girl Feng). Feng Xiangu, we are told, was a nun from "west of the Pass" (i.e., Shaanxi), who went to train in Dongzhou (environs of Luoyang) during the Huangtong reign era (1141–1149). Nobody knew her age or her real name, but everybody recognized that she spoke in a distinct Qin (Shaanxi) dialect. She went about begging with her hair disheveled and her face and body covered with grime and dirt. She feigned madness and slept in abandoned temples.[85] When Sun Bu'er came to train with her, Feng Xiangu had her live in the "lower grotto" near her own "upper grotto." In front of their grottos, the two nuns placed piles of bricks and stones. Whenever they saw men approaching their dwelling, they would throw the bricks and stones at them; such was their commitment to solitude and celibacy.[86]

This account is particularly interesting, because it tells us about a solitary female Taoist ascetic whose career began prior to the emergence of the Quanzhen movement. Also interesting is the fact that she originally hailed from Shaanxi. All of this seems to again suggest that Taoism in its solitary, ascetic mode was alive and well in the late twelfth century, particularly in Wang Zhe's home region in Shaanxi; furthermore, women also participated in it. The Quanzhen School seems to have inherited, perpetuated, and expanded this trend.

In sum, the "Seven Realized Ones" varied in their social and educational backgrounds. However, most or all of them had had prior interest or participation in some aspect of Taoist religion—whether philosophy, meditation, mystical experience, or the worship of immortals and deities. This was indeed a time when Taoist religiosity was alive and vigorous throughout diverse segments of society. In fact, as is well known, the Quanzhen School was not the only new Taoist school to emerge and gain prominence in northern China during this period. Both the Taiyi School (founded by Xiao Baozhen around 1138) and the Dadao School (founded by Liu Deren around 1142) emerged some decades prior to the Quanzhen School, and they enjoyed considerable prominence into the late thirteenth century.[87]

Also noteworthy is the small ascetic Taoist lineage started by Liu Biangong (a.k.a. Liu the Sublime [Gaoshang], 1071–1143) in Binzhou (Shandong), which Vincent Goossaert has recently brought to attention.[88] Liu Biangong gained fame for his many years of silent, secluded meditation in his tiny hut, a practice similar to what was carried out by Wang Zhe, Ma Yu, and many Quanzhen monks thereafter.[89] Ma Yu himself alludes to Liu Biangong as follows in his "record of sayings":

> Liu the Sublime lived in his meditation hut (*huandu*)[90] for forty years. He did nothing else but simply empty his mind and fill his belly, avoid what is elegant, forget about fame, abandon all profit, clarify his spirit, and complete his *qi*. His elixir (Radiant Spirit/ Real Nature) formed naturally, and his immortality was naturally accomplished. [91]

It is clear that Ma Yu admired this figure and drew inspiration from him. The same could well be true of the Quanzhen School as a whole.

The five congregations founded by Wang Zhe probably consisted primarily of lay believers. Through his Spartan teaching methods, Wang Zhe limited the number of his full-fledged disciples. However, by establishing lay congregations, he probably meant to provide a means by which people of lesser resolve and fortitude could gain spiritual benefits. Members apparently were not bound on a daily basis to the strict precepts demanded of full-fledged disciples but nonetheless convened periodically to engage in worship (and perhaps confession) and other practices to enhance their religious merit. Evidence in Wang Zhe's poetry suggests that members paid a monthly fee of four copper coins and perhaps met twice a month on the first and fifteenth days.[92] Wang Zhe's syncretistic tendencies seem to have been particularly strong when he ministered to the laity. One source tells us that Wang Zhe instructed people to recite specific scriptures central to each of the "Three Teachings," namely, the Confucian *Xiao jing* (Classic of Filial Piety), the Buddhist *Heart Sutra*, and the Taoist *Daode jing* and *Qingjing jing*. The same source also indicates that the five congregations each bore the words "Three Teachings" (*sanjiao*) at the beginning of their names ("Three Teachings Seven Treasures Congregation," "Three Teachings Golden Lotus Congregation," etc.).[93] Another source states that when instructing beginners, he first made them read the *Xiao jing* and the *Daode jing*.[94] Evidence from Wang Zhe's own writings also suggests that members of the five congregations received instructions on how to clarify and purify the mind and perhaps practiced some simple form of meditation (see chapter 2). It also appears that it was precisely in the area of mental and moral cultivation that Wang Zhe perceived the common ground between the "Three Teachings" (see chapter 2).

In the hagiographic accounts, the two traits of Wang Zhe that stand out the most are his eccentricity and miraculous power. One might question the sanity and emotional stability of Wang Zhe. His eccentric behavior could be favorably interpreted as a sign that he was an enlightened holy man free of all pride and vanity, whose ways eluded the comprehension of worldly people. Eccentricity is indeed one of the standard traits attributed to the protagonists of Taoist hagiography throughout the centuries. Some of the accounts concerning Wang Zhe's strange acts may well be embellishments meant to fit him into the classic model of the Taoist immortal. More troubling—and rather atypical of Taoist hagiography—is the volatile temper and abusive behavior manifested by Wang Zhe in his interactions with his disciples. His disciples and admirers would justify this as being the "tough love" or "skilful means" of a compassionate teacher, but perhaps it is part of a pattern of emotional instability and abusive behavior that tainted his character throughout his life. In one of his own poems, Wang Zhe reminisces about how he had squandered his family's fortune through his excessive drinking and had habitually abused his kinfolk verbally.[95] Whatever the case, it would appear that his religious conversion did largely cure him of his despondent state of mind. It is otherwise difficult to explain the great self-discipline and vigor that he manifested in the late years of his life.

The miraculous powers attributed to Wang Zhe in the hagiographies are manifold (as we shall see in chapter 6). Along with exhibiting clairvoyance on numerous occasions, Wang Zhe manifests his form in multiple locations, emits radiance from his body, heals diseases with talismans or by physical contact, makes a boulder stop in midair, throws an umbrella to a location 100 km. away, and so on. We also are told that he appeared before disciples and believers after his death. One source claims that his corpse still appeared "life-like" a full year after his death. This is all of course the typical stuff of hagiography in various religious traditions worldwide. While much of it probably can be understood as embellishment woven out of the pious imagination of hagiographers, we shall be seeing that the teachings and claims of the Quanzhen masters themselves were highly instrumental in engendering such stories.

The early development of the Quanzhen School took place under consecutive periods of foreign rule, first under the Jin dynasty of the Jurchen people and then the Yuan dynasty of the Mongols. The Jurchens gained full control of northern China after a long and bloody war with the Chinese Song dynasty that lasted from 1125 to 1142. The Mongols began to attack the Jurchens in 1210 and succeeded in conquering the entire region north of the Yellow River in 1215. The Jurchens, whose kingdom had dwindled to just the regions of Henan and Shandong, tried to make up for the territory that they had lost by engaging in another war with the Song, but they were unsuccessful. Pressure from the Mongols, the Chinese, and the Xixia kingdom in the west, combined with peasant revolts, brought the Jin dynasty to its demise in 1234. Conflict and bloodshed continued until the Mongols conquered all of China in 1279.[96]

The political and social circumstances of the time must have had a great impact on the development of the Quanzhen School. Wang Zhe and his older disciples probably witnessed some of the anguish and bloodshed of the Jin-Song war, which probably instilled in them an acute awareness of the evil and suffering that pervades the world. Also, a lack of good employment opportunities under the Jurchen government probably caused a high number of Chinese intellectuals such as Wang Zhe and Ma Yu to turn to religion. While the earliest years of the movement's existence coincided with a period of relative peace and stability, the movement seems to have grown at a phenomenal rate during the years of the Mongol conquest. The tormented masses in great numbers sought spiritual and physical help from the Quanzhen School, which provided ministry, ritual services, healing, and charity (especially free food; see chapter 8).

After burying Wang Zhe in Bianjing, Ma Yu, Tan Chuduan, Liu Chuxuan, and Qiu Chuji travelled westward to Shaanxi. There they met up with Shi Chuhou, Yan Chuchang, Liu Tongwei, He Dejin, and Li Lingyang and constructed a tomb and a small temple (*an*; hermitage) at the very site at Liujiang Village where Wang Zhe had burned his grass hut.[97] They then retrieved their master's body from Bianjing and interred it at the Liujiang temple. This temple, the Chongyang Gong, is regarded as the Patriarchal Garden (Zuting), the foremost sacred site of the Quanzhen tradition.[98]

For three years, Ma Yu, Tan Chuduan, Liu Chuxuan, and Qiu Chuji lived in mourning at the Liujiang temple, after which they parted ways to pursue their own training and preaching. The new leader, Ma Yu, evangelized in Shaanxi with great success, but in the winter of 1181, the Jurchen government started to view the growing Quanzhen movement with disfavor and suspicion and ordered Ma Yu to leave Shaanxi and return to Shandong. Ma Yu obeyed, leaving his Shaanxi ministry in the hands of Qiu Chuji.[99] Ma Yu died in 1183, but the movement continued to grow. In 1187, Wang Chuyi was summoned by Emperor Shizong for advice on how to seek longevity. Wang Chuyi told the emperor that the key to cultivating the body lay in the cherishing of seminal essence (i.e., sexual restraint) and completion of the Spirit. He further pointed out that sitting regally and doing nothing (non-intrusive governing) is the basic principle for ruling the empire.[100] Similar invitations eventually went out to Qiu Chuji in 1188 and Liu Chuxuan in 1197.[101] As the Jin kingdom began to receive the deadly blows of the Mongol war machine, the Quanzhen School seems to have grown more rapidly than ever with Qiu Chuji and Wang Chuyi as its most lauded figures. The fame of Qiu Chuji grew so much that Genghis Khan eventually heard of him and decided to summon him. Qiu Chuji (who was seventy-three *sui* at the time) complied and during the first lunar month (February 6–March 6) in 1220[102] embarked on a long westward journey from the Shandong Peninsula to the Hindu Kush mountains in present-day Afghanistan. He finally arrived there in the third lunar month (April 14–May 12) in 1222 and met with Genghis Khan. He urged the ruthless conqueror to be less brutal in his conquest tactics and instructed him in the basic principles of cultivating health and longevity. As a result of this mission, Qiu is said to have saved many lives. Furthermore, Genghis Khan decreed that all Taoist monks and nuns in his domain were to operate under Qiu Chuji's authority, and that their institutions would be exempt from taxation. This heroic journey is a great highlight in Quanzhen history that has made Qiu Chuji the most revered of all the Quanzhen masters.[103] After Qiu Chuji's death in 1227, the Quanzhen School continued to grow in prominence under the leadership of his disciple, Yin Zhiping (originally a disciple of Liu Chuxuan), who had been among the members of the party who accompanied him on the famous journey.

Under the Mongol Empire, the Quanzhen sect was clearly the largest and most influential Taoist movement in northern China. Goossaert has estimated that by the end of the thirteenth century, there were about 4,000 Quanzhen monasteries and 20,000 Quanzhen clerics, of which about a third were women.[104] One of the greatest accomplishments during this period was the restoration and expansion (completed in 1244) of the *Xuandu baozang* ("Precious Storehouse of the Mysterious Capital) in 7,000 volumes, the largest Taoist Canon ever compiled. Spearheaded by the erudite monks, Song Defang (1183–1247) and Qin Zhi'an (1188–1244), this was the only such project in history initiated and carried out by an individual Taoist school without government sponsorship.[105] However, less than four decades later, this canon was destroyed as a result of a very dismaying chain of events. The Buddhist monk, Fuyu, complained to the Mongol court that the Quanzhen School was printing and distributing the controversial *Laozi huahu jing* (Scripture of Laozi's Conversion of the Barbarians), along with illustrations known as the *Laozi bashiyihua tu* (Diagrams of the 81 Transformations of Laozi). This text propagated the infamous legend (which had been the focus of ugly Buddhist-Taoist debates way back in the sixth century)[106] in which the Taoist sage, Laozi, travels to India and creates the Buddhist religion as a lower doctrine fit for barbarians. The Buddhists further complained that the Quanzhen Taoists had occupied Buddhist temples and destroyed Buddhist images.[107] In response to the complaints, the government decreed in 1255 that the printing blocks for the slanderous texts be destroyed, and that thirty-seven temples be returned to the Buddhists. However, the Taoists were not fully compliant to these measures, which provoked further complaints from the Buddhists. Consequently, the emperor decided to resolve the issue by staging a debate between the Taoists and Buddhists in 1256. The Taoists, to his dismay, declined to participate. Debates eventually were held in 1258 and 1281. On each occasion, the Taoists were defeated and punished severely. In 1258, forty-five "false scriptures" were condemned to fire. In 1281, alas, the entire Taoist canon—excluding the *Daode jing*—saw the same fate.[108]

I would venture to surmise that Wang Zhe himself would have been perturbed by the conduct of his successors during this period. The attitude toward Buddhism reflected in his own writings and actions was consistently one of appreciation and conciliation. Yet it is also true that the larger *neidan* tradition held a particular polemical stance against Buddhism—a stance maintaining that the spiritual liberation won through *neidan* practice was inherently superior to that gained through the Buddhist path. This stance, which is not readily apparent in the teachings of Wang Zhe, can be identified in a particular text ascribed to Qiu Chuji (*Dadan zhizhi* [DT243/TT115]), as well as in the immortality lore that came to be promoted by the Quanzhen movement (see chapter 4).

Strangely, despite the humiliation and punishment that resulted from the debates, the Quanzhen School survived and even managed to regain the favor of the government. In 1310, Emperor Wuzong bestowed honorary posthumous titles upon the Quanzhen patriarchs (Donghua Dijun, Zhongli Quan, Lü Yan, Liu Cao, and Wang Zhe), the Seven Realized Ones, and fifteen other eminent Quanzhen monks.[109] While the Quanzhen School never regained the supreme status it held in the mid-thirteenth century, it has survived to this day as the foremost school of monastic Taoism.

## Preview of This Book's Contents

The purpose of this book is to provide a thorough description and analysis of the teachings and practices of the early Quanzhen masters. For this purpose, one must amply employ the voluminous writings left behind by the masters themselves. The vast bulk of this material—unfortunately, one might say—consists of poetry that is frequently difficult to comprehend due to its abstruse *neidan* symbolism. Fortunately, this material is supplemented and clarified by prose discourses (preserved largely in a genre of writing known as *yulu* or "records of sayings") that are much more straightforward. By employing these materials, my intent is to let the masters speak for themselves, and for this reason I beg the reader's indulgence with the frequency of direct quotes (some fairly long).

Quanzhen doctrine is remarkable for its balance and thoroughness. The Quanzhen masters taught a balanced and complementary cultivation of mind and body. Furthermore, in their view, personal religious attainment had to be supplemented and counterbalanced by compassionate action in the world. My plan thus is to provide a full exposition of the Quanzhen path of cultivation at both the mental and physical levels, followed by a discussion of the types of compassionate worldly action taught and practiced by the Quanzhen masters.

Chapter 2 will focus primarily on the mental aspect of the Quanzhen path. This first and foremost means the cultivation of inner clarity and purity attained not only through the diligent practice of seated meditation (*dazuo*) but through an inner vigilance that pervades all daily activities. Inner purity and clarity, if attained, are seen as conducive to naturally bringing about physical control and well-being, as well as a spontaneous capacity for compassion that manifests itself in altruistic deeds. Yet in the process of acquiring this all-important purity and clarity of mind, the Quanzhen masters maintained that conscious effort must be made to discipline the body and perform altruistic deeds.

Chapter 3 will focus on an aspect of the Quanzhen lifestyle that is so vividly portrayed in the hagiographies, namely, the rigorous asceticism. Here I will describe the various types of self-discipline and self-denial pursued by the Quanzhen masters and discuss the underlying motives and rationale of these practices.

Chapter 4 will focus on teachings concerning the maintenance of physical health and longevity. The Quanzhen masters ultimately saw the cultivation of mental purity and clarity as holding the key to immortality. They conceded the mortality of the ordinary physical body as inevitable and put their hopes in the immortality of the Radiant Spirit/Real Nature. Yet this did not eliminate the need for physical health and longevity, since the process for recovering the Radiant Spirit involved the refining and manipulation of the subtle essences and energies that animate the physical organism. Ultimately, a decrepit body was deemed to be an inadequate apparatus for the internal alchemical process. I will examine here the various theories of the Quanzhen masters pertaining to physiology and the various strategies recommended and employed for the curing and prevention of disease.

Chapter 5 will examine the various mystical experiences attested to by the Quanzhen masters, such as visions, locutions, and unusual bodily sensations and symptoms. These things were referred to as "signs of proof"—proof that the adept is making progress in his or her pursuit of immortality. Nonetheless, an ambivalent attitude existed in regard to these phenomena that could at times be harrowing, and even deluding. Mystical experiences were fervently desired for affirmation of one's worthiness yet were not to be too eagerly sought or anticipated.

Chapter 6 will deal with the issue of miracles. Many or most of the miracle stories in the hagiographies were certainly woven out of the imagination and evangelistic zeal of pious followers. The Quanzhen masters themselves were critical of Taoists who sought to infatuate the credulous with outlandish claims. Yet a deeper examination reveals that many such claims were logically consistent with what *neidan* cultivation purports to accomplish. Furthermore, an examination of the Quanzhen masters' own statements reveals that they themselves believed in immortals and their miraculous manifestations and furthermore sometimes confirmed the alleged miraculous feats of their brethren.

Chapter 7 will examine the issue of death and what it meant to the Quanzhen masters. Hagiographies preserve ample information on how the masters died, along with what they said and how they behaved in the face of death. The masters' own writings preserve specific insights regarding what death is and how one should prepare for it and face up to it. One may doubt whether their comportment in their final moments was as heroic as what the hagiographies portray. However, the early Quanzhen masters clearly intended to face death with equanimity and dignity and believed that this could be accomplished by fostering mental detachment from one's body and the world.

Chapter 8 will begin to examine the altruistic worldly involvement of the Quanzhen masters. Here we will examine how the Quanzhen masters, particularly in the years after Wang Zhe's death, actively engaged in charity and evangelism out of their fervent pathos for the plight of the world.

Another compassionate activity deemed essential was the performance of Taoist rituals. The tendency of some modern scholars, who deemed such rituals as representative of the irrationality of the "old Taoist religion," has been to maintain that such things were incongruous with the intent of Wang Zhe. In chapter 9 I will argue that Wang Zhe did not categorically disapprove of Taoist rituals; rather, he at times eagerly participated in them. When his successors eventually began to perform Taoist rituals frequently, this constituted not a deviation from the founder's vision but rather yet another facet of compassionate worldly activity. Particularly emphasized were rituals for the miserable souls of the dead, the number of which drastically increased during the Mongol conquest. Wang Zhe's disciples did at times express concern over excessive ritual involvement as well as disdain for the decadence and insincerity they saw in the religious rituals being performed around them. Their ultimate solution was, however, to reform rather than to abstain, and to extol purity and sincerity as the fundamentals of proper, efficacious Taoist rituals.

# Chapter 2

## Cultivating Clarity and Purity

Keep the mind rectified and give rise to no evil [thoughts].
The Three Teachings, when investigated, prove to be but one school.
When their meanings and principles are manifested, what difference is there among them?
When the marvelous mystery is penetrated, there is nothing to be added.
[You should] stop clinging to all the various things.
To be pure and clear [in mind] is the best thing of all.
The Real Person who spans the *kalpas* (*jie*)[1] reveals himself/herself once again;
Hereby you once again can mount the clouds and mists.[2]

The above poem by Wang Zhe states that the essence and common ground of the Three Teachings (Taoism, Buddhism, and Confucianism) are found in the practice of mental discipline. By maintaining clarity and purity of mind, one recovers the primordial, deathless Real Nature ("the Real Person who spans the *kalpas*") that has been obscured and lost amid the hassles and delusions of worldly life.

The path to this recovery is—or should be—a simple and straightforward one. One should not obsess over the abstruse utterances of teachers and scriptures. When questioned on the meaning of the technical internal alchemical words "dragon" and "tiger," Wang Zhe responded with the following poem:

Ask not about the dragon and the tiger.
The single point in your mind is your enlightened master.
When your *qi* is under control and your spirit (*shen*) is stable, this is what is called "the copulation."
The mind rectified in diligence and sincerity produces a warm glow.
To constantly serve all [sentient beings] equally is the Great Tao.
If [your mind is kept] pure and clear without relent, you will gain true compassion.
All becomes manifest to you as the circular light reaches completion,
Guiding forth the golden elixir and fetching the jade fungi.[3]

To make the "dragon and tiger copulate" means to keep one's spirit (conscious mind) and *qi* (the energy or breath that animates the body) under control. If one is diligent and sincere, then one can simply follow his or her own emerging intuitive wisdom. This intuitive wisdom is accompanied by a warm compassion that spontaneously compels one to serve all sentient beings. In another poem, Wang Zhe similarly states:

If you know the good visage, do not hold on to externals.
[Your] mind-spirit is your true teacher.
The problems and riddles (*gong'an*, a Chan Buddhist term)[4] posed by men of old should be investigated,
[But] your own school [of thinking] must be spread about.
Little by little you come to penetrate your past enlightened nature,
More and more you show forth your compassion of old.
When your compassion and purity are both [re-] established,
You will attain sudden enlightenment and absolutely nothing will bind you.[5]

The teachings of venerable masters are certainly to be consulted, however, one should not and need not rely on them once one's own innate wisdom and compassion emerge. Ultimately, one can do as one desires in an absolute state of freedom. The three poems we have looked at so far certainly seem to reflect a certain degree of inspiration from the Chan Buddhist tradition. Wang Zhe's attitude—and particularly his use of the phrase "the Real Person who spans the *kalpas*"—is strongly reminiscent of that of the famous Chan master, Linji Yixuan (d. 866). Master Linji taught his disciples to trust in the "Real Person of No Rank" (the intuitive wisdom of their innate Buddha Nature) rather than to rely on scriptures and teachers.[6]

In another poem, Wang Zhe describes the profound calmness of meditative trance and the prevailing serenity that results from it:

Resolutely yearn for the Tao and have nothing [else] that binds and enwraps you.
Isolate your body and sleep in solitude.
When stillness arises within the stillness, you will attain the wonders.
When calmness arrives within the calmness, you shall definitely unite with the mysterious.
Now you can act with free abandon, and know what it is to be relaxed and content.
Passing the days in refreshing coolness is the inborn saint.
Quit wishing for divine immortality; quit speaking of it!
Let yourself sit alone on the white lotus flower.[7]

Here Wang Zhe enjoins the reader to disengage from the world and single-mindedly cultivate inner calm. This culminates in "wonders" and a union with the "mysterious"—probably references to mystical experiences that occur in meditative trance. The blessed effect that prevails well beyond the transitory ecstasy is "coolness"—a state of supreme freedom, relaxation, and contentment. Indeed, one now need not wish for nor speak of divine immortality. The person who now abides in the coolness is none other than the "inborn saint"—one's Real Nature that always has and always will partake in life eternal. The life of the immortals can be lived right here and now. This insight was later echoed eloquently by Wang Zhe's disciple, Hao Datong, who said "A day of serenity is a day of immortality."[8]

The cultivation of inner peace and virtuous action lay at the heart of early Quanzhen Taoism. A broader and deeper study of Quanzhen writings certainly reveals beliefs in miracles, immortal beings, and a glorious afterlife. One also can find numerous testimonies of mystical experience and references to various physiological theories and practices. Much can be found that pertains to the supernatural or to the psycho-physiological intricacies that constitute the unique domain of Taoist religion. Nonetheless, it would appear that Wang Zhe most emphasized a path of mental discipline and morality that is simple and straightforward (albeit arduous). In this simple pursuit of inner peace and virtuous action, along with its underlying psychological principles, Wang Zhe perceived—quite aptly—a common ground with Confucianism and Buddhism.

Wang Zhe's simplified approach to Taoist training is most adamantly enjoined in a prose discourse directed to members of the lay societies that he had established in Shandong:

The reason why I established the Jade Flower and Golden Lotus Societies in the two prefectures was because I wanted all you gentle-

> men to recognize your Real Natures.[9] If you do not understand the true source, but [rather only] study all the small methods of subsidiary schools (*pangmen*), these are all but methods for creating good fortune and nurturing the body—they have absolutely nothing to do with the way of cultivating immortality. [Furthermore,] in matters of Nature and Life, if you make the slightest mistake, you could go away from the human path (be reborn in a subhuman state). Gentlemen, if you truly want to cultivate yourselves, [just] eat when hungry and shut your eyes when sleepy. Do not sit in meditation and do not study the Tao. You simply need to eliminate all trivial things [from your mind]. Your mind simply needs to be clear and pure;[10] anything aside from this is not cultivation![11]

Here Wang Zhe implores his followers to focus on recovering their Real Nature and maintains that this can be accomplished by simply maintaining a clear and pure mind. (Hachiya has pointed out that the phrase "[just] eat when hungry and shut your eyes when sleepy" resembles a passage found in the recorded sayings of the Chan master, Dazhu Huihai [fl. ca. 780]).[12] Prescribed training techniques and regimens of all kinds are denounced here. Physical practices aiming at better health are denounced, because they take one's focus off of the fundamental disciplining of the mind. Even seated meditation (the most time-honored technique of mental discipline) is discouraged for being artificial and unessential. Rather, Wang approves only of spontaneous, natural action.

Noteworthy is the fact that this discourse was directed at a lay audience. Rather than serve up a litany on piety, almsgiving, or basic morality—the staples of most lay religion—Wang Zhe describes the way by which immortality can be sought. In doing so, he is providing access to what might ordinarily be the exclusive privilege of monks.

In a much similar vein, Wang Zhe's top disciple, Ma Yu, made statements such as the following:

> Now, as for the [cultivation of the] Tao, it simply [consists] of [the following]: [Maintain] clarity and purity (of mind), and [practice] non-action. Wander carefree according to your will. Stay undefiled and unattached (*qingjing wuwei xiaoyao zizai buran buzhao*). If you are able to thoroughly chew and savor these twelve characters, you will be a person of the Tao who has fathomed the depths. Just believe this old man's (my) words. If you practice this, you shall certainly benefit. I am definitely not misleading you young people [by saying this].[13]

> The thirty-six *daoyin* exercises[14] and the twenty-four recycled elixirs, these are but the gradual gateways for entering the Tao. Do not mistake them for the Great Tao itself. When you fathom the [principles of the] stove and furnace or take your forms from the turtle and snake, you are giving rise to affairs where there are no affairs, and adding falseness your [hidden Real] Nature. All this is extremely misleading! Therefore the alchemical scriptures and the books of the various philosophers, the thousand classics and ten thousand treatises can all be covered up with one phrase—"clear and pure."[15]

So was the Quanzhen path of self-cultivation an easy path? This seemingly simple and straightforward approach to immortality advocated by Wang Zhe and Ma Yu might at first appear to be a means of accommodating the needs of the laity, whose worldly commitments rendered them incapable of concentrating on any sort of intensive program of self-discipline and meditation.

The Quanzhen masters certainly did not consider asceticism and meditation obsolete, as is obvious from the way they lived and practiced. While they exhorted all followers—clergy and laity alike—to pursue the mental cultivation that leads to the recovery of the Real Nature, much of their poetry implores people to abandon their families, possessions, and worldly pursuits. The easy, effortless mode of conduct described by statements such as "[just] eat when hungry and shut your eyes when sleepy" (Wang Zhe)[16] or "wander carefree according to your will" (Ma Yu) can really only be pursued after a prevailing state of inner purity and clarity is attained. Attaining this requires a sustained, strenuous effort that is probably only feasible for a monk or nun. This becomes clear when one reads the following two mini-treatises attributed to Wang Zhe that respectively bear the headings "Having a Sit" and "Subduing the Mind":

> Now, to "have a sit" (*dazuo*, to practice meditation) does not refer to the act of assuming the proper posture and closing the eyes. Such is but false sitting. [To practice] true sitting you must throughout the twelve [double-] hours, whether staying, going, sitting, or lying, throughout all your motion and stillness, make your mind be like Mt. Tai—unmoving and unwavering. Grasp and cut off the four gates of your eyes, ears, mouth, and nose. Do not allow outer scenery to enter in. If there is any stirring of thought even the size of a silk thread or a single fine fur, it cannot be called "quiet sitting." One who is able to be like this already has his/her name recorded in the ranks of the immortals, even though his/her body resides in the dusty world. He/she need not travel afar to consult another person. In

> other words, the wise sage (the Real Nature with its intuitive wisdom) is in his/her very own body. In a hundred years his/her merit will be full; shedding his/her shell, he/she ascends to Realization. The single pill of cinnabar is completed, and his/her spirit wanders the eight surfaces.[17]
>
> Now, in speaking of the ways of the mind: Always serenely the mind is kept motionless. Darkly, silently, you do not look at the myriad objects. Dimly, murkily, without an inside nor an outside, you have no thoughts even the size of a silk thread or a single fine fur. This is the stability of mind; it should not be subdued. If you follow your surroundings and give rise to thoughts, stumbling and falling while seeking now the head and now the tail, this is called the disorderly mind. You must cut if off immediately, and you must not follow its whims. It damages and destroys your Tao-virtue and it diminishes your Nature and Life. Whether staying, going, sitting, or lying down, you must diligently subdue it. What you hear, see, know, and understand is but a disease and [an] ailment to you.[18]

The mental regimen proposed is indeed demanding, as one must remain alert, concentrated, and self-vigilant throughout all situations and activities. Far from eliminating meditation from the Taoist's regimen, Wang Zhe is requiring that meditation take place incessantly, even when one is not seated in the lotus position. One can certainly see a parallel (and very likely a connection) here to the practice of mindfulness emphasized in Buddhism—Chan in particular. However, Wang Zhe enjoins the practitioner to cut off all external sense data and to concentrate inwardly ("Grasp and cut off the four gates of your eyes, ears, mouth, and nose. Do not allow outer scenery to enter in"). He says that one must not allow even the smallest stirring of thought, and that one should reside in a seeming state of entranced oblivion ("Dimly, murkily, without an inside nor an outside, you have no thoughts even the size of a silk thread or a single fine fur.") This would appear to be something different from Buddhist mindfulness practice in which the practitioner alertly, but in a detached and an objective manner, observes outer sense data, his or her own actions and his or her inner flow of thoughts.[19] If the above interpretation is correct, and if one was to faithfully follow Wang Zhe's directions, then it would indeed seem virtually impossible to remain engaged in the secular world. It also would explain why each of the Quanzhen masters underwent periods of self-imposed seclusion.

This ceaseless meditation of clarity and purity was perhaps the central, most definitive practice of early Quanzhen Taoism. Wang Zhe's top disciples also made noteworthy statements regarding it:

[In regard to your] daily sustenance, first you must never deceive and mock Heaven and Earth. Always train yourself diligently. Be jealous of each moment of time. Do not pass the day in vain. You should decrease your sleep [since] this also is something that people desire. You should reform your misdeeds, but this is not [only] to be done through seated meditation. You should keep your mind stable for a long time. Going, staying, sitting, and lying down (i.e., all daily activities—a phrase common in Chan discourse) are the practice of the Tao. Gentlemen, quit giving rise to thoughts! Quickly seek out your Nature and Life. If you can just clear your mind and abandon your desires, you will be a Divine Immortal. Acknowledge nothing else and stop having doubts! These are proper and true words. You only need to be constantly clear and constantly pure. Practice this diligently.[20] (Ma Yu)

What does it mean to "see your [Real] Nature"? Throughout the twelve [double]-hours [of the day] be clear and still in all your thoughts. Do not let your true source get obscured by your surroundings that you have cherished in the past. Always be like empty space and wander about freely. Naturally your spirit and *qi* will come together in harmony. If in your training you accomplish this single matter, what further lives and deaths will you have to fret over? What further transgressions and *karma* will you have to fear? If you give rise to even the slightest thought, you are not clear and still. In other words this [thought] has become a hindrance and you are not free. How can you arrive [at clarity and stillness]? I simply want you gentlemen to maintain your aspiration like a mountain, unmoving and unwavering. Advancing forward, go. [If you] encounter great demons who will put an end to this body, do not look back. What you anticipate ahead of you will certainly be accomplished. Realized Man Jin said, "For the mind to be clear and will still is the road to the halls of Heaven. For the thoughts to be confused and the mind depraved is the gate to hell."[21] (Tan Chuduan)

Practitioners throughout the twelve [double-]hours [of the day] should simply investigate their own shortcomings within. Thereby they can make their spirit and *qi* peaceful within. When the spirit and *qi* are peaceful, this is true merit. To not see the wrongs of people is true deeds.[22] (Liu Chuxuan)

To always make your entire mind limpid, to remain alert and aware throughout the twelve [double-] hours of the day, to not let your

> [Real] Nature become obscured, to make your mind stable and your *qi* harmonious, this is your true inner daily sustenance.[23] (Qiu Chuji)

> Your daily sustenance is to refine your *qi* when in quiet places and refine your spirit when in loud places. Going, staying, sitting, and lying down, these are all the Tao. Day and night do not get confused by what you see in front of you. If you sleep for one hour, you have accomplished nothing for that one hour. Day by day you will have merit. If you go without sleep for one thousand days, your training will be completed. Do not believe it when others tell you that you have bones of destiny.[24] (Hao Datong)

This daily self-discipline—referred to above by Ma Yu, Qiu Chuji, and Hao Datong as "daily sustenace" (*riyong*) because it is as essential to one's well-being as the very food that one eats—first and foremost involves keeping the mind clear and pure at all times. One must be aware of one's mental state at all times and in all activities. Constant effort must be made to rid the mind of wrong desires, thoughts, and feelings. When such inner blemishes arise (and they inevitably do), one must fully acknowledge them and repent of them. The task of cleansing the mind is an urgent one, and time must not be wasted. Since one is unable to tend to the task while asleep, and sleep is one among many objects of human desire, then one must reduce the amount of sleep. In fact, indulgence in all objects of desire needs to be curtailed. While the above discourses on daily self-discipline deal mainly with psychology, they also acknowledge that the mental state is intimately linked to the *qi* that animates the body and bears its impulses. When spirit and *qi* are out of harmony, then bodily impulses generate the desires that corrupt the mind. Thus Tan speaks of bringing the spirit and *qi* together in harmony, Liu speaks of making spirit and *qi* peaceful, Qiu speaks of making the mind stable and *qi* harmonious, and Hao speaks of the dual refinement of spirit and *qi*.

Yin Zhiping discussed somewhat more concretely the process of daily discipline:

> Those who have left their family (i.e., monks and nuns) must examine their minds and figure out how many evil thoughts they have had during the morning and the day. [Thoughts of] liquor, sex, wealth, and anger are not the only desires; all [thoughts of] things that you have been fond of up to now are all desires. If only just one thing at a time you should break off these wrongs. Naturally your mind will become easy to subdue and will gradually become peaceful. People all say that attaining the Tao is very difficult.

> [But if] a practitioner can break off his wrongs, his/her mind will be cool and pure and his/her training will become much easier. Without generating smoky fires (desires) nor discriminating between right and wrong or self and others, his/her merits and deeds will quickly be completed.[25]
>
> Barefooted Master Liu [Chuxuan] once said to me, "It figured that Master-Father Tan [Chuduan] would complete the Tao early on. In the past when we were begging for our meals together, he used to reflect within his mind every day. In the evening he would examine all the thoughts that had arisen [in his mind] since morning. In the morning he would examine all the thoughts that had arisen [in his mind] since the evening. Day after day [he continued this habit] without ever receding [in diligence]."[26]
>
> When our predecessors (Wang Zhe's first-generation disciples) trained themselves, during each and every single moment, they examined their thoughts. When they became aware of even a single bad thought, they always confessed it to others, in order to bring humiliation and shame upon themselves. [In doing so they] hoped never to give rise [to the same bad thought] in their minds. Students [of the Tao] nowadays act contrarily to this. If they have but a single good [thought or deed], they flaunt it and boast about it, fearing only that people will not come to know about it. [As for] their evil [thoughts and deeds] numbering in the thousands and tens of thousands, they keep them to themselves and forgive them themselves, fearing only that someone might find out about them. If somebody does get to know about them (the evil thoughts and deeds), they still are unable to do good [deeds].[27]

Yin Zhiping thus describes a gradual and systematic process of self-monitoring. He sternly maintains that all desires need to be suppressed. However, instead of attempting to eliminate all desires all at once, one should identify and eliminate the desires one by one. As the process progresses, it becomes easier. Tan Chuduan, it appears, monitored his progress by reviewing twice daily the quantity and quality of his thoughts in order to make sure that his desires were decreasing at a good pace. All of the first-generation disciples, we are further told, verbally confessed their inner flaws to their peers in order to more effectively chastise themselves and vanquish the pride that fears public disgrace.

Interestingly, however, Yin Zhiping also pointed out that while one wants to suppress desires, one must not become completely blank mentally:

> Who among people does not have any thoughts? You must discern what is evil and what is proper among your thoughts. What you want to eliminate are your evil thoughts only. Whatever depletes your vital essence (*jing*)[28] or damages your spirit and *qi* is evil. Students [of the Tao] do not understand this, and many of them grab onto [the notion that] it is good to eliminate all thoughts. If one practices according to this principle, their proper thoughts that enable them to accumulate merits and deeds will also be eliminated. If they lose these [proper thoughts], they are but dead objects. How can they correspond with the Tao?[29]

Yin Zhiping's concern is that in eliminating all types of thoughts indiscriminately, a practitioner might even eliminate his or her good thoughts, the thoughts that would compel him or her toward diligent self-cultivation (merits) and virtuous action (deeds). (The reason evil thoughts were believed to deplete the vital essence shall be made clear in chapter 4.) To "correspond with the Tao" does not mean to become like a dead object; the Tao is not followed nor attained by becoming inanimate and unconscious.

Yin Zhiping's views in this respect might seem to represent a departure from those of his predecessors, some of whose statements previously cited could easily be construed to mean that one should try to eliminate all thinking and activity. But such was apparently not their intention. For example, Ma Yu, much like Yin Zhiping, took care to note that the proper state of mind is not one of complete vacuity:

> [The state of] no-mind is not the same as the stupid mindlessness of cats and dogs or trees and rocks. Your task is to maintain your mind within the realm of clarity and purity, and to have no evil thoughts. Thus worldly people have no mind of clarity and purity, while people of the Tao have no mind of dust and defilement. [The state of no-mind] is not a state of complete mindlessness akin to that of trees and rocks or cats and dogs.[30]

Ma Yu here asserts that the so-called state of "no-mind" is a positive mental state that can be described as the mind of clarity and purity. In this state, one is not unconscious like a tree or rock, and one's consciousness has positive qualities exclusive to humans and higher beings. While he unfortunately does not specify what these qualities may be, one might conjecture that he is referring to the sincere will to persevere in one's training and the compassionate will to serve other beings.

Even Wang Zhe, who in a previously cited passage seemed to be saying that one should cut off all sense data, still all stirrings of thoughts, and reside in an entranced oblivion, seems to have acknowledged that one can interact with the external world without damaging one's inner state. One source records the following conversation between "Master-Father Ma" (presumably Ma Yu) and a teacher whom the text neglects to specifically name, but that teacher is most likely Wang Zhe:

> [Ma Yu] asked, "How does one see one's [Real] Nature?"
>
> [Wang Zhe (?)] answered, "You simply must be of no mind and no thoughts. Do not become attached to anything. Clearly, serenely, be free of affairs within and without. This is what it means to see your [Real] Nature."
>
> [Ma Yu] asked, "What does it mean to respond to objects without getting confused?"
>
> [Wang Zhe (?)] answered, "Even though you hear with your ears, see with your eyes, and speak with your mouth, you simply must not become attached with your mind."[31]

Unattached though one may be, in "responding to objects" the sense organs and conscious thought processes are certainly at work. If Wang Zhe—as the previously cited passage suggests—indeed recommended adepts to reside constantly in a disengaged, outwardly oblivious state, then he may have been specifically addressing disciples who were pursuing an intensified self-discipline.

Complete and permanent disengagement from the outer world was in fact unthinkable. The path of Quanzhen was a dual cultivation of "true merit" (*zhen'gong*) and "true deeds" (*zhenxing*). Wang Zhe explained this concept as follows, quoting as his authority the words of a now obscure pre-Quanzhen figure, Realized Man Jin (Jin Zhenren; Jin Daocheng[?]).[32]

> Realized Man Jin said, "If you want true merit, you must clear your mind and stabilize your will, disciplining your spirit and emotions. Without movement and without action, in true clarity and true purity, embrace the origin and guard the One, preserve your spirit and solidify your *qi*. This is true merit. If you want true deeds, you should cultivate benevolence and accumulate virtue, by relieving the poor and rescuing those who suffer. When you see people in strife, always put to action your mind [that desires] to help them. At times [you should] persuade good people to enter the Tao and engage in training. In whatever you do, put others first and yourself last. Be selfless [in your interactions with] the myriad things. This is true deeds."[33]

The Taoist needs to be engaged in the dual pursuits of personal training and virtuous action. The latter includes aiding people both physically and mentally through charity and evangelism. In interacting with others, Wang Zhe emphasizes humility and selflessness. By diligently engaging in personal training and virtuous actions one was thought to increase one's store of merits and deeds and consequently to move farther along toward the recovery of her or his Real Nature.

Ma Yu and Qiu Chuji also spoke of the personal and interpersonal aspects of self-cultivation, which they referred to, respectively, as "inner daily sustenance" (*neiriyong*) and "outer daily sustenance" (*wairiyong*):

> You every day must not forget the matter of your daily sustenance. Of daily sustenance there are two types; there is outer daily sustenance and inner daily sustenance.
>
> Outer daily sustenance [is as follows]: You are strongly forbidden to see the faults of others, boast of your own virtue, envy the wise and talented, give rise to the worldly thoughts that are the fire of ignorance, give rise [to] feelings of superiority over the masses, [discriminate] between self and other or right and wrong, or to speak of hatred and affection.
>
> Inner daily sustenance [is as follows]: Quit giving rise to doubtful thoughts. Always do not be forgetful of the inside. Whether wandering about or staying and sitting, you should clear your mind and discard your desires. Have nothing that hangs upon or hinders [your mind]. Do not get defiled and do not cling. In true clarity and true purity, wander about freely at your will. Consistently throughout the day, contemplate upon the Tao in the same way a hungry person thinks of food or a thirsty person thinks of drink. If you become aware of the slightest imbalance [in your thinking], you must correct it.
>
> If you train yourself in this way, you will definitely become a Divine Immortal.[34]

> You people, listen to my words. You must not forget your inner daily sustenance and outer daily sustenance.
>
> Outer daily sustenance [is as follows]: You are strongly forbidden to see the faults of others, boast of your own virtue, envy the wise and the talented, give rise to ignorant worldly thoughts, [or to commit] the various misdeeds of a desiring mind.
>
> Inner daily sustenance [is as follows]: Be truly clear and truly still. Do not become defiled and do not cling. Control your energy, and nurture your spirit. Wander about freely at your will. Secretly accumulate merits and deeds; do not seek for recognition from people,

but only wish to be observed by Heaven. A poem says, "[From the] Tao, human emotions are distant. Non-action is the basis of the wondrous origin. If in the world you have nothing that you cherish, confused thoughts will not ensue."[35] (Ma Yu)

Again [someone] asked [Qiu Chuji] about inner and outer daily sustenance. Qiu said, "To abandon your self and follow another person (humbly obey one's teacher), to overcome yourself and return to propriety, this is your outer daily sustenance. To forgive others and withstand insults, to eliminate all thoughts and worries, to put all things to rest in your mind, this is your inner daily sustenance."

The next day [someone] again asked about inner and outer daily sustenance. Qiu said, "To put others first and yourself last, to put yourself in accord with others,[36] this is your outer daily sustenance. To carry out your training in clarity and stillness, this is your inner daily sustenance."

He also said, "To always make your entire mind limpid, to remain alert and aware throughout the twelve [double-] hours of the day, to not let your [Real] Nature become obscured, to make your mind stable and your *qi* harmonious, this is your true inner daily sustenance. To practice benevolence and accumulate virtue, to make yourself suffer for the benefit of others, this is your true outer daily sustenance."[37] (Qiu Chuji)

As previously stated, "daily sustenance" (*riyong*) refers to that which is indispensable for one's life and well-being. At the personal (inner) level, it is the self-discipline that centers primarily upon maintaining the clarity and purity of mind. At the interpersonal (outer) level, it is the basic attributes of humility and selflessness that appear outwardly in conduct that is patient, tolerant, obedient, benevolent, and altruistic.[38]

Wang Zhe, in his discourse on "true merit" (quoting from Realized Man Jin), stated that you should "preserve your spirit and solidify your *qi*." Regarding "inner daily sustenance, Ma Yu proclaimed, "control your *qi*, and nurture your spirit," and Qiu Chuji spoke of making the mind stable and the *qi* harmonious. This now brings us back to the theme of the cultivation of *qi* that must accompany and complement the mental discipline. As previously noted, the Quanzhen masters were acutely aware that a person's mental state is intimately linked to the *qi* that animates the body and bears its impulses. When spirit and *qi* are out of harmony, bodily impulses generate the desires that corrupt the mind. Consequently, if the cultivation of *qi* is neglected, then bodily impulses will undermine the clarity and purity of mind and furthermore undermine one's capacity for virtuous action. (The Quanzhen masters also taught and practiced the cultivation of *qi* as a means toward good health and long life, as we shall see in chapter 4.)

For an illuminating, much more concrete elucidation of this idea, we can once again turn to Yin Zhiping. In a discourse on the suppression of all desires, Yin Zhiping singled out three desires as being most troublesome, namely, the desires for food, sleep, and sex. These three desires all pertain to very basic bodily needs and are mutually linked:

> Furthermore, among the things that harm one's training, three desires are the most serious (food, sleep, and sex [annotation in text]). If you do not limit your eating, you will sleep too much. [The problem with excessive] sleep is most serious; this is where passion and lust arise from. [Only after] a student [of the Tao] is first able to control these three desires, has he truly entered the gates of the Tao. People all know that this is so, but few are able to control them (the three desires). What controls them is the will, and what defeats it (the will) is *qi*. It is with the will that you control the *qi*. If the will is frail while the *qi* is vigorous, you cannot win. If you definitely want to control them (the desires), first decrease your daytime sleep. Spanning days and months do not seek for instant results. Naturally the dark and turbid forces (of drowsiness) will cease to arise, and gradually you will gain the power of awareness.[39]

Thus overeating causes oversleeping, which in turn causes lust. Yin Zhiping analyzes the struggle to suppress these urges in terms of the conflict of mind versus body. The desired harmony of mind and body is only achieved when the will (*zhi*) of the former controls the *qi* of the latter. When the body is overnourished and overrested, the *qi* overwhelms a weak will, making desires rampant. This is why austere physical discipline needs to accompany mental discipline. Yin Zhiping also stated as follows, regarding the relationship of mind and body:

> The single method of completing the mind includes within it the myriad deeds. Have you not seen how the various Realized Masters, [despite] receiving direct instruction from the Patriarch Master (Wang Zhe), still had to undergo a thousand polishings and a hundred refinements in order bring their minds under control? This is only because the [Real] Nature, once it has been cast into the midst of form and substance (the body), becomes encumbered by emotions and desires. Now the body is what is left to you by your father and mother. Made of the energies of *yin* and *yang*, it possesses the principles of motion and stillness. When a single good thought arises,

> you become influenced by bodily energies and are unable to put [your good intentions] into action. Therefore, gentlemen who have aspirations [for the Tao] should understand that their mind and [Real] Nature originally issues from the Tao, and should not let their bodily energies usurp their will. After a long while you shall prevail over them. Your *qi* and [bodily] form will together transform, interfusing and reverting to their Heavenly Nature. This is all brought about through the evenness of mind. When the mind is even, the spirit is stabilized. When the spirit is stabilized, the *qi* becomes harmonized, and the Tao is spontaneously born![40]

Here the focus is on how the bodily energies undermine one's innate capacity for virtuous action. Yin Zhiping implicitly maintains that our Real Nature that issues from the Tao is bestowed with a propensity for virtuous action. (This, of course, is consistent with Wang Zhe's assertion that the Real Nature possesses intuitive wisdom and spontaneous compassion.) However, the energies of our bodies that we inherit from our human parents obscure and hinder this potential. Fortunately, the mind that is kept clear and pure can have a transforming influence on the body and its *qi*. When the *qi* has thus been transformed and harmonized with the spirit, virtuous action will come about without hindrance.

This relationship between spirit (mind) and *qi* (body) and the transforming influence that a stable mind can have on one's *qi* was apparently also described by Wang Zhe in a reply to a question from Ma Yu:

> [Ma Yu] asked, "What are the Passage of Heaven and Pivot of Earth? How does one get them to guard each other?"
>
> [Wang Zhe (?)] answered, "The Passage of Heaven and the Pivot of Earth refer to the two words 'spirit' and '*qi*.' You should simply remain unattached and undefiled. If the mind is stable, the *qi* will be stable. If the mind moves, the *qi* will scatter. If the mind is motionless, the child and mother will guard each other."[41]

Elsewhere, Wang Zhe employs the child and mother metaphor as follows:

> When the *qi* and spirit bind together, this is what is called a Divine Immortal. The commentary to the *Yinfu jing* says, "The spirit is the child of *qi*, and *qi* is the mother of the spirit." When the child and mother meet each other, you can become a divine immortal.[42]

So why is the spirit the child and the *qi* the mother? What does the metaphor mean? Apparently the answer can be found by tracking down the passage that he quotes here. The passage he probably had in mind is found in the *Yinfu jing* commentary by Tang Chun, the Taoist of Jinling (Jinling Daoren). This seems to have been the preferred *Yinfu jing* commentary of the Quanzhen School.[43] The passage in question reads as follows:

> When the spirit is in the [Lower] Elixir Field (behind the navel), *qi* enwraps it and forms the womb. If the true *qi* does not scatter, divine radiance will naturally arrive. Thus spirit and *qi* guard each other; is this not the way to immortality? The spirit is the child of *qi*, and *qi* is the mother of the spirit.[44]

The *qi* is the "mother" because it enwraps the spirit and forms an embryo in which the spirit matures and acquires a "divine radiance." For this to happen, however, the spirit needs to be in the Lower Elixir Field located in the lower abdomen beneath the navel. What exactly does this mean? It means that one should concentrate one's mind on that special space in the belly, and in doing so, the spirit-child enters the belly and resides in the *qi* womb. This practice also is described in *Chongyang zhenren jinguan yusuo jue*, a text attributed to Wang Zhe:

> With your mind think of your spirit residing lengthily in your [Lower] Elixir Field, embracing and guarding the primal *qi*, without letting it get scattered and lost. This is the Method of Embracing the One.[45]

For a more thorough description of the method, we can turn to the words of Realized Man Jin, whose influence on the Quanzhen masters was undoubtedly great.[46]

> The study of the Tao from its origins has three [stages].
>
> [Stage] one: Concentrate your whole mind on the inside of the Cave of the Immortals in your Lower Elixir Field (located below the navel). Do not let your mind and will become scattered and disorderly. Embrace your primal *yang* Real *qi*. This is what is basic to the true way of long life. It is the way of escaping death and entering into life. It is the immortals' furnace for carrying out the creations of *yin* and *yang*. Inside this Elixir Field, clarify your mind and stabilize your will. Darkly and silently, constantly without ceasing, diligently maintain this for three to five years. Naturally within the crucible of the elixir furnace, the two energies (spirit and *qi*) will converge with each other, warmly becoming a single energy. [Further] worked upon, this becomes a soul of vacuous non-being. The womb's

immortal completes its vessel. The spirit in the heart naturally becomes numinous, jumping in joy, dancing and singing all by itself. The fact is that when the spirit acquires the *qi*, it becomes numinous. When the *qi* acquires the spirit, it becomes clean. The *Yinfu jing* states, "Holy merit arises from this. Divine light emerges from this." *Qi* is the mother of spirit. Spirit is the child of *qi*. Always make the child and mother guard each other without separating. Naturally, after many days, the spirit will become stable, and the way of immortality will be accomplished.

[Stage] two: Once this has been attained, let go of your four great elements (or limbs?)[47] [of your body] without restraining them. Cultivate yourself casually. Naturally, in the *qi* of the Tao, amid purity and clarity, the spirit ascends to the Upper Palace. Always do what is before your eyes, without ever turning to look back.

[Stage] three: Once you have attained the stability of spirit and harmony of *qi*, you should thus pass your years [allotted] by heaven. Let go your mind in casual abandon. Wander carefree at your will. Be pure and serene without affairs. Hereby the Great Tao Without Limits is accomplished. Clear and pure to the utmost, some day your merit will be accomplished, and your deeds will reach fulfillment.[48]

The important question that remains is how this visualization technique fit into the overall Quanzhen regimen of mental discipline. It would appear to be indeed a very useful technique for stilling and concentrating the mind and for disengaging the senses from outer stimuli. The typical Quanzhen adept in the intensified phase of his or her career perhaps spent a great deal of time on a specific simple meditation technique such as this. However, one probably would not use such a technique exclusively, since one also needed to make time for self-reflection and repentance. One can perhaps also surmise that such a visualization technique was used primarily or exclusively during seated meditation. Although, as we have seen, meditation was supposed to take place even when standing, walking, or lying down, one would surmise that simple mindfulness and self-vigilance could be made to suffice when one is in a more active mode. Perhaps most noteworthy here is that after the intense visualization of the Lower Elixir Field has been carried out for three to five years, spirit and *qi* will be blended and reconciled to the point where no more effort is necessary. A state of mental clarity and purity naturally prevails, and one does fine simply by acting freely according to one's will. Everything becomes easy once spirit and *qi* have been fully merged through years of sustained discipline. Wang Zhe also described this state as follows, in more abstract terms:

> Your [Real] Nature is spirit. Your Life is *qi*. When Nature meets Life it is like a bird that gets a [gust of] wind. It wafts up lightly, accomplishing its task with decreased effort. [When] the *Yinfu jing* says "the control of the bird is in the *qi* (or air)," this is [what it means to say].[49]

## Conclusion

The Quanzhen masters taught and practiced a path of self-cultivation that was simple yet strenuous. It consisted of keeping the mind clear and pure while carrying out virtuous acts of humility and compassion.

The path was strenuous because it is by no means easy to keep the mind clear and pure at all times. As much as one might intend to act virtuously, it indeed requires much self-discipline to act on one's good intentions. This is in large part due to the body and its *qi*, the desires and impulses of which too often obscure or contradict the good inclinations of one's Real Nature. Constant mindfulness and self-vigilance were considered essential, as was ascetic physical discipline—especially the controlling and limiting of one's food intake and hours of sleep (this point will be further examined in the next chapter).

Ultimately, though, the strenuous path would become easy. This would essentially be because one's Real Nature, which is innately wise and compassionate, emerges from obscurity to govern one's inner and outer life. Furthermore, the bodily *qi*, which had previously undermined and contradicted the noble impulses of the spirit, now is subdued by the spirit and fuses with it. Mind and body are in perfect harmony. The state of inner clarity and purity prevails, and all of one's actions follow one's intuitive wisdom and spontaneous compassion.

# Chapter 3

## The Asceticism of the Quanzhen Masters

"Ode on Laziness"
Ridiculing my own laziness I go by the [ironic] title, "the diligent."
In my dreams, with my brush, I record my good causes.
In returning the greetings of other people, how can I open my mouth?
Though I see food and feel hunger, I do not move my lips.
A paper cloak and hemp robe always clothe my body.
With messy hair and grimy face I am perpetually in complete Reality.[1]

[Set to the tune of] "Night Wandering Palace" (Yeyou gong)
My body resides deep in the mountains.
I stroll among the green peaks,
Randomly at my own will.
When cold, I wear a grass robe.
When tired, I go to sleep.
When hunger comes, I eat pine [seeds (?)].
When thirsty, I drink green water (stream water).

When I thoroughly nurture my spirit and *qi*,
I naturally no longer feel cold, get hungry, nor sleep.
I attain to the state of carefree wandering, the ground of clarity and purity.
I enjoy true serenity,
And enter into the red mist and yellow-green fog.[2]

In the above two poems, Wang Zhe describes his austere, unworldly lifestyle. The first poem describes his life of vagrancy and mendicancy amidst town and village folk. Wang Zhe makes no apology for the fact that he is lazy (a "bum," so to speak)—too lazy to hold a worldly occupation and practically too lazy even to bother to talk or eat. But despite his slothful comportment and squalid appearance, Wang Zhe is happy and content in his conviction that he is thus recovering his immortal Real Nature. The second poem describes the life of wilderness seclusion, where the barest of sustenance is drawn from nature. This life, Wang Zhe maintains, is blissfully serene and carefree. Furthermore, once mind and body are sufficiently cultivated, one becomes invulnerable to coldness, hunger, and fatigue—or so Wang Zhe claims.

One of the most prominent traits of the early Quanzhen School was its asceticism. Hagiographic sources and personal testimonies indicate that all of the early Quanzhen masters lived austere lives and underwent periods of intense self-denial. Throughout their lives they followed the ideal of "pure poverty" (*qingpin*) and relied on begging as their primary means of sustenance. Wang Zhe trained his disciples with the strictest of methods, and after his death, his disciples imposed various severe methods of discipline on themselves, such as self-confinement, wilderness seclusion, fasting, and sleep deprivation.

A good example of what is meant by "pure poverty" can be seen in the following descriptions of the lifestyle of Ma Yu, found in *Danyang zhenren yulu* (Record of Sayings of Realized Man Danyang [Ma Yu]):

> The master resided in a hut furnished only with a desk, a long couch, a brush, an ink tablet, and a sheepskin. It was empty without any extraneous objects. In the early morning he ate one small bowl of rice gruel and at noon ate one large bowl of noodles. Beyond this, never did fruits or spicy vegetables go through his mouth.[3]
>
> [Cao Zhen and Lai Lingyu (Ma Yu's disciples) said,] "The Master-Father wore only a single cloth garment in summer and winter. He was lazy about clothing and feeding himself, making what was meager suffice. In the snow and cold at the height of winter he had no fire in his hut, resolving to live in such a way for ten years. If he had not had the *qi* of the Tao in his belly, how could he have sustained himself [like this]?"[4]

In the same text, Ma himself discusses the importance of maintaining this simple lifestyle:

> A person of the Tao must not dislike being poor. Poverty is the foundation of nurturing life. If hungry, eat one bowl of rice gruel. If you

> become sleepy, spread out a grass mat. Pass the days and nights in tattered garments. Such is truly the lifestyle of a person of the Tao. Therefore you must understand that the single matter of purity and clarity cannot be acquired by the wealthy.[5]

By saying "poverty is the foundation of nurturing life," Ma Yu is implying that his lifestyle of poverty not only helps erase the desires and attachments that hinder spiritual progress, but that it is conducive to better health. (These two benefits were in fact completely interrelated in the Quanzhen view of things, as shall become particularly apparent in chapter 4.) Ma Yu's disciples, Cao Zhen and Lai Lingyu, furthermore claim that their master could withstand extreme cold because of his special physiology ("*qi* of the Tao in his belly"), acquired through his years of training. Further evidence in Ma Yu's poetry indicates that he vowed to himself not only to avoid using fire in the winter but also to not drink cold water in the summer. It also appears that he did not provide any light for himself during the night:

> "Vowing unto death to go barefoot, drink no [cold] water in the summer, and not face fire in the winter"
> I now vow unto death in my hut.
> I shall cut myself off from the cool stream in the summer,
> And shun the red [flame] and smoke in the winter.
> Thus I shall properly confirm the connection of water and fire in the elixir hearth.
> Wishing to repay my master's kindness, I diligently cultivate [myself].
> Refining the mercury and boiling the lead,
> My deeds are fulfilled and my merit is complete.
> I [thus] become a barefooted immortal of Peng[lai] and Ying[zhou] (two islands where immortals dwell).[6,7]

> "Living in the Hut"
> Even though I have no fire in the winter, I embrace the primal *yang* [*qi*].
> In summer I cut myself off from the clear spring water, but I drink the jade juice.
> Wax candles I do not burn, but I make bright the candle of my [Real] Nature.
> Garoo wood incense I have no use for, since I can burn my heart's incense (sincerity of will and devotion).

Three years barefoot, my vow of three years.
My one aspiration is toward the blue skies, and this one aspiration grows.
The mountain fool who keeps mourning is in his hut.
He still has done nothing to repay the Lunatic Wang [Zhe].[8]

In both poems, Ma Yu suggests that what he has deprived himself of externally (fire, water, heat, light, etc.), he can compensate for internally with the breaths, energies, and fluids that he nurtures and mobilizes during his intense *neidan* meditation regimen. The "connection of water and fire" most likely refers to the harmonizing of spirit and *qi* that results from proper training. In the cold of winter, Ma Yu's body sufficiently generates its own heat (primal *yang*). Though he drinks no cold water in the summer, he refreshes himself by drinking the fluids that plentifully well up in his mouth (jade juice). Though he lights no candle in his hut, he has no trouble seeing his radiant Real Nature within.

In both of the poems, Ma Yu speaks of how he is trying to repay the kindness of his master, Wang Zhe, and in the latter of the two poems, he expresses his intention to maintain this way of life diligently for three years. It would thus appear that the two poems, or at least the latter one, were written during Ma Yu's three years of mourning beside the grave of the deceased Wang Zhe. However, Ma Yu actually seems to have lived more or less in this manner for the remainder of his life. On at least two occasions, he is known to have confined himself in his tiny, meager hut for a designated period of 100 days.[9] This, as we have seen (see chapter 1), had previously been done by Wang Zhe, when he was in the process of trying to make Ma Yu and Sun Bu'er his disciples. (Also of note here would be Wang Zhe's two and a half years of secluded meditation in the "Grave of the Living Dead Man" at Nanshi Village.) Another source of inspiration for this practice may have been the aforementioned Liu Biangong (see chapter 1).

Whatever the case, the 100-day self-confinement in the hut (*huandu*) would be widely emulated by Ma Yu's many disciples, who in turn promoted the practice within Quanzhen monastic circles throughout the regions of Shaanxi, Henan, Shanxi, and Gansu. By the thirteenth century, it became common to find large Quanzhen monastery compounds dotted with such huts. (The development and spread of the 100-day *huandu* meditation within the Quanzhen School have been masterfully discussed by Vincent Goossaert.)[10] The elusive question concerns the specific meditative technique that was employed during the 100-day confinement period. A designated period seems to imply a specific technique that purports to bring about some specific desired effect in 100 days. Whether or not the technique entailed much more than simply emptying the mind and concentrating on the Lower Elixir Field beneath the navel is unclear. Some of the psychic and physical effects that were thought to occur over the lengthy course of solitary meditation will be examined in chapter 5.

Liu Chuxuan, in explaining why his school laid such importance on maintaining an ascetic lifestyle, pointed to the fact that the sagely men of past times were ascetics:

> Accomplished men of old, wanting to distance themselves from the dreams and mirages (the impermanent and illusory world), took on the outer appearances of fools. The Confucian Yan Hui (Confucius' favorite disciple) was pure and poor and [owned only] a rice bucket and a drinking gourd. The Buddhist Shakya[muni] (the historical Buddha) begged for food and took one meal [per day] by [begging from] seven [different] households. The Taoist Lü Chunyang (Lü Yan) was non-active. He lived like a quail (had no permanent home) and ate like a baby bird (ate only what was given to him without complaint).[11]

As paragons of the austere life, Liu Chuxuan points to outstanding figures from each of the Three Teachings. As we saw previously, Wang Zhe asserted the ultimate unity of the Three Teachings on the basis that they all conduce to inner peace and moral action. Here Liu Chuxuan asserts that they also share the austere life as a common ideal.

Quanzhen monks engaged in begging as their primary remunerative activity. For a newly initiated monk, begging was a humiliating activity. In *Danyang zhenren yulu*, Ma Yu points to the famous immortal, Liu Cao, as an admirable example of one who had overcome all greed and pride to live the life of a beggar:

> Sir Haichan (Liu Cao) was originally a minister of the land of Yan.[12] One morning he realized the Tao. Thereby he cut off his family connections. His poetry includes the words "I abandoned and left the 3,000 people of my household fires (domestic life and its attachments). I abandoned my personal troops which numbered one million." After this he supported his livelihood by begging. Wherever he came to an open area he put on a playful performance (acted in an eccentric manner when in the presence of other people?). He got to the point where he would go into brothels carrying barrels of liquor. He did not feel any embarrassment.[13]

Liu Cao, we are told, abandoned his great wealth and status to pursue the life of a beggar. He also acted like an insane person and associated unashamedly with the more unsavory elements of society; he was entirely free of vanity.

In the same spirit, Wang Zhe sometimes dressed up in funny outfits when he went out begging, and at times he made his disciples dress similarly; all of this was apparently for the purpose of maximizing the humiliation. *Chongyang quanzhen ji* tells us of an incident where Wang Zhe dressed up like a funny village youth (*bange*) and attached to his back a piece of paper bearing a poem coaxing Ma Yu to join him.[14] On a later occasion—after Ma Yu had become a disciple—Wang Zhe subjected Ma Yu to a similar embarrassment:

> When we returned to my home village and went to the streets [to beg] for the first time, the Patriarch Master (Wang Zhe) had us wear our hair in small horns (*xiaojiao'er*; a common hairstyle for small children) and put rouge on [our faces]. I thought to myself, "I don't care if children and friends see me; I only fear running into one of my relatives." While thinking thus, I arrived at the house of Fan Mingshi, and was about to take a short rest. [There] I saw my sister's father-in-law, who was in the house before [I got there]. I said to myself, "This time I should put a cease to being ashamed."[15]

Ma Yu—who had enjoyed much wealth and prestige prior to his conversion—understandably struggled with his vanity in his early days as a disciple, particularly when training in proximity to his family and acquaintances. On at least one occasion, this vanity provoked the violent wrath of Wang Zhe:

> The Patriarch-Master (Wang Zhe) one time ordered his disciples to go to Ninghai and beg for grain, coins, and rice. I (Ma Yu) wanted to have another disciple go for me [and thus said], "Make another older or younger brother [of mine] (fellow disciple) go." Later, [the Patriarch-Master asked me], "Why [do you want me to do that]?" [I answered,] "I, your disciple wish to not have to return to my home village [as a beggar]." The Patriarch-Master became furious and beat me continuously until dawn. Because of the many blows that I received, I had a regressing heart and I left him. But Master-Brother Qiu [Chuji] urged me into staying. Till this day, neither of us has forgotten [this incident].[16]

Wang Zhe's vehement reaction reflects how strongly he deplored vanity in his disciples. The same source records one other occasion where Wang Zhe pummeled his favorite disciple. On that occasion, Ma Yu's transgression involved greed:

> I picked up a donkey contract (*luqi*; a certificate of ownership of a donkey?) off the street. The Patriarch Master beat me continuously until dawn. Some scars were left on my head and face.[17]

While there is no evidence that Ma Yu himself was ever given to this kind of violent outburst, he also would have to cope with monks who were reluctant to beg, as is apparent from the following episode recorded in *Dongxuan jinyu ji*:

> Mr. Shi of Liquan (in Shaanxi) came to see me at the tea room by the eastern gate. I asked him what his name was. He said, "I am the Crazy Man Shi. I am also a disciple of the school of Realized Man Chongyang (Wang Zhe)."
>
> I had already sensed that this man was afraid of going into the streets and begging. Therefore I took him around with me. I wanted to share a round of drinks with this wise man. The master [of the saloon] hesitated to serve us (perhaps because of their appearance). Mr. Shi took some money out from his bosom. I said, "Do not use this money. You must go into the streets and beg for the money to buy the liquor." Mr. Shi stared [at me] and after a while finally went into the streets to beg. He returned with some liquor. I drank it [all] by myself.[18]

Thus whether through violence or by skillful means, a master had to somehow bring his disciple to vanquish his pride and beg.

This lifestyle of "pure poverty" supported by begging had to be maintained throughout one's life. However, the highest perfection sought by the Quanzhen masters involved even more. At times one had to toil and suffer in ways that exceeded normal human capacities. The word "suffering" is discussed as follows by Liu Chuxuan:

> To suffer means to suffer with the mind and body. The confused people of the world make themselves suffer by coveting life and entering into the road of death. Straining their minds they use their cleverness, and thus their [Real] Nature sinks into the land of punishments. One who understands the Tao makes himself suffer by training his body. In other words, it is like shattering a rock to take out a piece of jade. Straining his will power he forgets cleverness and therefore his [Real] Nature ascends the Nine Skies. The wise find enjoyment in the midst of suffering. The foolish suffer in the midst of enjoyment. For the wise, bitterness ends and sweetness arrives. For the foolish, enjoyment climaxes and then they are sad. A scripture

> (*Yinfu jing*) says, "Blessings are born from difficulties, and difficulties are born from blessings."[19]

Here Liu Chuxuan encourages the reader to renounce worldly benefits and pleasures in favor of the bitter, strenuous path that leads to eternal life. Only by tasting the bitterness can the true sweetness be savored. The metaphor of "shattering rock to obtain jade" can perhaps be interpreted simultaneously in two ways. To obtain what is truly valuable (immortality), one must engage in heavy labor (shattering rock). Also, in order to recover the Real Nature/ Radiant Spirit (jade) from the mortal body (rock), the latter must suffer through harsh training (be shattered).

The quest for immortality, as we have seen (chapter 2), was understood as an accumulation of "merit" and "deeds." In the following sermon, Qiu Chuji encourages strenuous, unrelenting effort in his disciples, based on the principle of accumulating merit and deeds:

> Generally speaking, in cultivating Reality and cherishing the Tao, you must rely on the accumulation of deeds and the stringing together of merit. If you do not strain your will power and have a determined heart, it is difficult to transcend ordinariness and enter into sacredness. To use your strength to perform a great amount of tiresome labor for the religion, to resolutely engage in merit (training methods), to completely abandon worldly affairs, to do nothing other than overcoming your self-consciousness and focussing your mind on the Tao, all of these things form the basis of bringing about blessings. However, the Tao envelops Heaven and Earth, and its greatness is hard to measure. Slight goodness and slight merit cannot bring results immediately. Therefore, it is said that the enlightenment of the Tao that takes place in an instant must result from training that spans over long *kalpas*.
>
> The sudden enlightenment of the single mind must rely on thorough cultivation and myriad deeds.
>
> The enlightenment of the Tao that takes place in this life is a result of one's having had merit during previous lives. Yet not knowing of the causes from past incarnations and seeing that they have toiled for years without success, [people nowadays] regard [self-cultivation] as hard labor that is but a hoax.
>
> Thus they give rise to laziness. What a shame! What they especially fail to understand is that even though their minds are reflecting upon the Tao within all activities, their mind's ground has not yet been opened up. As time elapses, everybody has one's accumulation

> of hidden merit. When one's merit is insufficient, then [one's unity with] the Tao is incomplete.
>
> Even if you have not yet acquired the Tao, if your roots of goodness are deep and solid, support from a holy sage will come to you in this life or the next. One who has no roots of destiny is far [from salvation] indeed! I only regret that the minds of people become regressing and lazy and that therefore the holy sages are unable to deliver and release them. If you do not backslide during this life, the next life or over the span of many lives, salvation [by the hands of a holy sage] will arrive suddenly, and you will accomplish and master [the Tao].
>
> I did not have bones of destiny (a significant amount of merit and deeds accumulated from past lives). [Thus] even though I have met an insightful master (Wang Zhe), I have not yet completed [my self-cultivation], [even though I have undergone] 10,000 sufferings and 1,000 harsh experiences. Danyang (Ma Yu) and Changzhen (Tan Chuduan) were predestined, and thus were able to rise and fly beyond the heavens at will after ten or five years. Even though I have not yet completed [my training], the difficulties that I have undergone surpass those of ordinary people.[20]

Here one might see a tinge of fatalism. Qiu Chuji says clearly that some people are destined to gain immortality during this lifetime, while others are not. Also, his words reflect a sense of reliance upon divine beings for one's ultimate salvation. Such fatalism and hope for divine intervention might conceivably undermine the impulse toward ascetic personal effort. But quite to the contrary, Qiu Chuji effectively uses these notions to enhance his exhortation toward relentless personal effort. Because the so-called "bones of destiny" are acquired through one's actions in past lives, Qiu Chuji maintains that it is essential to work hard and maintain one's faith in the Tao, even if this only serves to build a foundation for the ultimate salvation in some future incarnation. Although the aid and intervention of an immortal ("a holy sage"; this theme will be discussed further in chapter 5) is deemed a necessary step, Qiu Chuji reminds his students that this will not occur unless the aspirant has acquired the appropriate amount of merit and deeds.

The principle of accumulating merits and deeds also is demonstrated by Yin Zhiping in his narration of the following episode concerning Qiu Chuji's tutelage under Wang Zhe:

> In the days when the Patriarch-Master (Wang Zhe) was on Mt. Kunyu, the Master-Father Changchun (Qiu Chuji) had already been his disciple for three years and was 23 *sui* old. Because Master-

Father Danyang (Ma Yu) had an extremely great amount of merit and deeds from past lives, the Patriarch-Master always spoke to him about the profound wonders. But because Master-Father Changchun was still lacking in merit and deeds, he made him perform mundane labor without allowing him to rest for even a moment. One day, while the Patriarch-Master was discussing a method of breath control with Danyang behind closed doors,[21] the Master-Father eavesdropped from outside. After a while, he pushed the door open and entered, and [Wang Zhe and Ma Yu] immediately ended their discussion. The Master-Father thought about this and decided that breath control is marvelous, and that the arduous labor that he was doing contradicted it completely. Thus after this, whenever he could find time, he defiantly practiced the method that he had overheard.

The time of return (death) of the Patriarch-Master was imminent. Therefore, during the three years [that Qiu Chuji trained under him], he trained the four masters (Ma Yu, Qiu Chuji, Tan Chuduan, and Liu Chuxuan) with ever-increasing harshness. The work of each day was equivalent to that of hundreds and thousands of days in the past. As the seasons changed, his demands became more and more unreasonable, and nothing could gain his approval. Nothing they said or did ever went without blame and reprimand. The Master-Father silently thought to himself, "Since the time I began to follow the Master, I have been unable to understand what the Tao is. Everything that he has taught me (or made me do) has had nothing to do with anything." He had his doubts and wanted to question [Wang Zhe] about them but was afraid of the harshness of the Patriarch-Master. He wanted to obediently practice what he had been told, but his desire to seek the Tao was urgent, and he could not stabilize his will. Thus when his frustration came to a climax, he gathered up the courage to ask. The Patriarch-Master answered, "It is upon your [Real] Nature," and said nothing more. The Master-Father did not dare to ask anything more. Later, when the Patriarch-Master was on the verge of his death in the middle of the *la* month (the twelfth month), the four masters had gathered some money through begging. [Wang Zhe] made them buy some firewood and build a large fire in the room in which he was sleeping. The room was very small. He made Danyang and Changzhen (Tan Chuduan) stand inside the room. The heat was unbearable. He made Changsheng (Liu Chuxuan) and Changchun stand outside. The coldness was unbearable. He did not allow those inside to go outside and those outside to come inside. After a long time, Master-Father

> Changsheng could not stand the suffering any longer and thus ran away.
>
> On the fourth day of the first month, the Patriarch-Master was about to ascend [to immortality] (pass away), and the three masters stood by his bed. The Patriarch-Master said, "Danyang has already acquired the Tao, Changzhen already understands the Tao, and I have nothing to worry about [regarding them]. Changsheng and Changchun have not yet [acquired the Tao]. Changchun in studying should listen to Danyang's orders. Changzhen should look after Changsheng." He then said to Changchun, "You have committed one great sin which you must get rid of. In the past you thought to yourself that everything that you had been taught had nothing to do with anything. You never understood that that which has nothing to do with anything is the Tao."[22]

We can see from how Wang Zhe trained his disciples that one's method of training varied accordingly with one's store of merit and deeds. Wang Zhe somehow deemed Ma Yu far superior in his store of merit and deeds accumulated in past and present lifetimes[23] and as a result transmitted special breathing methods to him alone. Qiu Chuji had to enhance his store of merit by performing menial chores while maintaining a clear and pure mind. The ineffable Reality (the Tao) and its apprehension cannot be reduced to a verbal explanation or any specific technique. It is best to seek the Reality within one's own mind that has been thus kept pure and clear. Qiu Chuji's eagerness to be taught it was, ironically, hindering his progress.

One hagiography[24] further tells us that during the few days before his death, Wang Zhe subjected his top disciple, Ma Yu, to a very strange torture. One day he bought four carp at the market, brought them back to the inn, and boiled them in a pot of water together with two *jin* (approximately 1 kg.) of mutton.[25] He left the stew to sit and spoil for over a month. He then brought the stew out before all of his disciples and followers and ordered them to eat it. Everybody refused, on the grounds that they were obeying the precept against the eating of meat and fish. Ma Yu alone complied by saying, "If the master tells him to eat, the disciple must eat it." Wang Zhe rebuked him by saying, "Just because you are unable to abstain [from meat and fish], you lay the blame on me!" Wang Zhe then forced him to eat a whole bowl of the hideous stew and further proclaimed, "When you get to the west of the pass (Shaanxi), there will be none of this available; I give you this to eat." For the next several days, Wang Zhe made Ma Yu eat the stew for breakfast, after which he would send him off to the market to buy liquor and steamed honey-jujube treats, which Wang Zhe himself indulged in. He would then ask Ma Yu, "Can you get it?" Ma Yu failed to understand, and Wang Zhe would become even stricter. Night and day he flogged and berated Ma Yu, at the same time reassuring him, "Some day you will understand." Ma Yu would reply, "I receive your benevolent teaching, but have no way of repaying you." Wang Zhe would in return reply, "You can repay me simply through your training."

While Wang Zhe's actions were abusive, arbitrary, and nonsensical, Ma Yu humbly complied without giving rise to despair, resentment, and anger. (Wang Zhe's antics and enigmatic statements—it should be noted—bear some resemblance to the didactic ploys of Chan masters.) If the anecdote is true, then Wang Zhe's confidence in his chosen successor must have been greatly enhanced. Few people possessed Ma Yu's humble endurance. Another source indicates that it was indeed Wang Zhe's harshness that made his inner circle of disciples such a small, exclusive group:

> Because he frequently manifested his divine extraordinariness (performed miracles), people of the east (Shandong) all followed him. He cleaned off and parceled out the earnest ones and cut off the pretenders. Hundreds of times he whipped them, and angrily insulted them. The unworthy fled.[26]

After the death of Wang Zhe, it was up to the disciples to severely discipline themselves. Some of their ascetic feats are described as follows in the hagiographies:

> The teacher (Liu Chuxuan) hid his traces in Luojing (Luoyang) and refined his nature in the midst of the intermingling of the dust. He nurtured his simplicity amidst the clamor of the shops and market places. [Sounds of] wind and string instruments did not disturb his inner harmony. Beautiful sights did not arouse his essence. His mind was like ashes, and because of this he regarded coldness as a benefit. His body was like a tree, and therefore did not act in lewd ways. If people gave him food, he would eat. But if not, he showed no traces of resentment. If someone asked him something, he would answer with hand gestures.[27]

> After mourning [Wang Zhe's death] in a graveside hut for two years, [Qiu Chuji] entered the Panxi Gorge in the fall of the *jiawu* year (1174). He lived in a cave and begged for one meal per day, going about wearing a grass mantle. People called him "Mr. Grass Mantle." For six years he went day and night without sleeping. After this he hid himself in Mt. Longmen in Longzhou (in northwestern Shaanxi) and performed acts of suffering as he did in Panxi.[28]

After this, [Wang Chuyi] went back and forth between Deng[zhou] and Ning[hai] (both located on the north coast of the Shandong Peninsula). At night he would return to the Cloud Radiance Grotto (a grotto located on Mt. Cha) where he stood at the entrance on one foot facing the great sea on the east for nine years, not once falling asleep. People called him "Mr. Iron Leg." Realized Man Qiu [Chuji] praised him, saying, "In the summer he stood facing the sun. In the winter he slept embracing the snow." He trained his body like this for nine years and entered into the great marvelousness.[29]

The teacher (Hao Datong) roamed about Hebei. In the *yiwei* year (1175) he was begging in Wozhou when he suddenly understood the secret words of Chongyang (Wang Zhe). [His insight] widely opened up. Consequently he went to a bridge and sat silently and motionlessly upon it. When he got hungry or thirsty he did not seek [food or drink]. Amidst coldness or heat he did not change his attire. If people gave him food, he ate. If they did not give him food, he would not [eat]. Even when there were people who insulted and ridiculed him, he did not get angry. His will was [concentrated] on forgetting his body. He was like this for three years. People called him "Mr. Speechless."

One evening when the sky was dark, a drunkard accidentally kicked the teacher while crossing the bridge, knocking him down under the bridge. [Hao Datong] said nothing and did not come out from under the bridge for seven days. People did not know what had happened and thus wondered where the teacher was. It suddenly happened that when a travelling official was trying to cross the bridge on horseback, the horse became startled and started to buck and would not advance even when whipped. The traveler got off his horse and asked [people] left and right, "There must be something strange under the bridge. If not, why is my horse frightened?" He ordered [people] right and left to go and look [under the bridge]. They found a Taoist (Hao Datong) sitting properly (upright in a meditative position) in a relaxed manner. When they questioned him he speechlessly wrote on the ground with his hand, "I have not eaten for seven days." The commoners of the district heard of this and hurried forth to offer him food, burn incense, and beg him to come out [from under the bridge]. But he only waved his hand and refused. He just sat under the bridge for three more years. Water and fire overturned, *yin* and *yang* came together, and the Merit of Nine Cycles was completed.[30]

> For months, [Sun Bu'er] slept lying in the snow. Frostbite damaged her appearance, but she did not regard it as suffering.[31]

One can see that while all of the disciples trained very rigorously (exaggerated though the accounts may well be), the methods and environments they chose varied. This was probably due to their understanding that they each differed in their store of merit and deeds. It also is perhaps natural and appropriate that the youngest disciples took the harshest ordeals upon themselves; they probably possessed more stamina and were perceived (by self and colleagues alike) to be deficient in their merit and deeds.

How did they gauge their progress in their respective ascetic regimens? For a large part, the object was to maintain an "unwavering heart" (*budong xin*) in all situations. The lives of the Quanzhen masters were filled with trying circumstances that had to be faced with an "unwavering heart." If they failed to do so, it served as proof of their unworthiness. Tan Chuduan engaged in essentially the same training methods as Liu Chuxuan, begging in the streets of Erzu Town in Cizhou (in Henan) and exposing himself to all of the distractions and temptations while maintaining his composure in spite of them. The following incident was perhaps his greatest moral victory:

> A drunk man asked the master (Tan Chuduan), "Where do you come from?" Before he could answer, [the drunkard] suddenly punched [Tan Chuduan] in the mouth with his fist. His teeth were broken and blood was flowing, but with a very content expression he spat out his teeth into his hand and went off singing and dancing. People in the marketplace who saw this were furious. They made [Tan Chuduan] report this [incident] to an official. But all that the master said [to the official] was, "He was only drunk." At the time, Danyang (Ma Yu) was inside the Pass (Shaanxi). When he heard about this [incident] he praised [Tan Chuduan], saying, "[By receiving] a single blow, he has erased the karma of his entire lifetime!"[32]

In *Danyang zhenren yulu*, Ma Yu himself reminisces about a similar personal experience:

> The master said, "When I first came inside the Pass and was going about begging, I arrived at a saloon. There was a drunk man [at the saloon]. Amidst the insults [that he was saying to me], I received a punch from him. Thereupon I ran, but he dragged me back and punched me again. All I could do was take it and bear it. Have any of you ever met with this kind of demonic hazard?"
>
> A disciple answered, "No."

> The master said, "That's good. If you do encounter [such a situation], do not fight back."[33]

Life for a Quanzhen monk entailed "demonic hazards" that had to be met with equanimity. By living as beggars, the Quanzhen masters exposed themselves to frequent derision and abuse. Thus here we see virtually the same thing happening to both Tan Chuduan and Ma Yu, and Ma Yu warns his disciples that they may very well face the same situation.

While life among worldly people entailed many trials, the life of wilderness seclusion chosen by Qiu Chuji and Wang Chuyi also was full of difficulties. Yin Zhiping describes as follows the difficulties undergone by Qiu Chuji:

> My Master-Father, the Realized Man Changchun (Qiu Chuji), went about straining his will power and encountering evils. Fearing only that his merit was lacking, he went about carrying rocks on top of mountains in order to fight off his sleepiness. Only because he was yet lacking in good deeds was he unable to stabilize his mind. After this he encountered the evil of [near-] death twice. One time he purified his body (*jingshen*; castrated himself?) and almost died at his own hands. On another occasion, a flying rock hit him and broke three of his ribs and limbs. After this, he came close to death many more times. Demons of illness hit him and broke his arms three times. Amidst these demonic hazards, his heart did not waver. Throughout his life he strained his will power doing nothing but training himself.
>
> If people have determination, they will overcome the evils. If one has no determination, he will encounter no evils. [If such is the case one] should experience an evil in order to acquire one layer of good merit. [Each time you encounter an evil], you can enlighten your mind, and your [Real] Nature can become numinous.[34]

Qiu Chuji, we are told, deliberately exposed himself to life-threatening circumstances in order to create opportunities to accumulate merit. While some of the difficulties and dangers—such as the diseases and accidents—were caused by his natural surroundings, some of them were brought on entirely by his own zeal. He went to great pains to refrain from sleeping. (Today, at one of the two main sites where he trained, an interesting relic connected to this aspect of Qiu Chuji's training can be seen by visitors)[35]. As the reader may recall, Yin Zhiping recommended his disciples to limit their sleeping, because too much sleeping causes one to be lustful. In light of this, one wonders whether Qiu Chuji was having trouble subduing lustful passions (highly understandable for a young man) and hoped that eliminating sleep would eliminate lust. Our passage here appears to even say that he castrated himself—if he indeed did, then we can see how painfully (!) he struggled with his lust.[36]

Another life-threatening peril in the wilderness was wild animals, particularly tigers. Second-generation disciple Wang Zhijin (a disciple of Hao Datong and Qiu Chuji) tells us how Qiu Chuji dealt with this problem:

> In the past, when Realized Man Changchun (Qiu Chuji) was at the Panxi Gorge, there were always tigers and leopards coming and going at night. On this particular evening, as [tigers and leopards] went in and out, one of the people (who was there training together with Qiu Chuji) became horrified and in the morning wanted to build a wall (to keep the tigers out of the hut or grotto in which they were staying). [Qiu Chuji] thought to himself, "If one has a frightened heart and wants to guard and protect oneself in this kind of a situation, how can one hope to avoid life and death (*samsara*)?" Thereby he stopped [the building of] the wall and got rid of [the wall]. Firmly, with determination, he resigned himself to life and death (did not fear death). His fearful thoughts naturally no longer existed. Thus he got to where he was unwavering like a mountain amidst the surroundings of life and death. In a single moment he was emancipated from his various forms of attachment. This [is known as] "going to places which are difficult to go to."[37]

All fear, including even the fear of death itself, had to be overcome. Fear is a symptom of the ignorant state of mind that clings to the mortal flesh and all other impermanent things of the world. (We shall return to this point in chapter 7.)

Aside from the fear of life-threatening hazards of the mundane realm, a Quanzhen monk also had to conquer his fear of gods and demons. Apparently for Qiu Chuji, this type of fear was particularly difficult to conquer:

> [Qiu Chuji] himself said, "I am not scared by fierce tigers, but when I see a clay statue of a god slaying [evil spirits and/or sinners], I feel scared." Thus from time to time he went to look at it and sometimes stayed overnight in the shrine which housed that particular statue. It took him three years to overcome this fear.[38]

This fear of Qiu Chuji's—which may seem childish and irrational to some—reflects his deep, sincere belief in the spirit realm, as well as perhaps a deep-seated feeling of guilt and inadequacy. While such feelings may have the positive effect of inspiring piety and repentance, a fully realized Taoist master should ultimately be able to outgrow them. A Realized Man was supposed to not only possess eternal life (in the Real Nature/Radiant Spirit) but also wield dominance over spirits and demons (as we shall see in chapters 4 and 6).

To have a clear and pure mind meant to be in complete control of the body and its vital forces. A particularly traumatic and embarrassing failure for a Quanzhen monk was seminal emission, voluntary or involuntary. Such a mishap not only betrayed an impurity of mind but was also thought to bring detrimental effects to one's health (see chapter 4). The way in which a truly determined monk was to react to such personal setbacks was simple; more discipline, more suffering, and more hard work:

> Master-Father Changchun (Qiu Chuji) said, "Looking at all of the [other] masters, I realized that they were all superior to me in their countenances of blessing and wisdom. Finally I exerted my heart. After three years my ambition was to refine my mind to the point where it is like cold ashes. After ten years of aspiring, my mind was beyond control and could not be subdued. I myself realized that my merit was lacking. Again I increased in my determination. Wearing a pair of sandals I tied them and untied them over and over again at night and ran seventeen to eighteen laps in order to keep my Nature from getting darkened. After fifty days of doing this I had an unwavering mind. My perfected heart was like a crystal pagoda."
>
> One day, [Qiu Chuji] fell [asleep (?)] and gave rise to thoughts. The Master-Father wept and wailed. It was from this time that [he knew that] his merit was shallow. Later, when a military general in Chang'an summoned him to perform a *zhai* ritual,[39] he leaked [semen] three times during the night. The Master-Father himself realized that his merit was lacking and that he had been unable to accomplish the Tao. He experienced heavenly temptations and great temptations of the five emperors. Even when a flying rock broke three ribs and limbs, his heart did not waver. Later he reached the holy sages (the immortals took notice of his gallant efforts) and heard a human voice (of an immortal?) in the air say, "You will acquire the Tao on the 15th day of the second month."[40]

> Grand Master Yuyang (Wang Chuyi), from the time he was still living at home, did not know any erotic affairs. After leaving his home he never leaked [semen]. But later, one evening on Mt. Tiecha he suddenly had a leakage. He wailed and wept in extreme despair, and felt hungry. The [gods of] the various heavens thereupon spread about harmonious *qi*. Three days later he acquired his mind's ground. From then on he underwent a thousand rigors and a hundred

> ways of training. One time, he knelt in rocks and gravel until his knees became tattered to the bones. In mountains full of rough rocks and thorn bushes he went about with bare feet. This is why [people of] the world call him "Iron Legs." In three years his old *karma* disappeared.[41]

Qiu Chuji and Wang Chuyi, as they are portrayed in the above passages, epitomize the spirit of the Quanzhen School. They trained and punished themselves to the point where they could finally believe that they had attained Realization. For them, every day and every moment was a struggle to discipline their minds and bodies. By enduring their hardships, they proved to themselves and their believers that they were legitimate holy men. For Qiu Chuji, as we can see, affirmation came when he heard the voice of an immortal tell him that he would soon "acquire the Tao." Both men saw their involuntary seminal emissions as grave setbacks but did not relinquish their quest in the face of abject despair. The fact that Wang Chuyi felt hunger on such an occasion also is interesting, since it suggests a perceived (or an actual?) link between seminal retention and the capacity to survive on a limited diet.

The Quanzhen masters believed that in order to purify the mind, gain control of the body, erase bad karma, and accumulate merit, it was necessary to engage in extreme asceticism. As we saw in chapter 2, it was deemed essential to keep the mind (spirit) pure and clear, and that this required keeping the mind in harmony with, and in control of, the body (or its *qi*). No mediocre level of discipline could suffice in this effort; the corruptive influences in the world and in the body were considered far too numerous and formidable. Thus as we saw in this chapter, these attitudes translated into acts of rigorous self-denial. In the next two chapters, we will see in more detail how this severe asceticism was considered conducive to good physical health and mystical experience.

# Chapter 4

## Cultivating Health and Longevity

The womb is created, and the egg is moistened. [It] transforms and gives birth to a person.
If you are confused, how can you know the cause of your [incarnation into the] four provisional elements (*sijia*)?[1]
Truly this (body) is a ball of mud and a clod of dirt.
When gathered together, it becomes the body, and when it scatters, it becomes dust.[2]

Reincarnating in this world are many kinds of people.
Each are allotted their divine Nature, and each have their cause [for their present incarnation].
One hundred years is their greatest limit from the womb until death.
The five aggregates (*skandhas*)[3] will all return to the dust below the dust.[4]

In the above verses, Wang Zhe conveys a very disparaging view of the body. He points out that the body is but an impermanent conglomeration of "provisional" (impermanent and conditioned, lacking any inherent existence or self-nature) elements or aggregates that can stay intact for 100 years at the very most. People, all of whom partake in a higher, eternal Real Nature, are constantly being reincarnated into these "balls of mud" or "clods of dirt" for reasons that they are too ignorant to figure out.[5] (The Buddhistic tone of these verses is, of course, unmistakable.) When people ascend to enjoy eternal heavenly bliss, they do so without their fleshly bodies:

> [As for when I speak of] leaving the ordinary world, [I do not mean to say that] the body leaves. [In such cases I] speak of one's state of mind (lit. "mind's ground"). The body is like the lotus roots, and the mind is like the lotus flower. The roots are in the mud, while the flower is in empty space. As for people who have attained the Tao, their bodies are in the ordinary [world], but their minds are in the sacred realm. People nowadays who desire to be ever deathless and depart from the ordinary world are great fools who have not fathomed the Tao's principles.[6]

Thus it appears that in Wang Zhe's view, the human body could not ascend to the heavens, nor evade death. Equally noteworthy here is that in a spiritual sense, the enlightened adept already dwells in the heavens. The joy of heavenly immortality can be experienced now, and one need not await the death of the body and liberation of the Radiant Spirit. Elsewhere in Wang Zhe's writings, we can find statements such as the following:

> Amid stillness fathom the causes for the five agents (wood, fire, earth, metal, and water).
> Hereby you will be able to abandon the body [made of] the four provisional [elements] (earth, water, fire, and wind).
> Look back upon your original Real visage.
> Peacefully mounted upon the clouds is a single divine immortal.[7]

> Your original Real Nature is the golden elixir.
> The [body made of] the four provisional [elements] (earth, water, fire, and wind) is the furnace in which you concoct the pill.
> Without getting defiled (by impure thoughts) and without thinking, eliminate your delusions.
> Naturally [your Real Nature] will thrust out and enter the altar of the immortals.[8]

In these poems we see a clear contrast made between the Real Nature and the "provisional" body of flesh. Significantly, the immortal Real Nature is described by the adjective "original" (*benchu*, or *benlai*), meaning that it has existed eternally, prior to the formation of the mortal body. Through the cultivation of inner purity and serenity, one comes to enjoy and partake in an eternal life that one has unknowingly possessed all along.

However, can we thus conclude that the Quanzhen School was uninterested in bodily health and longevity? Were enlightenment and release from the cycle of rebirth regarded as strictly non-physical phenomena pertaining to the spirit? No, we cannot. Wang Zhe and his direct disciples were indeed interested in the makeup, functioning, and maintenance of the physical body, since it is—in Wang Zhe's own words—"the furnace in which you concoct the pill." Wang Zhe also wrote poems such as the following:

> "Sent to the younger brother of the military official who inquired about methods for ease and comfort (*anle*; good health)"
> If you want to seek ease and comfort [you should] receive good causes.
> You should detach your mind from grime and dust (worldly corruption).
> In loud places do not allow your *qi* to be encumbered and diminished.
> In stillness you should nourish and complete your spirit.
> Naturally you will recognize the excellence of the three lights.[9]
> Surely you will harmoniously penetrate the spring of four seasons.[10]
> The outer provisional [body] will be lustrous and bright, while the inner Real [Nature] enjoys itself.
> While ordinary people are unaware, you will have become a divine immortal.[11]

> "[Begging for Coins in Liquan] Fourth Poem"
> Matters of cultivation I shall set forth well in detail.
> On the outside [you should] practice the methods for ease and comfort of the four limbs (body).
> Inside [you should] observe the causes for the overturning of the five agents.
> Hereby you can attain complete Realization.[12]

Wang Zhe's attitude here seems to be that physical health (ease and comfort) can and ought to be attained by a Taoist practitioner. Wang Zhe appears to know methods and guidelines by which good health can be realized. While in the first poem he once again refers to the body as "provisional," he also seems to be saying that the body that gives repose to the immortal Real Nature is (or ought to be) a very healthy one.

The fact that the early Quanzhen masters did not take a morbidly disparaging view of the body is well reflected in an incident attested to in Ma Yu's poetry collection *Dongxuan jinyu ji*:

> Hermit Liu of Mouping District (in Shandong) wanted to burn his own body. Thus I wrote the following poem quickly in order to save his life:

Mr. Liu, listen to my exhortation.
Studying Buddha-hood and studying immortality,
Is to rely on one's knowledge and insight in order to cut off and abandon the mind's dust.
It is not to be accomplished by burning and abandoning the body.

Intricately cultivate, refine, and train the divine elixir.
Strive for the nine cycle completion of your merit and deeds.
Follow in the footsteps of Haichan, the brilliant Patriarch Liu [Cao].[13]

It is unclear who this Mr. Liu was—whether he was Buddhist or Taoist, and whether or not he was a disciple of Ma Yu. Somehow Mr. Liu had gotten it into his mind that he ought to burn himself to death. His motivation may have been related to the notion that the body is but fleeting and ought not be an object of attachment; such an idea may well have been taught to him by Ma Yu. However, in Ma Yu's mind, suicide was not a proper course of action. One reason perhaps is that the act of suicide and the despondent state of mind underlying it constitute harmful *karma*. However, another reason is that the process required for becoming a blessed Taoist immortal (like Liu Cao) involves the body as well as the mind.

Of course, information in the poetry collections regarding physiological theories and practices tends to be fragmented and difficult to comprehend. Much more complete and/or coherent discussions can be found in texts such as Wang Zhe's *Chongyang zhenren jinguan yusuo jue*, Ma Yu's *Danyang zhenren yulu*, Qiu Chuji's *Dadan zhizhi* and *Xuanfeng qinghui lu* (DT175/TT76; edited by Yuan official Yelu Chucai), and Liu Chuxuan's commentaries to the *Huangdi yinfu jing* and *Huangting neijing jing*.

It is important at this point to note that questions have been raised concerning the authorship of *Chongyang zhenren jinguan yusuo jue* and *Dadan zhizhi*—the two sources that will be cited most frequently in this chapter.[14] Neither text is mentioned in hagiographic sources. The fact that *Chongyang zhenren jinguan yusuo jue* deals so extensively with health and physiology—to a degree far surpassing Wang Zhe's other works—has brought forth speculation that it is a fabrication of some later period, or that it comes out of an early phase in Wang Zhe's ministry that preceded the development of his mature doctrine (the straightforward emphasis on clarity and purity of mind).[15] Yet in many ways its teachings are consistent with what one might expect to hear from Wang Zhe. *Chongyang zhenren jinguan yusuo jue* first and foremost extols inner purity and virtuous action, endorses a regimen of strict mind and body discipline, describes the body as "provisional" (yet nonetheless essential for cultivating what is "Real"), and extols the veracity and harmony of the Three

Teachings. While it speaks in unusual detail on matters pertaining to bodily fluids, internal organs, curing and preventing diseases, and the like, it also makes it clear that the mastery and application of such knowledge is but a preparatory—albeit an essential—complement to the recovery of the Real Nature. *Dadan zhizhi* appears to have been composed in its present form between 1269 and 1310—some four decades or more after Qiu Chuji died.[16] The question is whether or not—and to what extent—it truthfully conveys the utterances of Qiu Chuji. Interestingly, as we shall see in chapter 5, passages in another text contain quotes from Qiu Chuji that pertain to strange, marvelous mystical experiences of the kind vividly outlined in the *Dadan zhizhi*. We also shall see that evidence in the writings of other early Quanzhen masters reflects their belief in physiological theories and phenomena akin to what *Chongyang zhenren jinguan yusuo jue* and *Dadan zhizhi* describe. In sum, one cannot hastily reject these texts as spurious. We can at least say that our two suspect documents issue somehow from Quanzhen circles and can help shed light on the assumptions held by the early Quanzhen masters regarding the makeup, functioning, and maintenance of the human body. (The authors of *Chongyang zhenren jinguan yusuo jue* and *Dadan zhizhi* will hereon be tentatively referred to, respectively, as "Wang Zhe" and "Qiu Chuji".)

This chapter will discuss the early Quanzhen School's theories and methods pertaining to the body and its maintenance. The first part will summarize how the Quanzhen masters perceived the structure and mechanisms of the human anatomy. The second part will discuss what the Quanzhen masters considered the causes for disease and death. The third part will discuss the methods prescribed and used by the Quanzhen masters for combating and preventing diseases. Ultimately, as we shall see, mastery over the physical body—reflected in good health and a long life—had to complement and facilitate the recovery and liberation of the Real Nature/Radiant Spirit.

## The Anatomy

> Someone asked, "What is the marvelous principle of cultivating Reality?"
>
> ["Wang Zhe"] answered, saying, "First you must get rid of your nameless[17] confused thoughts. Secondly, give up coveting, attachments, liquor, sex, money, and anger. This is how to train yourself. A person's whole body completely has in it the principles of Heaven and Earth. Heaven and Earth contain and nourish the myriad things, and therefore the myriad things abound between Heaven and Earth. The highness, brightness, vastness, and greatness of Heaven and Earth have never been [completely] covered by the myriad objects. People

who train themselves, whenever responding to myriad affairs, must embody [this capacity of Heaven and Earth to encompass everything and yet not get overrun]."

[The questioner] doubted [and said], "Heaven (the sky) gets dark, Earth trembles, mountains crumble and erode, seas dry up, the sun and the moon wax and wane, and people have illness and impermanence (death). How can one cure this?"

["Wang Zhe"] answered, saying, "If you want to cure and get rid of these [difficulties], master the Most High [Laozi's] Method of refining the Five Agents."

[The questioner] asked, "What is this Method of the Five Agents?"

["Wang Zhe" said], "A lesson says that first you must uphold the precepts. Be pure and still, withstand humiliation, be merciful and compassionate, and practice goodness. Cut off and get rid of the ten evils (*shi'e*).[18] With skillful means, save and convert all living things. Be loyal to your ruler, and be filial to your father, mother, and [Taoist] teacher. This is the way to train yourself. After [doing all of the above], you can study true merit."[19]

This passage, which appears at the very beginning of *Chongyang zhenren jinguan yusuo jue*, conveys two basic notions regarding the body and its maintenance: (1) the body is a microcosm; and (2) the pursuit of health and longevity requires morality and mental discipline. Shortly later in the text, "Wang Zhe" reveals a detailed knowledge of the workings and maintenance of the microcosmic body. However, here he withholds such information and states that basic self-discipline and morality must precede the study and practice of any specific physiological theories or methods (which is what "true merit" [*zhen'gong*] seems to refer to here). That he should hold this view certainly makes sense since, as we shall see later, immorality and lack of self-discipline were considered principal causes for diseases. By living a moral, disciplined life, one already goes a long way toward gaining good health and a long life.

"Wang Zhe," after listing the essential prerequisites for learning life-nurturing methods, goes on to outline how the inside of the body functions:

A lesson says that *geng*, *jia*, *mao*, and *you* make up day and night.[20] *Jia* and *mao* are the *qi* of the liver. Among the eight seasonal transitions (*bajie*)[21] it [corresponds to] the beginning of spring. At the spring equinox inside the mouth it becomes *jin* saliva. *Geng* and *you* are the *qi* of the lungs. Among the eight seasonal transitions it [corresponds to] the beginning of fall. At the fall equinox inside the

> mouth it becomes *ye* saliva. *Kan* and *li* are coldness and heat.[22] The lead of *li* is the heart's *qi* inside the body.[23] Among the eight seasonal transitions it [corresponds to] the beginning of summer. At the summer solstice inside the body it becomes blood. *Kan*'s mercury is the *qi* inside the kidneys. Among the eight seasonal transitions it [corresponds to] the beginning of winter. At the winter solstice inside the body it becomes essence (*jing*).[24] Essence creates the *po*, and blood creates the *hun*.
>
> Essence is Nature (consciousness), and blood is Life (vitality). For a person to understand and master his or her Nature and Life, this is the true method of training oneself. A lesson says that essence and blood are the basics of the body of flesh. Real *qi* is the basis of Nature and Life. Therefore, it is said that those who have blood (i.e., all living beings) are able to produce Real *qi*. Those who have youthful and abundant Real *qi* can naturally for a long time bring together their essence and blood and constitute a shape.[25]

The human body is described as a mass of *qi* that circulates and transforms into many different forms (such as saliva, essence, and blood) by the cyclical functioning of the liver, lungs, heart, and kidneys that corresponds to the four seasons of nature.[26] Blood and essence (*jing*), generated out of the *qi* of the heart and kidneys, respectively, in turn generate the two categories of souls (*hun* and *po*) that give sentient life to the body by bestowing it with vitality (*ming*; Life) and consciousness (*xing*; Nature). The Real *qi* (*zhenqi*)—"Real" meaning primordial, uncorrupted, and everlasting—is the vital principle that creates and supports all life; it is the Real Nature viewed in its aspect as vital force. Terms such as *hun* and *po* or Nature and Life describe dual, differentiated aspects of it. Real *qi* is constantly generated and replenished if its dual aspects are nurtured and kept in harmony.[27]

Ma Yu, quoting the statements of a certain "little Immortal Ren," also compares the human body to the universe and speaks of maintaining—through the cultivation of purity and stillness—the harmony and solidarity of the vital principle in its differentiated aspects:

> Therefore a scripture (the *Qingjing jing*) says, "If a person is able to be perpetually pure and still, Heaven and Earth will all return." This "Heaven and Earth" does not refer to the Heaven and Earth that cover and carry. I believe that it refers to the Heaven and Earth inside the body. From a person's diaphragm and up is 'Heaven'. Below the diaphragm is 'Earth'. If Heaven's breath descends and the Earth's vessels circulate, above and below will be in harmony, and the essence

and *qi*[28] will naturally be solidified. This is what was spoken of by the little Immortal Ren."[29]

The dual aspects of the vital principle cited here are essence (that which nourishes and/or fertilizes [for reproduction]) and *qi* (that which animates). Unfortunately, no concrete description is given of how to make the "Heaven's breath descend," but this was most likely done by concentrating the mind inward and perhaps focusing on the Lower Elixir Field, much like what is described in the passages we examined in chapter 2.

Elsewhere in the same text Ma Yu gives a similar brief description of the internal physiological phenomena that an adept should try to bring about:

> One who studies the Tao should not concern himself with anything other than nurturing his *qi*. If the heart's fluid (blood?) descends downward and the kidneys' *qi* ascends upward and [each respectively] reaches the spleen, the primal (Real) *qi* will be vigorous and will not scatter, and the elixir will gather. [Organs] such as your liver and your lungs are the paths through which [the heart's liquid and kidneys' *qi*] come and go.[30]

Again, the basic idea is to solidify and reinforce the Real *qi* (the vital principle) by harmonizing and bringing together dual aspects of it from the upper and lower ends of the inner anatomy. The five viscera act as the prime agents and loci for circulating and transforming the *qi*.

Since Real *qi* in its various transmutations is the creator and supporter of all life, it is also present in the world outside us and can be drawn upon. Liu Chuxuan's commentary to *Yinfu jing* explains:

> Heaven has the proper breaths of the five directions [which] inside the human body become the mother of spirit. . . .
>
> People eat the five grains and nurture the body. The waste and filth (from the digested food) sink into the water and fire. [But] the essences of the five grains are preserved in the human body and become Life (vitality).[31]

Thus people breathe the air that comes from Heaven (the sky) and are nourished by the essence of the grains that grow out of the earth. "Essence," in other words, can be understood as the nutrition in the foods that we eat. The concept that breath becomes the "mother of spirit" relates to the concept that *qi* (the basic material constituting the universe) can be refined from heavy forms to airy forms and ultimately to spirit (that which bestows consciousness and intelligence). Breath is described as the "mother," because spirit is "born" from it.

The *Dadan zhizhi*, attributed to Qiu Chuji, contains a highly illuminating passage describing the processes of conception, gestation, and birth:

> At first, because the *qi* of the father and mother come in contact, feel, mingle, and merge, a pearl is completed which contains inside of it a single speck of primal *yang* Real *qi* and is surrounded on the outside by semen and blood. Its life stem (navel) is connected to that of its mother. After the mother is impregnated, she feels that there is an object [within her]. Every inhalation and exhalation that she makes reaches that place [where the fetus is] and makes contact with the primal *qi* which she received in the womb. First, [the fetus] develops its two kidneys and the rest of the viscera and bowels are produced consecutively one by one. In the tenth month [since conception], the womb is completed, and its *qi* is sufficient. Before it is born, the fetus has its two hands covering its face, and its nine orifices are unopened. It is nourished by the mother's *qi*. In a state of primordial chaos, it is completely pure and unblemished. This [*qi* that nourishes the fetus] is the *qi* of the time before creation. As soon as the breath abounds, the spirit is supplied, and the essence is sufficient, its navel will no longer accept any more of the breath and blood of the mother, and its life stem will separate from that of the mother. Its spirit and *qi* will move upwards, and its head changes its direction and faces downward, [causing the fetus to] descend and to be born. Once it has left the belly of its mother, its hands spontaneously uncover its eyes, and its *qi* begins to scatter from its nine orifices. It exhales and inhales through its mouth and nose. This [type of breathing] is of the time after creation.[32]

The *qi* received by the fetus in the womb is the *qi* of the time before creation. Once born, the human being carries out breathing that is "of the time after creation." Thus in keeping with the tendency to correlate the human body to the universe, the fetal condition is compared to the condition of primordial chaos. As such, it is seen as a time of purity, innocence, and unharmed vitality. In the fetal condition, the eyes are covered and the nine orifices are unopened. As soon as the newborn baby uncovers its eyes and begins to breathe, its orifices open up and *qi* begins to go out of them. As we shall see shortly, this was considered a serious problem, and the prescribed remedy was minimizing the depletion of *qi* while replenishing the store of Real *qi* in the Elixir Field.

This all-important Elixir Field was thought to exist in the belly, in the vicinity of the spleen and/or kidneys—the texts are somewhat vague and inconsistent on this matter.[33] This was thought to be the place where Real *qi* could be produced, replenished, and stored:

> 1.3 *cun* (about 3 cm.) inside the navel is where the primal *yang* Real *qi* is stored.
>
> The [area inside the navel] alone within the body is called the Central Palace, the Mansion of Life, the Spiritual Room of Primordial Chaos, the Yellow Court, the Elixir Field, the Cavity of Spirit and *Qi*, the Orifice for Returning to One's Roots, the Passage for Restoring One's Life, the Orifice of Primordial Chaos, the Cavity of 100 Meetings, the Gate of Life, the Spiritual Hearth of the Great One (Taiyi; the North Pole Star), the Original Visage. It has many different names. This place encloses the most exquisite [*qi*] which penetrates the 100 blood vessels and nourishes the entire body.[34]

A large portion of the life-nurturing methods involves visualizing this area behind the navel (which is sometimes clearly specified as the spleen, but not in the above passage) in order to preserve this priceless "primal *yang* Real *qi*" and replenish it.

Were all people considered anatomically identical and equal? Apparently not. Liu Chuxuan, in his commentary to the *Yinfu jing*, states:

> The nine orifices [of the heart] are the *yang* roads of the nine penetrations. [Their] not yet being open is [caused by] evil hindrances of the nine *yin*. Peoples' hearts are square and round (sort of oval shaped) and are empty and hollow. Inside they have spiritual light. Hearts of superior people have nine orifices. Middle quality people [have] seven orifices. Lower quality people [have] five orifices. If the heart has no orifices, [such a person] is called an ignorant person.[35]

The basic point here seems to be that a "superior" (wise) person is better able to control the impulses of the body with the rational mind (heart). Thus the most superior people have nine orifices in their hearts to correspond to the nine orifices of the body, and each heart orifice provides a passageway through which the heart's rational thinking capacity (spiritual light) can go out and control each external body orifice. (The heart—not the brain—was thought to be the primary thinking organ.) Thus Liu Chuxuan seems to be saying that wise people and ignorant people are anatomically different. But the phrase "not *yet* (emphasis added) being open" does seem to imply that a person born ignorant can open up more heart orifices and become enlightened.

In *Chongyang zhenren jinguan yusuo jue* is found one passage where "Wang Zhe" comments on the reason some people are not as good-looking as others:

> [Someone] asked, "What do you have to say about the reason why there are ugly people and handsome people?"
>
> ["Wang Zhe" replied], "A lesson says that the properness (handsome-ness) of one's appearance [occurs because] on the day [of conception] the father's and mother's two *qi* arouse and respond [to the] sun and moon before the *wu* (noon) hour and after the hour of *chou* (2 A.M.). Thereby, [the child will possess] rectitude, honesty, longevity, and prosperity. The appearance of [the child] will bring joy to the hearts of the father and mother. If conceived after the *wu* hour and before the *chou* hour, there will be [born] one whose appearance is not proper (is ugly) and may suffer from deafness or dumbness. His personality and intelligence will be inferior, and he will not win the hearts of people. His life span will be limited, he will not have prosperity, and his life span will not be long. These are basic principles of creation."[36]

"Wang Zhe" apparently believed that good or bad looks were a direct result of the time of conception. Here he seems to be following some system of chronological divination akin to what is found in the ancient day books (*rishu*)[37] or the popular almanacs still being produced today. Apparently, according to the system being followed here, those blessed with good appearance also tend to be more intelligent, more virtuous, and destined to better fate.

## The Causes of Disease and Death

> I (Wang Zhe) took [Ma] Yu [with me] and stayed at the Smoky Mist Grotto on Mt. Kunyu. Because his mind had not yet died (his mind had still not gotten rid of confused thoughts), [Ma Yu] got ill. He suffered aching throughout his head, and the pain was unbearable. [It was] as though he was being hacked at with an ax. I ordered him to descend from the mountain and treat [his headache] at his home. But [after he had gone home] the pain became even more severe. A man came up the mountain and reported [Ma Yu's condition] saying, "[At this] moment at which I have arrived here, Mr. Ma has [most probably] already died." Upon hearing this I clapped my hands,

> laughed loudly and said, "I came [to Shandong] wanting to make him into an immortal. I appreciate your telling me about his [supposed] death. He caught this disease because of his lack of faith."[38]

Wang Zhe, as we saw in the previous chapter, was notorious for subjecting his disciples to harsh discipline. Here we see an occasion where the hardships had gotten the best of his top disciple, Ma Yu, who had to be sent down from the mountain. Ma Yu's inability to rid himself of his confused thoughts and his lack of faith are cited here as reasons for his severe illness. "Faith" here probably means faith in the guidance of Wang Zhe, faith in himself,[39] or both. (Evidence elsewhere suggests that Ma Yu, after being sent down from the mountain, had aggravated his headache by drinking an alcoholic beverage with some medicine.[40] This violation of the precept against alcohol only deepened Wang Zhe's disappointment in his disciple, making Ma Yu's reacceptance much more difficult. It also appears that Wang Zhe treated Ma Yu's illness with "ritual water" [*fashui*] or "talisman water" [*fushui*, which one source claims cured him][41] and entrusted him to the care of "Immortal Lu"[42] [the abbot of the monastery that Ma Yu had built in Ninghai; see chapter 1], who was skilled at medicinal remedies.[43,44])

Fortunately, Ma Yu did recover from his illness. The narrative quoted above is followed by poems exchanged between Wang Zhe and Ma Yu during these events. In the first poem, Wang Zhe admonishes Ma Yu for being of shallow faith and thus vulnerable to disease, telling him, "because of your lack of faith, your whole head ached", and "your sweet heart[45] continued to long [for worldly comforts] and thus you entered the pond of confusion." Ma Yu, in his reply, repents by saying, "I limitlessly thank you, my master, for profoundly teaching me to repent." When the fully recuperated Ma Yu begs to return to the mountain, Wang Zhe turns him down, saying, "When you [come to] live in the mountain, I will descend from the mountain. My heart always dislikes the ignorant and the stubborn." He also expresses his regret over the fact that all that he had taught Ma had gone to waste by saying, "In past days I wasted one thousand mouthfuls of breath."[46] (Ma Yu, in fact, never made it back to Mt. Kunyu. Ma Yu finally gained Wang Zhe's forgiveness and reacceptance some months later [on 10/1/Dading 9] in Wendeng, where Wang Zhe's party was sojourning after having left Mt. Kunyu two months earlier.[47])

Ma Yu's disease, in Wang Zhe's opinion, was thus caused by lack of faith and mental discipline. Elsewhere in early Quanzhen literature, the causal relationship between an ignorant, undisciplined mind and disease is drawn out in more concrete physiological terms. Qiu Chuji, in *Xuanfeng qinghui lu*, states:

> If your eyes see colors, your ears hear sounds, your mouth enjoys flavors, and your nature follows your emotions, you will scatter your

> *qi*. You are like a ball filled with air. If a ball is full of air, it is firm. If the air scatters (leaks), it is not firm. If people make their *qi* their masters (rather than being masters over their *qi*), they will follow objects, give rise to thoughts, and their primal (Real) *qi* will scatter like the air scatters from an air-filled ball.[48]

Thus it is explained that the Real *qi* gets depleted little by little every time the mind gives rise to worldly desires, emotions, and thoughts. Here it appears that the Real *qi*—*qi* in its most subtle form—departs invisibly. However, Qiu Chuji, elsewhere in the same text, also indicates that the precious, life-sustaining *qi* transmutes into various liquids and can be depleted when these bodily fluids are wasted:

> When *qi* goes through the eyes, it becomes tears, when it goes through the nose, it becomes phlegm, and when it goes past the tongue, it becomes saliva. When it goes outside, it becomes perspiration, when it goes inside, it becomes blood, when it goes through the bones, it becomes marrow, and when it goes through the kidneys, it becomes semen. If your *qi* is complete, you live. If your *qi* is lost, you die. If the *qi* is vigorous, you are youthful, and when the *qi* declines, you age. Always cause your *qi* to not scatter.[49]

Thus it follows that the retention of these various bodily fluids is essential to health and longevity. This idea also is conveyed by "Wang Zhe" in *Chongyang zhenren jinguan yusuo jue*:

> Someone asked, "As for people who do not die, why [can they manage to avoid death]?"
>
> ["Wang Zhe"] answered, "As for one who does not die, his body is pure and still without defilement, and [he] cherishes his Real *qi* inside his Elixir Field. His/her essence and blood do not decline, and he/she does not die."
>
> [The questioner] doubted and said, "I often see men nowadays who are pure and still who divorce their wives and yet are not able to accomplish the Tao. Why [is this]?"
>
> ["Wang Zhe"] answered, "Such people, while being pure and still, have not yet accomplished the merit of true purity and stillness. Such people, while their whole body is pure and still, are not yet able to stabilize their essence and blood, and nurture the Real *qi*. As for such people, their bodies are pure, but their minds are impure. Their bodies are still, but their will is not still. . . . According to the treatises, as for those who are truly pure and still, inside their eyes are no

> tears, inside their noses is no phlegm, inside their mouths is no saliva, and they do not produce solid and liquid waste. The men nurture their essence (semen), and the women stabilize their blood. The myriad evils return to correctness, and the myriad diseases do not arise."[50]

In the above passage, "pure and still" (*qingjing*) is used by both "Wang Zhe" and his interlocutor to refer to celibacy. Through celibacy, men hoped to retain their essence (semen), and women hoped to retain their blood (that would otherwise be lost in childbirth), to maintain the Real *qi* in their Elixir Fields. The interlocutor, however, points out that even celibate monks often do not "obtain the Tao." To this, "Wang Zhe" replies that there is indeed a condition of "true purity and stillness" that one must aspire to, which entails more than just celibacy. Celibate adepts in fact often fail to stabilize their essence and blood in spite of their celibacy (how this is so shall be discussed later). Furthermore, to be truly "pure and still" means not only that one no longer leaks semen or blood but also emits no substances whatsoever from the body's orifices. This total control over the body's functions comes from a state of mind that is completely pure, disciplined, and in control of bodily impulses.

Of course, one wonders whether Wang Zhe actually deemed anybody capable of this (after all, as we have seen, he did concede that the flesh was ultimately mortal). He probably just wanted his disciples to set high standards for themselves and to not get complacent simply because they were celibate. What seems especially peculiar here is the notion that one could end all bowel movements. In the process of moving the bowels, was it thought that Real *qi* was somehow wasted? Perhaps it was. However, the more important implication here seems to be that the accomplished adept completely conquers the impulse of hunger, thus he or she no longer eats and no longer has bowel movements.

The fact that such a notion was current among Taoists of this general period is reflected in a story found in the *Lishi zhenxian tidao tongjian* (a massive hagiographical work compiled in the late thirteenth century; the story itself seems to be set in the Northern Song period, ca. eleventh century). The story is about Zhang Gong, who, we are told, was a failed *jinshi* degree[51] aspirant living in the capital (Bian; a.k.a., Kaifeng). There he tried to support his wife, children, and aging mother by operating a drugstore, but with little success. One morning he was visited by a strange Taoist (*daoshi*) whom he first mistook for a crazy person, but he soon came to recognize him as a wise teacher. When the Taoist asked Zhang Gong what sort of special wisdom or power he wished for, Zhang Gong replied, "My family is poor, and I have trouble feeding them consistently (lit. "the porridge does not continue"). If I could just become able to satisfy my hunger without eating! [This is] what I wish for in this worldly life." To this, the Taoist replied, "Divine immortals consider the avoidance of grains to be not so (the meaning of this sentence is unclear). When you eliminate grains you have no waste-filth, and when you have no waste-filth, you do not leak (*bulou*).[52] From here you can enter the Tao. It was in the remote past that people such as Zhang Zifang cured their hunger with elixir medicines. If you want to acquire this Way, you must abstain from sex from now on. Are you able to? When people abstain from sex, their worldly thoughts naturally stop. Once their worldly thoughts have stopped, they become immortality material." The Taoist then took seven jujubes, blew on them, and gave them to Zhang Gong to eat, telling him that these would enable him to stop eating. The immortal then told Zhang Gong that once he had fulfilled his obligations as a son and householder, he could leave the world and cultivate full immortality in the secluded mountain crags. The immortal then walked away and disappeared.

The story goes on to say that after eating the jujubes,[53] Zhang Gong started to become nauseated by just the smell of food. Within two years, he got to the point where he no longer ate and no longer excreted any feces or urine. At the same time his strength and endurance increased phenomenally. He ended all sexual relations with his wife, whom he now viewed as "a person on the street" (*luren*). His wife, who was "violently emotional in temperament (*xing gang*)," died in a fit of anger.[54] When Zhang Gong reached age sixty, he still looked like a man in his prime. Eventually his mother passed away, whereupon he left society and was never seen or heard from again.[55]

Largely fictitious though this story probably is, it certainly suggests that some Taoists (how many, or what percentage of Taoists is uncertain), prior or contemporary to the Quanzhen masters, considered it desirable to eliminate bowel movements, and that this was to be accomplished by not eating. Furthermore, the story conveys the notion that an adept who attempts this also should be celibate and should become free of worldly thoughts. The usage of the phrase "do not leak" sheds light on an otherwise puzzling passage from Quanzhen hagiography that reads, "when someone (apparently a disciple or lay follower) boasted about the master's [Wang Zhe] non-leakage, [Wang Zhe] relieved his bowels in front of the prefectural administrative building."[56] Wang Zhe's admirer was apparently proud of his hero's supposed "non-leakage," because it meant that he had perfected the art of fasting. The motive for Wang Zhe's subsequent action is not quite as clear. Perhaps out of modesty (!) or for didactic purposes, Wang Zhe wanted to disabuse his admirer of his fawning, vicariously boastful attitude. Or perhaps he was intentionally admitting through his actions that even outstanding adepts cannot, while still in the body of flesh, fully acquire the ideal traits of an immortal.

Wang Zhe probably did not consider it possible to stop eating completely for the rest of one's life. However, as was already seen in chapter 3 (particularly in the case of Hao Datong), the Quanzhen masters indeed appear to have at times engaged in very strenuous fasts. Celibacy was apparently thought to complement fasting, since by retaining "essence" (*jing*), a Taoist was supposed to be providing the nutrition necessary for his digestive system. This is an idea that can in fact be found in material that could date as far back as the Latter Han dynasty,[57] and it also seems to be conveyed in the episode where Wang Chuyi is said to have felt hunger after his involuntary seminal emission (see chapter 3).

As I discussed in a previous book, some early Taoist texts convey the belief that total fasting can confer physical immortality and heavenly ascension.[58] Wang Zhe, it would appear, did not believe this. Still, he and his disciples seem to have strongly believed that fasting was conducive to longevity. Interestingly, we have evidence that the Quanzhen School took note of the fact that obese people tend to die sooner. *Chongyang zhenren jinguan yusuo jue* contains the following verbal exchange:

> Someone had doubts and said, "Why do people who are fat decline sooner?"
>
> ["Wang Zhe"] answered, "Fat people cultivate the outside and do not cultivate the inside. Inside their bones they have no marrow, and their Elixir Fields allow their Real *qi* to run out."[59]

In other words, people who nourish their bodies heavily with food are those who are neglecting to preserve and replenish the Real *qi*. Not surprisingly, Quanzhen Taoists had a tendency to become very thin. One poem by Ma Yu, entitled "Friends of the Tao Marvel over My Pure Thinness," was apparently written in response to lay believers who had expressed concern over his gaunt physique:

> [My] thinness is thinness that accords with the Taoist teachings.
> I am not allowing my skin to wrinkle.
> The body of the crane and the shape of the pine tree,
> Are the venerable elders of the woods and springs.[60]

Thus he adamantly insists that he is healthy and points to the crane and the pine tree (traditional symbols of longevity) as examples of how slender forms prevail.

We must now return to the problem of why celibate adepts lose essence (semen) and blood in spite of their celibacy. "Wang Zhe," in *Chongyang zhenren jinguan yusuo jue*, explains as follows:

All men and women [in their] minds give rise to lustful pleasures, and [thus] covet and long for objects in their surroundings. During daylight they do not cut off their nameless confused thoughts and in the surroundings of night time are unable to get rid of the Three Corpses and *Yin* Demons. [As a result], men lose their semen, and women lose their bloody *qi* (menstrual blood). . . .

If men are pure and still (celibate) for 64 days, their seminal *qi* will be abundant. If women are pure and still for 49 days, their bloody *qi* will abound. Things which climax will return [to their opposite]. Purity gets overturned by filth. Stillness gets overturned by movement. The mind and will thus scatters and loses [*qi*]. The nine orifices allow the Real *qi* to run out. Defilement of *qi* causes the monthly water (menstrual blood) of women to come out in large quantities. Men at night dream of *yin* (evil, erotic) surroundings, and their seven valuables and eight treasures get stolen. This is why people have illnesses.[61]

Here, of course, he is describing bodily functions that modern medicine considers entirely harmless and involuntary. "Wang Zhe," however, saw them as a prime cause of disease and death and linked them to an impure, undisciplined state of mind.

In light of this, one can understand why, in the episodes cited in chapter 3, Qiu Chuji and Wang Chuyi were so humiliated and traumatized by their involuntary seminal emissions. We also saw how Qiu Chuji and Wang Chuyi resorted to extreme measures to stay awake at night. Perhaps the main reason for this was to prevent the wet dream.

Nuns, on the other hand, were supposed to try to shut down their menstrual cycles. A hagiographic story indicative of this fact is found in *Chunyang dijun shenhua miaotong ji* (DT304/TT159)—an early fourteenth-century collection of legends concerning the immortal Lü Yan, compiled by a Quanzhen monk, Miao Shanshi. There we are told about a sixteen-year-old girl who entertained the lofty ambition to become a Taoist immortal. Because her parents were about to force her to get married, she ran away from home and hid herself in Mt. Siming (located in Zhejiang Province). There she got lost and soon became hungry. Luckily she found a chestnut on the ground. As soon as she had picked it up and eaten it, there appeared before her an old man with shiny blue eyes, whose whiskers and eyebrows drooped down to the ground. The old man (who was in fact Lü Yan in disguise) pointed at the girl's belly and said, "I have already slain the Red Dragon for you. Because of this, you can now enter the Tao." The old man then transmitted "the profound meanings" to her. She thanked him for this, and then said, "But I have not yet overcome my attachment to food. Can the Tao actually take the place of

[food]?" The old man then gave her a luscious and ripe-looking chestnut about the size of a crossbow pellet to eat. After she ate it, "she no longer enjoyed cooked food; she ate only fruits and drank only water. She no longer menstruated, and she moved about like a god. [Therefore], her father and mother no longer tried to force her to get married." The girl went on to become the Realized Woman Guan.[62]

When and where this story originated is unclear. The fact that it takes place in Zhejiang suggests that it first circulated among southern *neidan* practitioners and/or Lü Yan devotees and is not, properly speaking, a Quanzhen story. However, the fact that it appears in an early fourteenth-century Quanzhen text suggests that the message of the story was compatible with Quanzhen doctrine and practice. The story conveys the notion that it is desirable for a female adept to avoid marriage (and be celibate), restrict her diet, and terminate her menstrual cycle. One strongly suspects that the stoppage of the menstrual cycle, when it was indeed achieved, was an effect of malnutrition. This endeavor to terminate the menstrual cycle was undoubtedly extremely arduous. This difficulty seems to be reflected in how it takes a miracle by the compassionate Lü Yan to "slay the Red Dragon (the menstrual cycle)." One wonders whether real-life female adepts prayed to Lü Yan for this very purpose.

The Quanzhen masters considered the leakage of the body's vital *qi* the prime cause of disease and death. This leakage, in turn, was blamed on ignorance and lack of discipline. Was a person therefore considered solely responsible for his or her troubles? Such was not entirely the case. Diseases also were understood to occur as a result of outside influences or circumstances beyond one's control.

> [Someone] doubted and said, "For what reason do children [who are (by definition)] pure and still (celibate) and do not lose their three treasures (essence, breath, and blood) have illness and death?"
>
> ["Wang Zhe" said], "A lesson says that a child who has a disease has in the past while in his mother's belly, received his mother's ten-month womb *qi* insufficiently due to the fact that her bloody *qi* was feeble and weak. Also, [the mother] may have violated wind, lewdness, heat, or dampness (acted in a lascivious way or exposed herself to adverse weather conditions?) and did not avoid the four gatherings (what this refers to is unclear) when she conceived. Children therefore have illness and death."[63]

Thus it was understood that a mother needed to act responsibly during conception and pregnancy, for the sake of the unborn child's health. (As seen previously "Wang Zhe" cited the time of conception as a factor in determining a child's physical fate.) Also mentioned here are the forces of nature that, if one is not careful, can cause harm. *Chongyang zhenren jinguan yusuo jue* contains two different passages that discuss two different theories on the harmful forces of nature:

> A lesson says that the myriad diseases are all born from the improper breaths of the eight seasonal transitions. . . .
>
> These breaths within the eight seasonal transitions (*bajie*) that cause people to enter into wickedness are hunger and satiation, labor and work, wind and coldness, and heat and humidity. When hunger comes, they fill themselves painfully (overeat). When coldness climaxes, their minds become troubled. When they travel far, they become tired. In extreme coldness or heat, their bodies become drunk. Thus they become unable to practice merit, and instead give rise to severe diseases.[64]

So without proper caution, people were deemed vulnerable to hazards such as severe weather, lack of food, or overexertion. When that happens, they become debilitated and incapable of performing the life-nurturing methods that the Quanzhen masters would prescribe:

> The five agents include metal, wood, water, fire, and earth. In the spring, wood is vigorous. If the internal wood (the liver) is not vigorous, people will ail greatly from eye diseases. In the summer, fire is vigorous. If the internal fire (the heart) is not vigorous, people will have a lot of diarrhea. In the fall, metal is vigorous. If the internal metal (the lungs) is not vigorous, people will have a lot of coughing. In the winter, water is vigorous. If the internal water (the kidneys) is not vigorous, people will suffer from many hernias.[65]

Thus the forces of nature (expressed in terms of the five agents theory) make it necessary during each season for a particular part of the body to be taken special care of, otherwise the body becomes vulnerable to certain diseases that are common during that particular season.

The Quanzhen masters also believed that evil spirits—who lived inside the body as well as in one's external surroundings—could cause diseases. The *Chongyang zhenren jinguan yusuo jue* passage quoted earlier mentions the "Three Corpses and *Yin* Demons," which seems to imply that these demons who live in the body tempt and delude adepts into having wet dreams. The concept of such internal demons (known usually as the Three Corpses, Three Worms, or Three Corpses and Nine Worms) is an ancient one in the Taoist tradition, and allusions to it are not uncommon in Quanzhen literature.

The fact that the Quanzhen masters did not deny the existence of ghosts is indicated by another passage in *Chongyang zhenren jinguan yusuo jue*. There the interlocutor asks "Wang Zhe," "Suppose that I met with a vengeful ghost. How do I control it?" "Wang Zhe" responds by describing a method with which to overcome the demonic hazard and prevent or cure the disease that the ghost could cause (see discussion later in this chapter).[66]

The Quanzhen masters themselves were believed to possess immunity from the power of evil that in theory gave them the power to combat the demons that victimized ordinary people. The diseases cured by the Quanzhen masters were attributed to a wide variety of evil forces. For example, *Tixuan zhenren xianyi lu* (The Record of Real Man Tixuan's Manifestations of His Extraordinariness) tells us that Wang Chuyi had a talent for discovering and pointing out the source of his patient's affliction. One time, Wang Chuyi's close friend and drinking companion, Sun Fu, was afflicted with a severe case of bloody diarrhea. Wang Chuyi cured him by destroying an animal-shaped roof tile whose resident spirit had been causing the disease.[67] In Laiyang (also in Shandong), he allegedly healed the wife of an innkeeper by making the innkeeper and his wife burn one of the figurines on their Buddha altar that had been causing the disease.[68] Another story has Wang Chuyi chopping down a tree next to the local shrine of the Yang Master God (*yangzhushen*) and destroying the bed of the patient in order to cure a severe case of diarrhea.[69] On another occasion, Wang Chuyi resurrects a certain Lady Li who had died suddenly after eating dog meat during a sacred Taoist ritual (*jiao*).[70] The belief conveyed in this last episode is that disease or death can sometimes ensue as just divine punishment for evil conduct.

The Quanzhen masters realized that the world was full of evil, danger, and misery. However, they believed that one could become largely invulnerable to such things through proper self-discipline. Yet they recognized that most people were incapable of this, and thus they saw it as their duty to heal and protect them. We shall now examine the various methods by which the Quanzhen masters combated diseases.

## How the Quanzhen Masters Combated Disease and Death

> I (Ma Yu) had been in my hut in Zhongnan with windy (bare) thighs and bare feet and with no fire or light for just six years. Suddenly my mind was moved. Trusting my steps, I wandered westward, arrived at Huating, and took up residence in a hole in the clay (*yaokong*).[71] By accident I became poisoned by a fiery poison inside some muddy fluid,[72] vomited blood, and was afflicted with a coughing disease. A

> crowd came to the scene very quickly. Many friends of the Tao gave me medicine. I bowed and received it but refused to take it. [The friends of the Tao] said to me, "You must eat raw onions and strong vinegar in order to antidote the poison." I thought about this over and over. [I came to the conclusion that] when a Taoist has a disease, no other people are able to cure it, and that I must cure myself by cultivating and refining the priceless treasures in my body. [Eventually], the disease healed itself.[73]

In the above episode Ma Yu falls ill yet refuses common medicinal remedies. Rather, he cures his diseases by relying solely on his own recuperative powers, which he perhaps mobilized through some sort of *neidan* technique. His rationale for taking this approach is based on the fact that he is a Taoist and therefore ought to be different from ordinary people. If he has made proper progress in his years of training, he ought to have the ability to cure his own disease without the help of medicine. Furthermore, he seems to say that ordinary medicines do not work on Taoists, since their bodily makeup and the types of diseases that they are liable to encounter are altogether different from those of ordinary people. The poisoning at Huating was a trial during which Ma's legitimacy as an adept was at stake. (Interestingly, various hagiographic sources allege that Wang Chuyi was immune to poison and describe how he survived even after imbibing some liquor containing the deadly poison of the *zhen* bird.[74])

"Wang Zhe," in *Chongyang zhenren jinguan yusuo jue*, enumerates various methods for curing diseases:

> Concerning the myriad diseases that people have; for each illness there is a method of true merit (exercise) for curing it to which [the disease] naturally responds. First there is the Method of Greatly Refining and Returning the Elixir in Nine Cycles, the method of the Yellow Sprouts and the Holes in the Knees, the Method of Shooting the Nine-Layered Iron Drum, the Method of the Prince Travelling to the Four Gates. There is the Method of the Golden Whip and Ring. There is the Method of the Bulrush Straw Holes in the Knees. There is Xuanyuan's (the Yellow Emperor) Method of Treading Fire. There is the Method of the Jade Girls Massaging the Body. There is Zhongli [Quan]'s Method of the Sword on the Back. There is Venerable Lü [Yan]'s Method of Angling Fish. There is Chen Xiyi's Method of the Great Slumber.[75]

Unfortunately, descriptions of the methods enumerated above by "Wang Zhe" are not to be found in any extant text, as far as I know. However, both

*Chongyang zhenren jinguan yusuo jue* and *Dadan zhizhi* contain lengthy descriptions of methods designed to ensure good health and long life. Some of these passages are quite cumbersome to read in full translation and thus will only be summarized in our discussion that follows.

*Chongyang zhenren jinguan yusuo jue* describes a method that is carried out as follows: The practitioner begins by sitting or standing still and removing his attention from all external sense data brought in through the eyes, ears, mouth, and nose. He or she then knocks his or her teeth together—perhaps to arouse and mobilize the vital forces within—fills the mouth with saliva, and swallows vigorously. By repeating this three times, the adept mixes the saliva with the *qi* beneath the heart and the diaphragm and causes the *qi* of the "dragon" (liver) and "tiger" (lungs) to come together. After these preliminary procedures, the adept simply concentrates his or her mind inward and visualizes the inside of his or her Elixir Field in the lower abdomen. This inner concentration and visualization is to be sustained during the whole day throughout all activities, whether one is "going, staying, sitting, or lying down." The *qi* in the body descends when the adept exhales and ascends when he or she inhales. Concentrating on the Elixir Field causes the *qi* in various modes from various organs of the body to converge and rotate within there and prevents the *qi* from leaking out of the body's openings.[76]

For the "dragon" and "tiger" to come together means that the heart's *qi* (which is blood when in its crudest form) and the kidneys' *qi* (which is semen when in its crudest form) come together. The reader may recall from the *Chongyang zhenren jinguan yusuo jue* passage quoted earlier that in the scheme of the body's "year" of *qi* production and circulation, the kidneys, liver, heart, and lungs correspond to winter, spring, summer, and fall, respectively. In other words, the liver's *qi* (the dragon) goes through the heart, and the lungs' *qi* (the tiger) goes through the kidneys before the adept brings them together at his spleen (Elixir Field). The reader also may recall that the previously cited quote from *Danyang zhenren yulu* states that the liver and the lungs are the routes through which the heart's liquid (blood) and the kidneys' *qi* (vaporized semen) pass through in order to come together at the spleen.

*Dadan zhizhi* describes a method that is very similar, in that it primarily involves concentrating on the Lower Elixir Field and bringing the "dragon" and "tiger" together. However, the procedure must be carried out while sitting in the lotus position, and the adept also is told to hold up his "outer kidneys" (testicles) in his left hand and cover his navel with his right hand (clearly "Qiu Chuji" has only male adepts in mind here). Also, by breathing very softly while visualizing the "Central Palace" (Elixir Field), the adept brings the air into the Elixir Field and replenishes the primal *yang* Real *qi*. (Elsewhere in *Dadan zhizhi*, "Qiu Chuji" laments how ordinary people—who do not practice Taoist methods and are afflicted by worldly emotions and desires—are not able to make their breath reach the Elixir Field. Their breathing, alas, reaches only as far as the lungs.[77]) The air eventually finds its way to the tailbone. There it enters the spine (through a hole believed to exist there) and rises up into the head and out of the nose. Apparently, as the adept continued to breath in this way, it was understood that Real *qi* (the tiger) from the kidneys would rise up, and liquid (the dragon) from the heart (the blood) would come down; then the two would "copulate" in the Elixir Field. Through this internal "sexual intercourse" of the body's own constituents, the adept hoped to become "pregnant" with an "embryo" that he had to keep intact. Then, through further engagement in more advanced methods, the adept was to eventually give birth to an eternal Radiant Spirit. The immediate good results were thought to be the attainment of youthful health and appearance.[78]

As the adept continued this controlled respiration and mental concentration over a long stretch of time, he or she would experience various physical sensations. The *Dadan zhizhi*, in a section bearing the heading "The Firing Times of the Revolving of Heaven" (*zhoutian huohou*), describes the mind's capacity to generate heat (this goes on simultaneously with "the Copulation of the Dragon and Tiger" and continues on after "the medicine has been gathered") and describes some of the sensations that this brings about. The mind of the adept is supposed to somehow generate heat as it visualizes the Elixir Field. Apparently, by visualizing the Elixir Field, the hot *qi* from the heart is supposed to be made to descend into it. Eventually this causes the "medicine" (the heart's liquid and kidneys' *qi*, brought together at the Elixir Field by the breathing method of "the Copulation of the Dragon and Tiger") to boil over and spurt up into the spine and up into the brain. During this process, the body of the adept is supposed feel increasingly warm, with the warm sensation gradually spreading out from the Elixir Field and the kidneys. (In his exposition, "Qiu Chuji" employs hexagrams from the *Yi jing* [Book of Changes] to designate the stages of the waxing and waning of the heat.) Eventually, streams of saliva start to gush out into the mouth of the adept, and as this happens, the body cools off. This saliva is supposedly the "medicine" that has been transformed inside of the brain.[79]

In light of the extreme ascetic tendencies of the Quanzhen masters, this notion of creating heat and/or coolness through meditative procedures is interesting. As we saw in chapter 3, the Quanzhen masters sometimes exposed themselves to extreme heat or cold. Perhaps their mastery of methods such as the aforementioned helped them endure such ordeals. Indeed, such seems to be the claim that both Wang Zhe and Ma Yu make in the poems previously cited in chapter 3.

*Chongyang zhenren jinguan yusuo jue* similarly comments on the methods of controlling and adjusting the hot and cold forces of the body:

> When you practice merit, eat metal food when hungry, and drink jade juice when thirsty. When you are cold, advance fire. When hot, advance water. Fire is true *yang*, and water is true *yin*. This is the Method of Adjusting by Extracting and Adding and Increasing and Diminishing. "Extracting" means to gather Real *qi* from above (transforming it into saliva inside the head and drinking it?). "Adding" means to advance warm *qi* from below (semen from the kidneys vaporized by the power of the "fire"?) and make it enter the Elixir Field. If a person's Kidney Palace is warm, the myriad diseases will be eliminated.[80]

It appears that here the swallowing of saliva also is thought to have the property of relieving thirst and hunger. "Metal food" and "jade juice" both probably refer to types of saliva that are swallowed. This property would then presumably have come in handy when the Quanzhen masters fasted. The following statements by Liu Chuxuan in his *Huangting neijing jing* commentary definitely indicate that the swallowing of saliva was thought to relieve both thirst and hunger and suggest that both "jade juice" and "metal food" refer to types of saliva that are swallowed:

> (*Huangting neijing jing*): Eventually reach non-hunger, and the Three Worms (evil spirits that tempt a person to desire food) will perish.
>
> (Liu Chuxuan's comment): Jade liquor and metal food; with three swallows [of them] you forget hunger. With the worms and corpses already scattered, [your Real] Nature's manifest radiance shines.[81]

> (*Huangting neijing jing*): Visualize and wash the five sprouts and do not hunger or thirst.
>
> (Liu Chuxuan's comment): The womb's immortal bathes. Wash with gold, the jade sprouts. Inside, you will not hunger or thirst. Always drink the smoky mist.[82]

> (*Huangting neijing jing*): Bland and without taste is the food of the Heavenly man.
>
> (Liu Chuxuan's comment): Unselfishly and quietly, the holy spring can quench hunger and thirst. Completely wash away ordinary emotions and completely master [the Tao].[83]

The practice of swallowing saliva as a means of alleviating hunger is indeed an ancient one within the Taoist tradition, and the text that Liu Chuxuan is commenting on here as his authority dates back to the early fourth century C.E.

As we saw previously, "Wang Zhe," in *Chongyang zhenren jinguan yusuo jue*, cited the depletion of semen and blood as the prime cause of disease and premature death for monks and nuns, respectively. In this sense, one could say that their celibacy was their essential means of health maintenance. Naturally they also thought that laypersons could improve their health greatly by cutting back on their sexual activity as much as possible. In *Xuanfeng qinghui lu*, Qiu Chuji repeatedly warns Genghis Khan about the dangers involved in his excessive enjoyment of his harem. His prescription for him is to try sleeping alone for one month, reasoning that just one night of solitary slumber is more beneficial than 1,000 days of medicinal treatment. He also tells him about Emperor Shizong of the Jin (Jurchen) dynasty, whose sexual overindulgence had made him so weak that he had to be carried to his throne every morning. Qiu Chuji then reassures Genghis Khan that by taking his advice and cutting back on his harem activities, Emperor Shizong fully recovered his strength and managed to reign for twenty more years.[84]

Sexual yoga, it appears, also was condemned within the Quanzhen tradition. This attitude is conveyed particularly strongly in the *Chunyang dijun shenhua miaotong ji*, the early fourteenth-century Quanzhen compilation of Lü Yan legends. There we find a story (#85) about a certain Lou Daoming who was an expert at sexual yoga. He always surrounded himself with pretty, buxom young ladies and would regularly make love to ten of them at a time. He was ninety-seven years old but looked like he was only fifty years old. Thus he claimed to be a Realized Immortal. He did not realize that over the years his sins had greatly accumulated, and he had actually been exhausting the Real *qi* in his Elixir Field. Because he also happened to be a great philanthropist and had done many good deeds in that respect, Lü Yan had the sympathy for him to at least come to warn him of his fate. The next day, Lou Daoming suddenly got a sick feeling, coughed up several bushels of a silver-colored oily liquid, and died.[85]

As we have seen, "Wang Zhe," in *Chongyang zhenren jinguan yusuo jue*, cited the involuntary leakage of semen as the prime cause of disease and premature death for celibate monks. Ma Yu, in *Danyang zhenren yulu*, offers some brief words on how to prevent the wet dream:

> The secret to preserving your *qi* lies in keeping your semen (*jing*) complete. More than anything else, you must prevent [leakage] during your sleep. When you want to go to sleep, make proper thoughts appear and completely get rid of the myriad concerns. Curl up your body and lay sideways, breathing long and soft breaths through your nose. [If you do so], your *hun* will not move within you, and your spirit will not roam outside of you. If you do like this, your *qi* and semen will stabilize themselves.[86]

Unclear here is the precise meaning and relationship of "spirit" (*shen*) and "*hun*"; they are perhaps synonymous. However, the basic meaning of the passage seems clear enough. By clearing the mind, lying down, and breathing in a proper manner, it was thought that the mind could be kept stable throughout the night, and the wet dream was thus prevented.

*Chongyang zhenren jinguan yusuo jue* also describes—albeit in a very cryptic manner—what seems to be a technique for retaining the semen within the body:

> [Someone asked], "Suppose the White Ox (semen?) is about to leave. How can I capture it?"
>
> ["Wang Zhe" answered], "A lesson says. 'When the White Ox is leaving, close and knock on your Dark Passage, close the Four Gates and quickly use the Method of the Immortal Angling Fish. Also use the Three Island Hand Signals and cause the Yellow River to flow backwards. Hold from above the Golden Passage and store it away with the Jade Chain. If people gouge out their eyes (stop looking at arousing sights?), the White Ox will of its own accord not run away. This is the Method of the Inner Function Leaving the Water and Climbing to the Other Shore.' There are ten methods of stabilizing one's Nature and Life. A lesson says, 'One is called, 'the *Samadhi* of the Golden Passage and Jade Chain.' A second is called, 'the *Samadhi* of Replacing Death and Returning to Life on the Three Islands.' A third is called, 'the *Samadhi* of Nine Curves of the Yellow River Flowing Backwards.' These [states of concentration] are called, 'Non-leakage.' Those whose fruits [of non-leakage] are complete have all completed the way of immortality. When the treasures have been stabilized, quit. [Or else you will] paralyze your hips and legs and blind your eyes."[87]

It is perhaps impossible for us to arrive at a reliable interpretation of the above passage. However, there is cause to suspect that it is describing something along the lines of the ancient arts of the bedroom (*fangzhongshu*; sexual yoga).[88] It seems to describe a situation where the adept is not asleep, and the semen (if this indeed is what "White Ox" refers to) is about to be emitted. By doing some sort of holding with his hands, he "makes the Yellow River flow backwards." In other words, it sounds as though the adept is resisting ejaculation and attempting to send his semen upward through his spine and into his brain, in the manner typically described in sexual yoga manuals. Perhaps the adept is supposed to arouse his "essence" by himself through some means of auto-stimulation rather than by engaging a woman in intercourse. Such seems likely in light of the fact that we are dealing here with a celibate monastic tradition.

However, one nonetheless cannot rule out the possibility that "Wang Zhe" here is speaking of sexual yoga. But why would he speak of such a thing? One can only speculate. We perhaps have our strongest reason here for questioning the authenticity of the *Chongyang zhenren jinguan yusuo jue*. Or perhaps this portion of the text represents views held by Wang Zhe at an earlier phase of his career, which he later modified or abandoned. Another possibility is that he condoned the practice of sexual yoga for married laypeople, or for accomplished adepts whom he deemed mentally disciplined to the point of being invulnerable to lust, even during sexual intercourse.

*Chongyang zhenren jinguan yusuo jue* goes on in the same cryptic style to describe a procedure for transporting and circulating *qi* from the lower abdomen, downward into the hips, legs, and feet and upward through the spine and into the head.[89] While these passages are too long and unintelligible to be worthwhile examining here, in one place we find a brief but interesting description of a method to be used specifically by women:

> The third [method] is called the woman's transporting of the treasures. Place [and burn (?)] frankincense (*ruxiang*; lit. "milk fragrance")[90] before you, and frequently advance the true fire.[91] Carrying out the exercise like this can in one year cause a woman to become like a young boy.[92]

Here it is to be noted that another (perhaps similar) training method for women is described in a short discourse by Jin Daocheng, who was probably one and the same as the "Realized Man Jin," whose teachings—preserved in the *Jin zhenren yulu*—greatly influenced the early Quanzhen movement:

> Women should concentrate their minds, not letting [their mental concentration] detach from the inside of their breasts, the inside of the floating flesh (apparently a description of [the] swollen shape of the bosom). In a year, you will have fully augmented your Real *qi*, and your merit will be the same as that of a male person.[93]

It would appear that female adepts were taught to concentrate their mind on their breasts for the purpose of mobilizing and utilizing the vital forces thought to be stored in them. Whereas for male adepts much emphasis was put on retaining and recycling seminal essence, it would appear that women were thought to possess a corresponding store of vital energy in their bosoms. If drawn upon, this energy was supposed to augment the female adept's bodily energy to the point where it lacked nothing in comparison to that of the male adept. "Wang Zhe" states that the woman's body becomes like that of a young boy. A hint as to what specifically he may have meant is provided in a hagiographic story about a Song period male adept, Wang Quan. There we are told that Wang Quan saw a rustic woman eating a melon and noticed that "her breasts were even with her belly." From this he realized that she must be an "extraordinary person" (*yiren*). When he asked her name, she replied that it was Xiao Sanniang, and she offered him a bite of her melon. When Wang Quan accepted unhesitatingly (and thus showed no revulsion for the "filth" of a country bumpkin), Xiao Sanniang deemed him "teachable" and brought him to the renowned immortal, Liu Haichan (Liu Cao) for instruction.[94] If the phrase "her breasts were even with her belly" means to say that her breasts did not stick out any farther than did her belly (i.e., she was flat-chested), this perhaps is also what "Wang Zhe" was referring to by the phrase "like a young boy." If so, there seems to have been the notion that an accomplished female *neidan* practitioner draws vital energies out of her breasts and into the rest of her body, and in doing so, she loses the most prominent external symbol of her femininity.

During its cryptic descriptions, *Chongyang zhenren jinguan yusuo jue* describes briefly a method for "Flying the Metal Crystals behind the Elbows" (*zhouhou fei jinjing*):

> Visualize the two pearls of lead and mercury. Shoot them at Penglai, and the back of the brain will open. The gate of Heaven will open on its own as the red mist clears. Real *qi* enters the Ocean of Marrow, which becomes naturally warm. This causes a person's white head [hair] to become black again.[95]

This is essentially a method for sending Real *qi* (generated by combining the "lead and mercury")[96] from the abdomen, through the spine, and into the brain. The result to be gained is rejuvenation. *Dadan zhizhi* describes in more detail a similar method, known as "Flying the Metal Essence behind the Elbows" (*zhouhou fei jinjing*):

> This method is entitled, "Flying the Metallic Essence behind the Elbows." [For] this method use the time after the *zi* hour (midnight) and before the *wu* hour (noon). This is the time when the *qi* is produced. Spread open your garments (for more mobility in the upper body), sit properly (with the back straightened to its "proper" posture), tighten your fists, and preserve your spirit (clear the mind and concentrate it). After first preserving [your spirit], stretch your

body. After first stretching [your body], lean back, making your chest stick out and your spine curve in. This opens the middle passage (located at about the center of the spine). From a level seated position (relaxed posture), lift your head. This opens up the upper passage (located at the part of the spine at the bottom of the neck). After first stretching [your body], preserve [your spirit]. [With your] hips and from your belly (using the strength of the stomach and the hips?), gradually raise your hips and stretch your body, making your chest stick out and your spine curve inwards. This opens up the lower passage (located at the bottom of the spine at the hip). After this, when the heat of the *qi* climaxes and rises up to the bottom of the passage, you should raise your hips, stretch your body, and sit properly. The hot *qi* will thrust through all three passages, supplementing the marrow in the brain. Naturally, your complexion will become rosy, your bones will become strong, your skin will become white (apparently this was considered healthy), and your body will become light. This is called "Returning to Youth from Old Age" and is a method of long life and immortality. If a young person practices this, he/she will not age. If an old person practices this, he/she will return to youth.[97]

Thus by simple physical movements, the passage through the spine was cleared for the *qi* to rise up. Again, rejuvenation is mentioned as the prime benefit of the method. Shortly later on in the *Dadan zhizhi*, "Qiu Chuji" explains that the three methods of the Copulation of the Dragon and Tiger, the Firing Time of the Revolving of Heaven, and Flying the Metal Crystals behind the Elbows should all be practiced together for attaining maximal results.

Generally speaking, what is superior is based on what is inferior, and what is profound begins from what is shallow. If people only practice the Copulation of the Dragon and Tiger, they can only supplement what they lack, benefit their *qi*, vitalize their blood, and send it to their faces. If people only practice the Firing Times, they can only bring joy to their skin and invigorate their sinews and bones. If they practice [only] the method of Flying the Metallic Essence, they can only return to youth from old age, strengthening their bones and lightening their bodies. If they are able to put into practice all of these lessons, they will greatly receive benefits. It is so that when the dragon and tiger intermingle and produce an object the size of a grain of rice or millet that moves around inside the Yellow Court; if you do not use the Firing Times you cannot refine and solidify it. As for

> [those who practice only] the Firing Times of the Revolving of Heaven; they will only have vacuous *qi* in their Elixir Fields and will be unable to make the dragon and tiger copulate. As for the Profound Pearls (semen?), they will be unable to make them stay peacefully. These two methods complement each other. In using [the method of Flying the Metal Crystals] behind the Elbows to extract the kidneys' *qi* [to make it] enter the brain; if you do not complete the *yang* inside the *yin* (extract the *yang qi* from the kidneys by means of the other two methods), you will cut up and violate the pure *yang* elixir [which is] the [most] profound amidst the profound, the marvel among marvels.
>
> [If you practice all three together properly], after 100 days, you will produce sweet *jin* saliva in your mouth, your body will have spiritual light [emanating from it], your bones will be strong, your face will be rosy, your skin will be white, and your belly will be warm. After 200 days, you will gradually come to dislike spices and meats, you will always smell an extraordinary fragrance, you will walk like you are flying, and when you sleep, your dreams will naturally decrease. After 300 days, your drinking and eating will naturally stop, coldness and heat will naturally become tolerable, your saliva, perspiration, and tears will naturally become non-existent, and diseases and misfortunes will naturally be eliminated. When amidst stillness (during meditation?) you will hear sounds of music in the distance, and a brilliant red radiance will gradually appear in the dark room. If you see these sights, do not regard it as strange. These are but minor effects. If you practice this with utmost sincerity, the divine and extraordinary effects [which will result] cannot be sufficiently listed (there are too many of them).[98]

Each of the three methods, if practiced alone, is supposed to greatly benefit one's health, however, if practiced together in a complementary fashion, these methods are said to enable one to become more than just an ordinary healthy human being. After 300 days, the practitioner is said to acquire extraordinary powers and qualities (a "non-leaking" body; immunity from hunger, heat, coldness, diseases, and misfortune) and to experience various strange sights, sounds, and smells. All of these were considered "signs of proof" (*zhengyan*) that one had gained—or was close to gaining—eternal life and the status of Realized Being.

*Chongyang zhenren jinguan yusuo jue* has a number of interesting passages that present adepts with solutions and remedies for specific crises. As mentioned earlier, "Wang Zhe" in one passage instructs his interlocutor on how to deal with threats imposed by vengeful demons:

[Someone] asked saying, "Suppose I met with a vengeful demon, how can I control it?"

["Wang Zhe" answered], "A lesson says that you should be pure and still. Within fearful agitation steal calmness (be calm during the normally frantic situation), and within calmness take stillness. When a person is in danger he/she should quickly avoid the heart-king (mental distractions?) and should use the Method of Irrigating (drinking saliva) and Visualizing. Quickly command your spirit-will to enter the Spiritual Palace of the Niwan (brain). Sit properly and visualize in front of your eyes the male and female immortals each playing the music of the immortals. Knock your teeth together and stabilize your will. See the scenery of Mt. Kunlun. See above you an ox, sheep, deer, horse, and jade rabbit. The mind visualizes [the brain] above, grabs, keeps, and ties up [the animals]. When your merit is stabilized, you will suddenly visualize a single treasure tree above you. On the tree is a flower. The flower blooms and produces a seed. With your mind, pluck it off and swallow it. One who is able to ingest this will eternally acquire a long life of peace and joy."[99]

"Wang Zhe" here does not appear to question the existence of vengeful demons, however, he clearly does not regard them as entities imposing any tangible threat that cannot be managed by a disciplined adept. The visualization method he recommends here is more a method for calming and soothing the mind than one for combating or evading an assailant. Perhaps adepts who engaged in extended periods of secluded meditation and ascetic discipline tended at times to be in a mental state susceptible to horrific hallucinations. "Wang Zhe" perhaps knew that such occurrences were common and not worthy of alarm.

In *Chongyang zhenren jinguan yusuo jue*, "Wang Zhe" also describes two methods for anticipating physical problems. His basic theory was that serious disease was imminent when the Real *qi* inside the Elixir Field was getting depleted or declining in vigor. The depleted condition of the Elixir Field could be detected through the color of the urine and the content of one's dreams:

As for one whose urine is yellow, his/her Elixir Field is empty and damaged, and he/she is losing the Real *qi* of the lower origin. He/she must quickly use the Method of Penetrating the Nine Curves, which is also called the "Nine Cycle Digging of the Small Intestine's Nine Penetrations." Real *qi* will enter the Hall of the Kidneys, and his/her urine will naturally become a bluish-white color, and the whole body will acquire ease and comfort.[100]

> At night, if you often dream of releasing an ox on top of a mountain and that ox is a red ox or a blue ox, or [if you dream of] immortals, Taoist monks, temples and monasteries, nice rooms and large roads, tall chariots and nice trees, or at night see little boys and girls and great officials, this is because the *qi* in your Elixir Field is vigorous. If you dream and see small roads, rough thorn bushes, evil people running about, ruined houses, buildings, towers and graves, trees falling down, or dream of being frightened while crossing a river, this is all because your Elixir Field's *qi* is declining and is weak.[101]

The Quanzhen masters possessed and transmitted a great deal of knowledge on how to prevent, cure, and anticipate diseases. With this knowledge they expected to be more or less immune from disease, or at least capable of curing their own diseases strictly through yogic techniques—without the aid of a physician or medicines. However, the Quanzhen masters also saw it as their responsibilty to heal the diseases of others. In their capacity as healers, they resorted to more standard, non-yogic methods.

Wang Zhe, in *Chongyang lijiao shiwu lun*, had the following to say about medicines:

> Medicine is the outstanding breaths of the mountains and rivers and the excellent essence of the grasses and trees. One kind [of medicine] is warm and the other is cold. You can nourish [the body] or excrete [bad *qi* that is causing the trouble]. One kind is rich in taste, and the other kind is bland. With the medicine, you can bring the disease out and scatter it. Someone who is knowledgeable in medicine can save the lives of people. If one is a blind physician, he will damage the bodies of people. People who study the Tao must not be ignorant [regarding the subject of medicine]. If they are ignorant, they will lack the means to help the Tao. But you must not be preoccupied [with medicines]. [If you are preoccupied with medicines], you will thereby damage your hidden merit. Externally you will covet wealth, and internally you will hinder your cultivation of Reality. [Even if your sins] are not bad enough to bring misfortune in this life, beware of the retributions in the life to come. High disciples within my gates must be thoroughly aware of this.[102]

The above passage suggests that Wang Zhe had considerable knowledge of medicines and expected the same of his disciples.

Actually, however, Wang Zhe seems to have had greater expertise in talismanic techniques of healing. In *Chongyang jiaohua ji* (Chongyang's [Wang

Zhe] Collection of Instructions) is a poem, "Ordering [Ma] Yu to Descend from the Mountain and Join in Companionship with Immortal Lu." This most likely was written during the aforementioned occasion when Wang Zhe temporarily sent the ailing Ma Yu back home and entrusted him to the care of Immortal Lu, who was knowledgeable about medicines. The first line of the poem reads, "I practice [the art of] talisman water,[103] and the master [Lu] practices medicine."[104] Wang Zhe seems to have first personally administered talisman water on his suffering disciple before entrusting him to the medicinal care of Immortal Lu.

In the passage quoted above from *Chongyang lijiao shiwu lun*, Wang Zhe expresses the reservation that excessive involvement in medicinal healing can lead to greed and create bad karma. This is probably because healing was sometimes done for remunerative as well as humanitarian purposes. Wang Zhe did in fact include healing among the few acceptable remunerative activities for Taoist monks:

> When training yourself, there are only three things by which you should rescue your hunger and coldness (feed and clothe yourself). Begging is superior [to the other two things in terms of desirability]. The practice of talismans is in the middle [in terms of its desirability as a remunerative means]. The administering of medicines is inferior [to the other two means in its desirability as a means for remuneration].[105]

In Wang Zhe's mind, the most commendable means of support was begging, probably because it helped foster humility. Remunerative healing was probably condoned by him due to the humanitarian purposes it served, and also because alms could be hard to come by. Why he rated talismanic healing higher than medicinal healing is unclear; perhaps he had greater confidence in talismans. In any case, it would appear that he did not want his disciples to accumulate any resources beyond what was necessary for subsistence. Their transgression in such a case would be even worse if they did not have proper mastery of their healing methods. In "Chongyang zushi xiuxian liaoxing bijue," Wang Zhe harshly criticized such greedy charlatans:

> How can those who are hateful and vicious possibly understand the profound truth? [They] envy the wise and resent the talented, bringing about misfortunes. [They] covet life and fear death, thus committing sins. [They] write talismans and sell their techniques and thus deceive people. [They] administer medicines and heal diseases [in order to] receive heavy remuneration.[106]

Accounts of healing—often miraculous—are frequently found in Quanzhen hagiography. In some cases the healing occurs by talismans or medicines. However, there also are some accounts where healing forces somehow seem to radiate out of the master's body. Wang Chuyi, we are told, could heal a serious disease by feeding his leftovers to the patient.[107] More amazingly, we are told, he could resurrect the dead simply by blowing on them.[108] Wang Zhe, we are told, healed the chronic rheumatism of Tan Chuduan by making him sleep for one night cuddled up against his legs. The accounts tell us that the incredible warmth emitted by Wang Zhe's body on that freezing winter night soon caused Tan Chuduan's shivering body to flow with perspiration. When Tan Chuduan washed himself the next morning, it was as though he had never been sick.[109]

## Conclusion: Nurturing the *Qi* and Completing the Spirit

In its totality, the completion and recovery of the Real Nature/Radiant Spirit was as much a physical process as it was a mental one. It was a process of "nurturing the *qi* to complete the Spirit" (*yangqi quanshen*), which Ma Yu describes eloquently in *Danyang zhenren yulu*:

> If you want to nurture your *qi* and complete your Spirit, you must completely get rid of your myriad attachments. Be pure and still on the surface and within. If you remain dedicated and devoted for a long, long time, your spirit will be stable, and your *qi* will be harmonious. If you do not leak for three years, your lower elixir will be brought together. If you do not leak for six years, your middle elixir will be brought together. If you do not leak for nine years, your upper elixir will be brought together. This [condition] is described [by the phrase], "the Three Elixirs Are Competely Sufficient and the Merit of Nine Cycles Is Completed." The bones and marrow will solidify, and the blood vessels will bring about Realization. Inside you will be complete, and outside your overflowing brightness will penetrate clearly. Calmly and motionlessly you will respond to and move with 1,000 changes and 10,000 transformations without limit. Sitting, staying, standing, or going, your 36,000 numinous spirits (that dwell in the body and together comprise the Spirit) will dance and jump and roam throughout the world under Heaven and the Three Realms, commanding and predicting. In the midst of the eight crises, the 1,000 misfortunes and 10,000 poisons will not be able to extinguish you. When the [era] arrives at the Transformation of the Great *Kalpa*

> and floods devastate the four directions, your Spirit will fill up the great vacuity and have no obstructions.[110] Therefore, Heaven has a [predetermined] time when it will fall down, Earth has a time when it will cave in, the mountains have a time when they will crumble, and the seas have a time when they will dry up. Everything that has a form will end the *kalpa* in destruction. Only those who study the Tao will reach the stage where their Spirit will reside together with the Tao and thereby be indestructible forever, and also have the power [which is strong enough to] raise nine generations of ancestors to [the Realm of] Upper Purity.[111]

Thus if one nurtures the *qi* and completes the Spirit, the Spirit will not only be eternally indestructible but will also possess the power to know anything, go anywhere, withstand and control all other forces, and rescue the souls of the dead. Going by the logic of the above passage, the body has form and is thus doomed to death, unlike the Spirit. However, the immortal Spirit cannot be recovered and completed without "nurturing the *qi*" and maintaining a state of "non-leakage." The meaning of "leakage" is unclear. Ma Yu is probably referring to the leakage of Real *qi* from the Elixir Field, a subtle phenomenon that can be caused by any sort of mental confusion or distraction (and in this sense is somewhat similar to the original Buddhist meaning of the term; see note 52 for this chapter). However, he may be referring more specifically to the loss of "essence" through seminal emission, involuntary or otherwise. If this latter interpretation is correct, then it certainly underscores the great efficacy attributed to celibacy within the Quanzhen tradition.

"Wang Zhe," in *Chongyang zhenren jinguan yusuo jue*, outlines as follows the relationship between body and mind and between physical practices and mental discipline:

> Only the Single Numinous [Nature] is Real. The body of flesh [made of the four elements (earth, water, fire, and wind) is provisional. Borrow and refine the provisional to complete what is Real. Move and combine and become one. A lesson says that [the methods that deal with] the ease and comfort of the present body are of the Lesser Vehicle. But all such methods are the roots of the Greater Vehicle. The Dharma mind of the initial ground is the Lesser Vehicle that bears fruit to create the Greater Vehicle. The Lesser Vehicle is the root, and the Greater Vehicle is the stem. A lesson says that the stems and branches borrow (rely on) each other. The stems borrow (rely on) the roots and are thus born. Practitioners of nowadays do not understand what the body acquires its Nature and Life from and how it

> got to be born. A lesson says that everybody is not separate from what is created by the *yin* and *yang*. You must borrow (rely on) your father's semen and mother's blood. These two things are the basics of your body. People nowadays who train themselves all do not cherish their father's semen and mother's blood. [They] waste and scatter their Real *qi* and damage their primal *yang*. Therefore they have aging, the aging have diseases, and within diseases, they have death.[112]
>
> For the practitioner to always be pure and still is the fundamental method of the Greater Vehicle. Those who want to practice the Greater Vehicle must begin by seeking and following the Lesser Vehicle.[113]

In chapter 2 we saw how Wang Zhe endorsed the simple cultivation of purity and stillness as the only true way toward recovering the Real Nature and gaining eternal life. This is the Greater Vehicle. However, this inner serenity needs to be built upon a foundation of sound physical health. This foundation is built through the more complicated physical practices of the Lesser Vehicle. As we have seen elsewhere, Wang Zhe sometimes seems harshly critical of the various physical practices, referring to them as "small methods of subsidiary schools" (*pangmen xiaofa*). Perhaps there was some inconsistency or change in his attitude on this issue (or one could question the authenticity of *Chongyang zhenren jinguan yusuo jue*). However, the seeming inconsistency perhaps occurs because the various discourses of Wang Zhe address different audiences and situations. Some of his followers perhaps tended to content themselves with pursuing the petty details of physical exercises, failing to attain true inner purity and stillness in the process. Others probably suffered health problems that hampered their spiritual progress.

It appears that the Quanzhen School and the larger internal alchemical movement maintained that it was by his or her mastery of the body and its energy that an accomplished internal alchemist could be deemed superior to his or her Buddhist counterpart after his or her liberation from the body. The liberated Radiant Spirit was deemed capable at will of assuming a clearly visible form with solid, corporeal properties. The liberated Buddhist adept, on the other hand, was said to become nothing more than a *yin* spirit incapable of appearing before mortal eyes or exhibiting corporeal traits.[114] This belief is clearly reflected in a legend about Lü Yan, recorded in *Chunyang dijun shenhua miaotong ji*. There we are told of an alleged occasion where Lü Yan and the spirit of a prominent, deceased Buddhist monk visited a home where a vegetarian feast was being held. Lü Yan was fed immediately by the hosts but had to ask for another serving for the Buddhist spirit, whom the hosts were unable to see. Lü Yan ended up eating both servings himself, since the Buddhist spirit was incapable of eating his (he could only suck on air).[115]

This concept also is discussed in *Dadan zhizhi*. In one passage, "Qiu Chuji" alludes to methods of active imagination allegedly used or endorsed by prominent immortal brethren for bringing about the final liberation of the Radiant Spirit from the body:

> This method is called "refining the body to merge with the Tao, abandoning the shell to ascend to immortality." This method has no [specific] time [for carrying it out]. Clearly it has five methods. Master Haichan (Liu Cao) [used the method of] the crane rising to the gate of heaven. Amid stillness (trance), he made his Real Nature—in the manner of a crane rising to the gate of heaven—exit outward. Naturally, he got to have a body outside the body. Patriarch Wang [Zhe (?)],[116] the Twelfth Realized Man of the Western Mountain, said, "In the manner of a blooming tree, exit amid stillness. In the manner of a blooming tree, gaze back without error. Your Original Nature will have already come out, and naturally you will divide your form outside your body." The Yellow Emperor exited in the manner of a fiery dragon.
>
> Amid stillness he transformed into a fiery dragon and jumped up, and naturally he had a body outside the body. This is called the "pure and clear Dharma Body." The two Realized Men, Zhong[li] Quan and Lü Yan, used the red tower to exit. Amid stillness, they climbed the three-storied red tower stage by stage. After climbing to the top, they leaped, and naturally abandoned their shells.[117]

This passage is followed by some commentary (anonymous):

> What is described above is "the Exercise of Refining the Spirit and Merging with the Tao, Abandoning the Shell, and Ascending to Immortality," which arrives at self-so-ness. As for Buddhist monks who enter into *samadhi* and die while seated in meditation, and Taoists who enter into stillness and thus send out *yin* spirits, these [spirits that they let out] are [nothing but] ghosts of pure vacuity and are not pure *yang* immortals. They are distantly faint with no appearance and in the end have no place to go to. Why do people who study [the way to immortality] make these mistakes? They especially do not understand that pure *yang qi* is born after the essence is refined and made into an elixir. After you refine the *qi* and complete the Spirit, the Realized Numinous Divine Immortal transcends the ordinary and enters into sacredness. You abandon your shell and ascend to immortality, and this is called "transcending and escaping." This is the

method of divine immortals that has not changed for a hundred million years![118]

Shortly later on in the text, "Qiu Chuji" himself says:

Generally speaking, if you have a body, you will have suffering. If you have no home, you will have no attachments. In the past and present [wise men] all say that arduous effort arrives at non-action.[119] How can [one who has arrived at non-action through arduous effort] bear to love his body and not leave it? Thus he abandons his shell and ascends to immortality by coming out from the top of his head. Refining his Spirit, he transcends ordinariness and becomes an immortal. People of the world do not like to cultivate and refine but only want to abandon their shells and thereby complete the way of immortality. How mistaken they are! With their bodies in a dark room, they sit still, eliminate their thoughts, and forget ideas without allowing outer surroundings to enter and inner surroundings to exit. They are like withered trees, and their hearts are like dead ashes (completely devoid of emotion or thought). Their spirit-consciousness protects the One inside, and their minds are not distracted. Amidst their *samadhi*, they let out their spirits which are but *yin* souls. Dark and without appearance, they are not pure *yang* immortals.[120]

The essential point is that no matter how thoroughly one has mastered mental methods of trance, one can only produce a feeble *yin* spirit if one has not trained the body and its *qi*—this in fact is a mistake that Taoists as well as Buddhists tend to make. Thus anxious as one may be to leave the body and this dusty world, one must not do so hastily, before both body and mind have been sufficiently trained. The full freedom and power of the immortal Spirit cannot be recovered without the proper care and training of the body.

# Chapter 5

## Visions and Other Trance Phenomena

### Introduction

The early Quanzhen masters cultivated meditative trances and hoped to gain visions, locutions, and other sensory and physical signs indicating that they were making progress in their training. They, along with other internal alchemists of their times, referred to these things as "signs of proof" (*zhengyan*), "signs of response" (*yingyan*), or "news" (*xiaoxi*). They regarded the "signs" as "proof" of their spiritual progress and the veracity of their beliefs in eternal life and immortal beings. The Quanzhen masters also found comfort in their belief that friendly immortals guide, aid, and protect diligent adepts.

In this chapter we will examine the testimony of the early Quanzhen masters regarding "signs of proof." By doing so, we hope to shed light upon how the Quanzhen masters viewed the nature and significance of these phenomena. We will begin by looking at one very unique testimony regarding a trance vision that was brought on entirely spontaneously and inadvertently. We will then proceed to examine some testimonies regarding communications from immortals of past and present and some of the other sensory and physical trance phenomena that were cited as "signs of proof"—both auspicious and baleful—in the testimonies of the Quanzhen masters and in the literature of the larger internal alchemical tradition of the time. Finally, we shall examine some testimonies and anecdotes uttered by Quanzhen masters regarding some of the struggles and frustrations involved in seeking "signs of proof."

## A Remarkable Incident from the Childhood of Yin Zhiping

Yin Zhiping (1169–1251), the eminent monk who succeeded Qiu Chuji as the leader of the Quanzhen School, had a rather extraordinary childhood experience. The incident occurred when he was only five years old, during the Cold Food festival.[1] The little boy, Yin, in keeping with the custom of his clan, went with a group of over 100 people before sunrise to offer sacrifices and pay respects at the clan cemetery. When the ceremony ended, everybody dispersed and went home—except for the little boy, Yin, who fell into a deep reverie. Roughly sixty years later, Yin Zhiping would describe the experience to his disciples in the following way:

> I alone had something that I felt. I privately thought about my ancestors of the remote past and of how I knew not where they went. People die, but I did not know where they return. Rapt in my thoughts, I sat under a large mulberry tree. Gazing above and below I inquired as to why heaven and earth were established and why the myriad things came to life. Above heaven and below earth, what thing is there that covers and carries [them]? What object sustains them? As my pondering and observations came to their limits, I arrived at non-thinking. No longer did I know of the vastness of heaven and earth, nor of the numerousness of the myriad things. All I saw was a watery vapor that pervaded above and below in the shape of an eggshell. Darkly and murkily, while unaware, my mind and body were both lost. Some of my relatives eventually came to look for me, and called and wakened me [from my trance]. It was already evening.[2]

The little boy, Yin, thus unintentionally entered a trance state of self-oblivion. What exactly was this "watery vapor" that he saw? Was it perhaps the creative, life-giving *qi* of the ineffable Tao? Unfortunately, Yin himself does not offer an interpretation. However, he goes on to state, "I at first did not yet know why it [the vision] was so. Later, after I had entered the Tao and encountered the Masters [and the] Realized Ones (*shizhen*), I came to understand the significance of this oblivion of mind."[3] Thus Yin Zhiping regarded this childhood experience as a foretaste of what he later came to experience and know as a Quanzhen monk.

Yin Zhiping seems to have been precociously gifted with a propensity for mystical experience—a propensity that would manifest itself intermittently later in life. However, his trances in his adult years would be induced through rigorous self-discipline and seated meditation, thus falling into a pattern much more typical of the Quanzhen school and larger internal alchemical tradition.

## Communications from Realized Beings of Past and Present

Yin Zhiping, in his reminiscences, goes on to state that at age seven he met "Grand Master Wang from the west of the Pass" and immediately felt an affinity for him. Initially this would seem to refer to Wang Zhe, who indeed hailed from "west of the Pass" (Shaanxi). However, this would be an anachronism, since Wang Zhe died the year after Yin Zhiping was born. The identity of this Taoist master, and his connection (if any) with Wang Zhe's movement, remains a mystery.[4]

Yin Zhiping's entry into the Quanzhen School came about through the influence of Wang Zhe's disciples. At age fourteen, he met Ma Yu and became a Quanzhen monk, despite the disapproval of his father. At age nineteen, he was forced to return to lay life (apparently due to pressure from his father), and he was locked up inside of his family's home, where he took to the nightly habit of bowing 1,000 times in prayer beneath the Pole Star. One day, from outside of the central gate, he overheard the voice of Liu Chuxuan conversing with a guest about the Tao. Yin Zhiping knelt and listened, rapt in attention and oblivious even to the rocks and sand that wounded and penetrated his knees. On three different occasions, Yin escaped from his home before finally gaining permission to join the Quanzhen order.[5]

Later, while residing at a hermitage west of Changyi County (in Shandong), Yin Zhiping—now a disciple of Liu Chuxuan—took to the practice of sitting in meditation at night under a peach tree. Yin Zhiping reminisces as follows:

> One night during the fourth watch (2–4 A.M.), a man suddenly came [before me]. He had the bones of the Tao and the wind of immortality (i.e., bore the impressive appearance of an immortal); [he] was not a man of the dusty world. He bore a golden radiance and jade-like luster that together glowed forth. I took one look at him and thereupon rectified my mind and made it motionless. I knew that he was the Realized Man Changsheng (Liu Chuxuan). When he arrived [before me] he wielded a sword and cut off my head; still my mind remained motionless. The master then cheerfully placed it (the head) back [on my body]. When I awoke [from my trance] my mind had an enlightenment; I understood that the master had replaced my worldly head and visage.

> Ten days later he came again and cut out my heart, and I understood that he had removed my worldly heart.
>
> Another ten days later he came again, holding a plate of deep-fried cakes.
>
> He offered them all to me to eat, and I overate until I [felt like] I was going to die. The master then cut open my belly and emptied all its contents. The fact of the matter is that I by my nature tend to put myself too high (and consequently overindulge?). When I put myself too high, I do damage [to myself]. Thus [Perfected Man Changsheng] removed that which had been damaged [in me].[6]

Here Yin Zhiping describes a different sort of trance vision from what he had experienced at age five. He encounters his teacher, whose strange and drastic actions provide him with verification that he is successfully undergoing the transformation from a secular to a spiritual man. The visions occur intermittently during his diligent, daily practice of meditation. Yin Zhiping probably also means to imply here that Liu Chuxuan possessed the power to manifest himself in the trance visions of others.[7] He thus, it seems, attributes much of his own spiritual progress to the compassionate power of Liu Chuxuan at work in him. Regarding his experiences while locked up in his family's home, Yin's account does not make it entirely clear that Liu Chuxuan was physically present outside of the gate. The discussion of the Tao that he overheard may have been an audition induced through his strenuous daily worship regimen. But if so, Yin's interpretation would again be that Liu Chuxuan had—out of his kindness—used his miraculous powers to manifest his voice outside of the gate.

Yin Zhiping sums up his reminiscences with the following words:

> Ah, utmost sincerity moves the deities; this truly is not empty talk! If you are able to practice the Tao with your whole heart, the Holy Sages will not be far from you. I have never before spoken of these things to people. Now that I have openly confessed [these things] to this gathering, [you] in this gathering must not take these as empty words and carelessly fall lax in your practice![8]

It would appear that Yin believed sincerely in the reality of his experiences, which were of deep personal significance. He understood such experiences as the workings of divine beings—whose ranks include Quanzhen masters of past and present—who sympathetically aid and guide those who are sincere and diligent in their religious quest.

Yin Zhiping's predecessors had similar experiences. Qiu Chuji, in a statement quoted by Yin Zhiping, claims to have had visions of his deceased teacher, Wang Zhe, that served a function similar to Yin's visions of Liu Chuxuan:

> One evening in my surroundings I saw the Patriarch-Master (Wang Zhe, who had passed away several years prior to this) with a child approximately 100 days old seated on his knee. When I woke up [from my trance (?)/dream (?)], my mind had an enlightenment; I realized that my Tao nature was still shallow. Half a year later, I again saw surroundings similar to the previous one. The child had already reached about two years in age. I awoke with the realization that my Tao nature was gradually growing, and later became aware that I no longer had any evil thoughts. One year [later], I saw the same surroundings again. The child was now three or four years old and was able to walk and stand by itself. After this I no longer saw this [vision]. Thereby I realized that [divine] aid had come directly to me and that I myself had the means by which I could stand on my own.[9]

The child thus represented Qiu Chuji, who under the fatherly gaze of his deceased mentor was daily making spiritual progress.

Ma Yu enjoyed similar didactic posthumous visions of Wang Zhe; such at least seems to be the claim made by Ma Yu in his poetry collection, *Dongxuan jinyu ji*:

> Coming out of my shack on the lower origin day (fifteenth day of the tenth month) of the *dingyou* year (November 7, 1177)
> Dancing I acquired the true exhortations that came before me.
> I have come to know my original true countenance.
> My Master-Father and Master-Uncle came to the lower realm.
> Joyfully I anticipate direct instructions in the northwest.[10]

While confined in his small meditation shack (*huanqiang* or *huandu*), he had apparently seen a vision or heard the voices of his "Master-Father" and "Master-Uncle," and this had enabled him to know his "original true countenance" (innate Real Nature). He was inspired to travel to the northwest, and he anticipated another encounter. The very next poem in the collection tells us that the anticipated encounter took place, and the comments added, along with the title, reveal the identity of the "Master-Father" and "Master-Uncle":

> Meeting Again—*[With] Master-Father Chongyang (Wang Zhe), the Realized Man of Merciful Transformations and Marvelous Deeds and Master-Uncle Yuchan, the Realized Man of Universal Light and Clear Calmness* (Ma Yu's note)

> Just as I was going by Fufeng (east of Xianyang, Shaanxi Province), I received instructions to turn my head,
> And especially visit Qiyang (in northeastern Shaanxi), to flaunt my blind eyes.
> Again I met my true master and acquired the Great Elixir.
> The [Quanzhen] school shall be established in the east, west, south, and north.[11]

Thus the "Master-Uncle" who appeared with Wang Zhe (sobriquet, Chongyang) was He Dejin, who had trained with Wang Zhe in Liujiang Village (see chapter 1). Apparently, when Ma Yu was going through Fufeng on his northwestern mission, he had another encounter during which Wang Zhe and He Dejin told him that he must change his direction and go eastward to Qiyang.

For Ma Yu, such communications practically became routine affairs—or so it would appear from the following incident related by Qiu Chuji:

> [Qiu Chuji] also talked about the time when the Master-Father Ma was still present (living) and there was a person who came to talk about matters of staying in the world and extending one's years. Suddenly out of empty space a person said, "You are nothing but small vessels (people of limited abilities). The Chan (Buddhist) school says that the two characters, 'pure' and 'still,' are the two chariots (guidelines for proper training). The body, which has a form and is but manure and dirt, has always had its limit. Emotions and desires are vast and limitless. Confused people are like the bees that covet honey. Deluded people are like butterflies that love flowers."
>
> Realized Man Danyang (Ma Yu) said, "In other words, the roots of *karma* are deep and heavy. If the *karma* is so limitlessly deep, can the Tao be hoped for? Furthermore, there are the techniques of joining battle in the bedroom. These only expend and confuse the spirit, injuring virtue and confusing the masses. It causes one's name to be recorded on the demon registers so that one falls into the [purgatory of] Fengdu. A scripture (*Huangting neijing jing*) says, 'To live long you must be careful of the dangers of the bedroom. Why engage in the doings of death and cause your spirit to weep?'"[12]

The basic message conveyed by the mysterious voice (is it Wang Zhe?) is that one must focus on maintaining inner purity and stillness rather than get engrossed in longevity techniques. To this admonishment Ma Yu adds his own injunctions aimed more specifically against sexual yoga. The seeming nonchalance with which Ma Yu responds to the voice that came out of empty space would make it seem as though such auditions were commonplace for him. What is even more unusual here is that the voice was supposedly audible by others present.

Evidence of a similar strange locution is found in Wang Chuyi's *Yunguang ji*:

> Friends of the Tao had gathered and were conversing at Mt. Danzao, north of Wang Yuan Village in Fushan County. When their discussion began to pertain to this mountain, and to the fact that this was the site where [Wang] Fangping (the famous ancient immortal Wang Yuan)[13] had trained, there was suddenly a response from midair. I therefore wrote [the following poem].[14]

Wang Chuyi, in his poem that follows in the text, describes these "responses" as the "melodious tunes of the superior immortals of the Three Heavens."[15] Again, the claim here seems to be that all of the "friends of the Tao" present heard the sounds (in fact, it is not entirely clear whether he himself was there to witness the blessed event).

Of course, Quanzhen hagiography tells us that the founder, Wang Zhe, turned to the religious life as a result of encounters with famous immortals such as Lü Yan, Zhongli Quan, and Liu Cao (see chapter 1). These, according to hagiographical accounts, were not trance visions or locutions; we are told that he encountered them in the flesh, in normal, waking consciousness. It is difficult to determine whether Wang Zhe himself actually believed and claimed that he had had such experiences—and if he did, maybe the encounters were actually trance visions or locutions. However, *Chongyang fenli shihua ji* (a collection of poems exchanged between Wang Zhe and Ma Yu) records comments by Wang Zhe in which he explicitly refers to a personal encounter with Lü Yan.[16] (Yet oddly—as Kubo and Hachiya point out—in some poems he mentions a momentous encounter with a certain teacher, but he does not say nor seem to imply that the teacher was Lü Yan or any other immortal.) The hagiographic accounts of his miraculous encounters appear to have been at least in part based on his own claims, although it still bears questioning whether his claims were made sincerely or simply concocted by him long after the time of the alleged events.[17]

As noted previously (chapter 1), Wang Chuyi is said to have encountered the ancient immortal, Donghua Dijun, in his childhood; he himself confirms this event in his *Yunguang ji*:

> When I was seven *sui* I encountered Donghua Dijun. From amid empty space he exhorted me to not allow myself to become confused and ignorant. In the *wuzi* year of the Dading [reign era] (1168), I

> again had an encounter, [this time with] Master-Father Chongyang (Wang Zhe). I thus wrote this poem to attest to these facts.[18]

From what is related here, it is not clear whether he saw Donghua Dijun (or so claimed) or merely heard his voice. Interestingly, he seems to have regarded his meeting with Wang Zhe (who was still alive in his mortal body) as an equally marvelous event. Apparently, in his mind, Wang Zhe was a divine being even prior to his death and apotheosis.

One must note that the Quanzhen masters did not claim any exclusive privilege to having encounters with the famous immortals. For example, a passage in the *Dongxuan jinyu ji* tells us that Ma Yu rejoiced greatly when a certain Mr. Liu received secret lessons from Liu Cao in a dream.[19] Ma Yu appears to have entertained no doubts that the famous Liao dynasty immortal had truly manifested himself. In *Qinghe zhenren beiyou yulu*, Yin Zhiping describes an occasion where Qiu Chuji was visited by a stranger who claimed to have undergone conversion through a direct encounter with Zhongli Quan. Qiu Chuji (and Yin Zhiping) in no way seems to have disdained the visitor's claims. However, Qiu Chuji was apprehensive that the extraordinary privilege of encountering the famous Han immortal might make the visitor complacent and boastful and advised him simply to train diligently, perform virtuous deeds, and refrain from "flaunting" (boasting of his encounter with Zhongli Quan?).[20]

Liu Chuxuan went as far as to say that all diligent practitioners, whether they know it or not, have encountered Lü Yan and Zhongli Quan:

> Master-Father Changsheng (Liu Chuxuan) used to frequently say, "People within the school today who advance upon the Way (Tao) with utmost sincerity all met the Perfected Men Zhengyang (Zhongli Quan) and Chunyang (Lü Yan) in their previous lives."[21]

Thus while most practitioners may be under the impression that they have never encountered the immortals, this—Liu Chuxuan claimed—could simply be because they lack the ability to remember their past lives.

## Miscellaneous "Signs of Proof": Sights, Sounds, Tastes, and Sensations

Nonetheless, the reality remained that in their conscious experience, most practitioners never had beheld the countenance or heard the voice of a Lü Yan, Zhongli Quan, Liu Cao, or Wang Zhe. However, in the course of their regimens of harsh self-discipline and meditation, practitioners would experience extraordinary sights, sounds, tastes, and sensations that were interpreted as resulting from the aid of kind immortals:

> Liu Daojian asked [Qiu Chuji] about training, "When the kidneys are hot and the heart is cool, and a fever arises throughout the body, what am I to make of this?"
>
> Qiu [Chuji] said, "The holy sages (*shengxian*) have given their aid. Afterwards, what you see in your eyes and hear in your ears you must not become attached to." [Qiu Chuji] also said, "Amid empty space you will only see a human head fall down. Thus the golden elixir will be completed."[22]
>
> [Qiu Chuji] also said, "What you hear in your ears and what you see in your eyes, all of this you must not become attached to. If you train conscientiously the holy sages will aid you from the dark (i.e., without directly manifesting themselves), as in whenever a person arrives at a state where his spirit is stable and his energy is harmonious, he feels his kidneys become hot. [The heat from the kidneys] steams his four extremities and dissipates in one or two hours. There then appears the forms of mountains, streams, the sun, and the moon."
>
> [Qiu Chuji] also said, "I wait until I have thrust into the gate of heaven three times. With the sun and moon right below me, I see the myriad forms (heavenly bodies) spread out before me." After saying this, he regretted [that he had said it] and [thus] said, "You must not look at it."[23]

Qiu Chuji was thus deeply familiar with certain strange phenomena that would set in during meditation. In the midst of a deep meditative calm, the adept feels unusual body sensations that will be followed by various visions and auditions. These phenomena are gifts from the "holy sages" that provide the practitioner with verification of his progress. As the adept continues his efforts, he will progress toward the highest mystical experience, an encounter with his immortal Real Nature (which is what the above-mentioned "human head" seems to represent). Yet Qiu Chuji is at the same time apprehensive of the visions, auditions, and sensations; they also can be harmful distractions that can prevent the adept from gaining the highest enlightened vision.

In the above-quoted passages we find Qiu Chuji acting as a guide to disciples who are beginning to explore the mystical realm for themselves. While perhaps aware that the experiences of individual adepts may differ somewhat in their details, Qiu does expect a certain conformity in their experiences and thus feels qualified to guide them based on his own knowledge.

However, his knowledge of these strange phenomena was probably not founded solely on his personal experiences. Rather, within the internal alchemical tradition there seem to have been certain established theories concerning the phenomena that an adept could expect in the advanced stages of meditation. This becomes particularly apparent when one reads tenth- or eleventh-century "Zhong-Lü school" texts such as *Zhong-Lü chuandao ji*, *Lingbao bifa*, and *Xishan qunxian huizhen ji*. Also instructive in this regard are three essays, "Jindan zhengyan," "Lun baguanjie" (which replicates a portion of "Jindan zhengyan"), and "Lun liutong jue," found in *Zhuzhen neidan jiyao* (DT1246/TT999), a collection of miscellaneous internal alchemical writings compiled by a certain Xuanquanzi.[24] *Dadan zhizhi*, which—as we have seen—records teachings attributed to Qiu Chuji contains the following passage under the heading, "Signs of Response during the Practice of the Exercise (*xinggong yingyan*)":

> At first you will gradually feel as though there is something in your Elixir Field-Yellow Court (the lower *dantian* in the lower abdomen) that is soft and warm. Your Real *qi* (*zhenqi*) will rise up, and your ears will hear the sounds of wind and rain. Gradually inside your head there will be the sounds of harps and of gold and jade. Within the gate of your jaws—which is called the Heavenly Pond—the Metal Liquid will gush out like a cool stream and flow down. Some of it will flow onto the face, some of it will flow up into the brain, some of it will be in a pearly dew-like form, and some of it will enter the mouth through the upper gums. Its flavor will be sweet and delectable.
>
> After a long while, inside the head there will be the sounds of *sheng* lutes, *se* and *qin* harps, and bamboo chimes. Also there will be sounds such as a crane's call, a monkey's cry, and a cicada's chiming. These various sounds of nature have nothing that is comparable to them.
>
> However, when you first practice this, amid your dreams (trances?), you will hear the noise of ferocious thunder. This is your Real *qi* thrusting open the head's *yang* bone (the base of the skull?) and then penetrating the Nine Palaces [inside the skull]. When [your internal] spirit(s) first enter the room (the Central Palace, the Lower Elixir Field in the belly), they will after a short while jump upwards. You will naturally be frightened. While you are sitting with your eyes closed, sometimes a single big object will jump up in fright. But when you get up and open your eyes, it is gone. This [happens because your] Radiant Spirit is not yet mature. When it is not yet mature, it is essential that you do not become frightened and give rise to thoughts.

> After a long while the spirit will become mature, and there will naturally be no more [frightening experiences]. [Your Radiant Spirit will] conceal and manifest in unfathomable ways. Its changes and transformations will be limitless. The future will spontaneously be known, and you will have no attachments to anything you see or hear. Only give heed to the self-so-ness. If you become attached to appearances, these are but illusions.[25]

As is indicated in the passage's heading, the strange phenomena described here are regarded as "signs" that the adept is progressing nearer to his goal of recovering his Real Nature, described here as the Radiant Spirit that emerges from the Real *qi* mobilized within the body. The delightful sensations, tastes, and sounds are to be taken as encouraging signs that the Real *qi* has begun to be mobilized properly. However, the adept also sometimes experiences visions or sensations that will frighten him. If he fails to maintain his composure, this is due to the immaturity of his Radiant Spirit.

Later on in the same text, "Qiu Chuji" describes a procedure for producing Real *qi* and radiant *yang* spirits out of the five viscera. Here he draws attention also to the internal demons and the harmful visions that they create:

> In accordance with the proper day and time, refine the five viscera. The reality of energy will spontaneously appear, and the reality of spirit will come out on its own. Illuminate both of them (visualize and concentrate on them), and they will ascend and enter the Heavenly Palace (the brain). Defend yourself against the *yin* demons and external devils who confuse the truth by means of what is false. At this time, the *qi* will follow the spirit and rise, and the spirit, adhering to the *qi* will rise from the Central Field (heart) into the Upper Field (the brain). *Yin* demons wish for people to age quickly, and external devils do not rejoice when people are at peace. [Thus] they falsely create [illusions of] armies and deceitfully give rise to floating flowers (visions of wealth and grandeur). They also disguise themselves as *yang* spirits, mingling and rising up together with them (the real *yang* spirits). It will thus be confusing and hard to distinguish between who is a real form and who is a false form. The sound of flutes will surround you, and chariots and horses will together arise.
>
> If you wish to tell them apart, nothing is better than to arouse the perfect fire (concentrate the mind) inside the vermilion (the heart). One [type of burning] is called "burning the body," a second is called "subduing the demons," a third is called "expelling the Three

> Corpses,"[26] a fourth is called "chasing away the seven *po*,"[27] and a fifth is called "gathering the *yang* spirits."
>
> Amidst stillness, visualize inside and naturally [the distinction] will be clear. Just look at the people mingling with each other amidst the fire. In a short while, the ones who rise up singing music will be your *yang* spirits, and the ones wailing and sobbing and going away will be the *yin* demons in your body.[28]

Thus much of what the adept can expect to see in the trance vision is an illusory creation of demons seeking to undermine his or her training. "Qiu Chuji," therefore, prescribes a method for arousing one's inner "fires" to burn away the demonic phantoms.

However, ultimate victory and dominance over evil is not attained until the "external devils" also are overcome. "Qiu Chuji" tells us that after the *yang* spirits have prevailed over the internal demons and have ascended into the brain, a vast panorama of mountains and rivers appears before the eyes of the adept as the "fire" (mental concentration) is extinguished and a "clean and cool" sensation is experienced. Aside from this vast natural scenery, the adept must make sure that he ignores everything else, because "ten devils" from outside of the body will try to deceive him by creating ten tempting visions or sensations. The temptations by the ten devils—which are virtually identical to those described in the *Zhong-Lü chuandao ji*—are as follows (here I paraphrase from the text):

1. The devil of the six desires: Flute music, beautiful flowers, sweet flavors, excellent fragrances, and good feelings.
2. The devil of the seven emotions: Nice breezes, pleasant sunshine, violent thunder and lightning storms, nice music, and pathetic wailing voices.
3. The devil of wealth: Sights of various luxuries.
4. The devil of nobility: Sights of royal and military pomp and gallantry.
5. The devil of love: Sights of family and relatives undergoing severe difficulties and tragedies.
6. The devil of calamities: Sights of one's own body facing various hazards.
7. The devil of swords and soldiers: Sights of armies engaging in battles.
8. The devil of the Holy Sages: The sight of the Three Pure Ones, the Jade Emperor, and other supreme deities.[29]
9. The devil of female entertainment enjoyment: Sights of Immortal Beauties and Jade Girls dancing and performing music.
10. The devil of women and sex: Sights of gorgeous women trying to seduce you.

As discussed previously (see chapter 4), some skepticism is in order as to whether the teachings in *Dadan zhizhi* are truly those of Qiu Chuji. However, as we have already seen in this chapter from evidence in *Zhenxian zhizhi yulu*, Qiu Chuji did indeed know and speak enthusiastically—albeit cautiously—of special trance experiences. If he ever spoke in further detail on such matters, he perhaps uttered something similar to what we find in the *Dadan zhizhi*.

It is relevant here to mention some other types of special phenomena known to internal alchemists. The aforementioned "Jindan zhengyan" ("Golden Elixir Signs of Proof")[30] describes phenomena that will occur during a 100-day period of solitary meditation confined to a "quiet room," perhaps a practice similar or identical to the solitary *huandu* meditation of the Quanzhen School that also was typically carried out for 100 days. The text states that within three to five days of practice, the adept will gain a stability of mind and harmony of *qi*. From this point on, various auspicious phenomena can be expected to appear as "proof" of his progress. Suddenly his[31] heart-fire will descend, and his kidney-water will ascend (apparently he feels a certain inner sensation that he interprets in this way). He will smell strange odors, and his tongue will produce a sweet fluid. He will become able to go without food and drink and will have no need for sleep. He will feel harmonious energy flow throughout the channels of his body, and his seminal essence will flow backward (thus nourishing the body rather than being emitted). He will obtain extraordinary vision that will allow him to see things clearly in the dark, and even through solid objects. He will foresee future events and be able to look into the "heavenly pavilions above" and "the infernal prisons below." A red mist will wrap around the top of his head, and he will emit a circular light from between his eyebrows.

At the same time, however, "Jindan zhengyan" warns of hazards, temptations, and diseases that can afflict the adept and that need to be overcome before the above-mentioned benefits can come about. At times, the adept may feel his "wise spirit leap and dance," and this will cause him to dance and sing spontaneously, to utter crazy words from his mouth, or to write poems incessantly, without being able to control himself. This disorder, the text tells us, is caused by the evil Three Corpses[32] and can completely undermine the fruits of all previous effort if not prevented or brought under control. The Three Corpses also can cause the adept to be prone to excessive moods of joy or sorrow and compel him to constantly engage people in jovial conversations and discussions of the Tao. The adept may experience various physical disorders such as excessive or insufficient appetite, vomiting, bad breath, an endless flow of foul mucus from the nose, rumbling in the belly, "leakage in back and front" (involuntary seminal ejaculation, bowel or bladder excretion or flatulence?), foul-smelling excretions, discolored urine, weakness, lethargy, doubts, anxiety, nightmares, evil visions, and fever.[33]

In the *Chongyang quanzhen ji*, one can find poems by Quanzhen founder, Wang Zhe, that pertain to "signs of proof" such as those described in "Jindan zhengyan" and *Dadan zhizhi*. In one poem (previously quoted in chapter 3) he states, "When you have thoroughly nurtured your spirit and *qi*, you will no longer feel cold, get hungry, nor sleep."[34] Thus he affirms the assertion made in "Jindan zhengyan," that an adept can become invulnerable to hunger, thirst, and fatigue. The Quanzhen masters were indeed renowned for feats of fasting and sleep avoidance, as we have seen in chapter 3. While the hagiographies may exaggerate these feats, it is undoubtedly true that Quanzhen adepts made conscious efforts to decrease their food intake and sleep. Naturally they would have cherished the notion that the body can—theoretically at least—overcome all need for nourishment and rest. Various other poems by Wang Zhe seem to attest to various trance phenomena akin to what is described in texts such as *Dadan zhizhi* and "Jindan zhengyan":

> Dwelling in a realm of refreshing coolness,
> Remotely I open up a new school.
> I attain serenity,
> And in this serenity is the true sweetness.
> The sweet dew of delectable taste comes forth,
> Cleansing my three burners, six bowels, and five viscera,
> They all become resplendent.
> Flowing and circulating with no obstructions,
> Overturning and all interpenetrating.
>
> White *qi* fills the intestines completely,
> Helping me give rise to my original being.
> You simply must plumb deeply,
> And await from time to time.
> Clearly in the coming and going discern east and west.
> Thereby you get to know your wise countenance,
> And this form emerges upon the arch of the heavens.
> Manifested completely, it emits its radiance that brilliantly illuminates,
> As it eternally dwells in the clear sky.[35]

Here Wang Zhe speaks of a cool sensation, profound peace, sweet flavors, and the activity of fluids and energies that cleanse, circulate, and nourish the body. This all culminates in the emergence of his original Real Nature that radiates brilliantly and mounts the skies.

Before noon and after midnight, you should join the spears in combat.
Seize the golden essence, and manifest your merit in battle.
A single human head will come down.
Hold it up joyfully and present it to Sir Ding.[36]

The ten thousand stalwart spirits vanquish the devilish troops.
They defeat the thousand evils in battle without employing a guest.
Alone manifest a radiance as brilliant as the sunshine.
Hereby know that there is a precious pearl in this place.[37]

Call forth your origins and observe in detail.
Glowing and complete is the purple-gold elixir.
Clearly brilliant, complete, and wondrous, it is without compare.
Five rays of misty radiance converge into one.[38]

It would appear that Wang Zhe himself in his meditative trances witnessed—or expected to witness—a conflict between inner spirits and inner demons similar to that described in *Dadan zhizhi*. He also mentions the coming down of a "human head," the phenomenon that his disciple, Qiu Chuji, would describe as a sign of the completion of the "golden elixir" (see previous discussion). Also noteworthy is the description of the "elixir" (the immortal Real Nature/Radiant Spirit) as being formed by the convergence of five rays, which seem to represent the five spirits of the five viscera, which—according to the *Dadan zhizhi*—merge to form the singular immortal Spirit.

There also is some reason to wonder whether Wang Zhe may have been afflicted with some of the problems mentioned in the "Jindan zhengyan." As noted previously, that text warns that inner demons (the Three Corpses) can cause the adept to dance and sing spontaneously, to utter crazy words from his mouth, or to write poems incessantly. It also says that mood swings and talkativeness can be symptoms of such demonic influence. Think what one may of the notion of the Three Corpses,[39] one wonders whether Wang Zhe's eccentricities were caused by mental disorders brought on by the rigors of self-denial and meditation. As we have seen, hagiographic records tell us that Wang Zhe answered to the nickname "Lunatic" (Haifeng), which he had earned as a result of his drunken, erratic deportment (this was particularly marked during the first few years after his conversion in 1159). He frequently danced and sang like a crazy man in public, and he uttered strange words that people usually took merely as mad ravings. He once set fire to his meditation hut and was found singing and dancing wildly by the fire, to the bewilderment of those who had come to his rescue. Later, after he had begun to attract a significant following, he took to frequently physically and verbally abusing his disciples (to test their sincerity and will power). On one occasion (as we saw in chapter 4), he relieved himself in front of the county government offices, right after an admirer had extolled him for being "without leakage" (*wulou*).[40] Interestingly, there is one poem in the *Chongyang quanzhen ji* where Wang Zhe says, "I always must compose poetry, and my brush does not stop."[41] However, it is not made clear as to what compelled him to write, and whether this compulsion in any way eluded the control of his rational will. Whatever the case, it should be duly noted that neither Wang Zhe nor his hagiographers admit to anything pathological or demon-influenced in his conduct.

## Difficulties and Frustrations Involved in Gaining "Signs of Proof"

Apparently "signs of proof" did not come easy—even for the Quanzhen masters. Even for the precociously gifted Yin Zhiping, the "signs" came, but rarely, at least during his early years of discipleship:

> This fool [Yin Zhiping (referring to himself)] one day while in stillness (meditation) felt a stage of *qi*. [*Qi*] spurted up to my head, making a noise as my head split open. Sweet liquid cascaded down. After this there was no particular news (signs of proof) to speak of, and thus I gave rise to doubts. I went to the residence of the Master-Father (Qiu Chuji) for consultation. Whenever any of the residents there consulted him regarding their doubts, they would be angrily scolded by the Master-Father. What he meant to say was that in studying the Tao, how can there be any further doubts?
>
> However, the Master-Father knew that this person (I, Yin Zhiping) was sincere, thus he entertained his inquiries. . . .
>
> After this the Master-Father inquired [of me] from time to time as to whether there had been any more news. When he found out that there had been no more news, he made [me] live in the monastery and accumulate merits and deeds (*gongxing*) by [performing the duty of] welcoming and waiting on [guests and visitors]. From this we can know that even if one engages in bitter training, without merits and deeds, one cannot succeed.[42]

Interesting here is how Qiu Chuji takes great interest in the trance sensations of Yin Zhiping and anxiously waits to see if he has any more "news." When it becomes apparent that no further "news" is forthcoming, he assigns Yin Zhiping to menial chores so he can accumulate "merits and deeds" (*gongxing*). The moral of the anecdote is that harsh self-discipline and meditation must be combined with service toward others before one can be blessed with "signs of proof." Qiu Chuji felt that Yin Zhiping might move closer toward earning such blessings by providing humble service to monastery guests.

Another episode related by Yin Zhiping indicates that Qiu Chuji also had great difficulty trying to receive "news":

> Master-Father Changchun (Qiu Chuji) was at Panxi and Longmen for close to twenty years. His will and energy pervaded Heaven and Earth and moved the holy sages. He was permitted [to partake in] the Tao. But later all news became distant [from him]. The Master-Father persevered harder than ever, and only then [re-] gained it (the "news" from the Tao). Not long thereafter, it was taken away from him again. This was all because his merits and deeds were insufficient. The Masters and Realized Beings are [thus] also like this. Much more is it the case with everyone else! Students must simply train and make progress in their merits and deeds without seeking for manifest signs. Do not give rise to doubts. When your actions have been sufficient, you will spontaneously have an opening up of insight.[43]

Apparently Qiu Chuji alternated between phases where he frequently enjoyed special trance phenomena and phases where he received no "news" at all. The "news" was considered a blessing that the holy sages (immortals) would bestow upon those they deemed worthy based on their merits (intensity and duration of self-discipline and meditation) and deeds (number of virtuous actions). The blessing could be bestowed or withdrawn at their will, and Qiu Chuji's merits and deeds were as of yet insufficient to sustain their favor.

Of particular interest is an episode related by Yin Zhiping in which a certain disciple of Qiu Chuji's witnessed in trance the coming down of a human head. This, as previously dicussed, is a vision that Qiu Chuji himself mentioned as being a sign that the "golden elixir" was complete. Naturally, then, the disciple sought out the master for validation of his experience:

> In Shandong there was a Mister Zhang who had sat [in meditation] in his enclosure for several years. When sitting he would see a single shorn hemp stem fall down in front of him. He took notice of this about three or five times and then stopped paying attention to it. Suddenly one day a human face came falling down from the ceiling. It stood on the ground before him and emitted a long mouthful of breath. Mr. Zhang wondered whether it was his body outside the body (Real Nature/Radiant Spirit). He thus came out of his enclosure and came to the residence of Master-Father Changchun (Qiu

> Chuji) in order to consult him on these ponderings. When he saw the Master-Father he bowed in respect, knelt before him, and was about to speak of the visions he had had in his enclosure. [However], the Master-Father already knew, and said, "When a practitioner does his work (meditates), he must not acknowledge and look at anything he sees with his eyes. Even [if he sees] a Master-Father, no. Even [if he sees] a Buddha, no. Even [if he sees] a god, no. Even [if he sees] a demon, no. Even [if he sees] a human, no. Even [if he sees] a dragon, no. Even [if he sees] a tiger, no. Even [if he sees] all the stars and planets in the heavens above, no. Even [if he sees] all the birds and beasts on the earth below, no."
>
> Mr. Zhang still had doubts, and could not help but think [that he had seen his] body outside the body. Thus he went to see Master-Father Changsheng (Liu Chuxuan) and told him about the visions he had seen. Master-Father Changsheng said, "What brother Qiu told you is correct. As for the visions that practitioners have, if you become attached to them they are evil. Amidst all types of visions, you should not become influenced or attached. When your efforts have been sufficient, the Tao will naturally respond, and you will have no doubts [as to the veracity of the Tao's response]." Zhang bowed and thanked him.[44]

The passage thus tells us that Qiu Chuji—who with his clairvoyant powers already knew what Mr. Zhang had seen—did not deem his vision an authentic manifestation of the Real Nature/Radiant Spirit. Quite to the contrary, he admonished him strictly to heed no vision, however marvelous and auspicious it may seem. Asked for a second opinion, Liu Chuxuan confirmed the view of Qiu Chuji, but he also offered him the kind assurance that an authentic experience will come some day when his efforts have proved sufficient. When this true enlightenment experience happens, Mr. Zhang will simply know beyond a doubt. The lack of certainty that compelled Mr. Zhang to seek validation from Masters Qiu and Liu was thus to them a revealing sign of the falsity of his vision and his spiritual immaturity.

All of the above episodes bear as a common moral the notion that diligent training and virtuous behavior are eventually rewarded, and that the "signs of proof" in meditative trance are among the rewards. However, one rather exceptional passage in the collected sayings of Yin Zhiping takes into account a factor that is quite beyond the control of even the most diligent and virtuous:

> This is something that Master-Father Changsheng (Liu Chuxuan) used to speak of often. I once personally heard this [from him]. [Liu

> Chuxuan] said, "Training needs to correspond with the proper time. It is now the auspicious autumn of the *jiazi* year of the heavenly plane (1204?).[45] Once this time passes, training will become very difficult."
>
> When I first heard this, I did not really believe it. This was because my understanding was not yet deep. It has now been a long time since I entered the Tao, and I believe that the significance of the times is great. Looking back on the early years of Master-Father Changsheng's (Liu Chuxuan) [Quanzhen] School leadership, [I recall that] when adepts dwelled in silence and did their exercises (meditation), they would have news upon their heart not long after beginning their practice. Cases such as this were frequent and numerous. But in these later years, why do we never see anybody attain this? It is because the times are wrong.[46]

The above passage attests to an apparent decline in the Quanzhen School. This is not, of course, a decline in the size of the movement; the movement was, in fact, at the height of its influence and popularity. The perceived decline, rather, is in the frequency of "news" among Quanzhen adepts. But rather than blame his followers here for any lack of effort and virtue, Yin Zhiping laments that the "times" are bad. While the underlying theory is not explained here, Yin Zhiping had come to believe that progress in self-cultivation could be hindered by cosmic processes altogether beyond human control. But if he understood the cosmic process as being cyclical (which seems to be implied by the apparent reference to the sexegenary cycle), then he may have upheld hope that the "times" would eventually improve—although perhaps not during his own lifetime.

## Conclusion

In early Quanzhen Taoism, visions and other trance experiences were valued as "signs of proof"—evidence that one's merits and deeds were sufficient to move the "holy sages" (the immortal Taoist brethren who benevolently watch, aid, and guide adepts). The holy sages were thought to then either manifest their countenances to the adept or make their presence and power apparent in some other marvelous way. However, the "signs of proof" also were seen as hazards and distractions. Some, in fact, were thought to be of demonic origin. By and large, one needed to avoid being overly anxious to experience them and needed to ignore them when they occurred. So how was one to distinguish demonic trance phenomena from the work of the holy sages? What "signs of proof" truly signified the complete recovery of one's immortal Real

Nature? These, according to the Quanzhen masters, were superfluous questions. When the "signs" are authentic, one simply knows, and this inner certainty is the best proof of their veracity. Thus one need not worry about these things but simply strive to accumulate "merits" and "deeds." The central message of Quanzhen is extremely simple: keep the mind clear and pure (*qingjing*, which confers "merits"), and practice humility and compassion (this confers "deeds"). "Signs of proof" should eventually come as a result of this endeavor but should not be consciously anticipated or sought out.

The fact is, however, that the Quanzhen masters were deeply concerned and troubled when "signs of proof" failed to appear to them or their disciples. Ultimately they recognized that no noble human endeavor—whether self-disclipline, morality, or meditation—can be fully guaranteed to bring the desired "signs of proof." Thus the "signs of proof" had to be interpreted as something conditioned by forces beyond human control, such as the will of the holy sages or the "times."[47]

# Chapter 6

## The Miraculous Powers of the Quanzhen Masters

> The Dharma Body (*fashen*) is an appearance without form. It is not emptiness, and it is not being. It has nothing after it, and it has nothing before it. It is not beneath, and it is not high. It is not long, and it is not short. If used, it has no place where it does not penetrate, and if stored, it is obscure and silent without a trace. If you acquire this Tao, truly you should nurture it. If you nurture it much, your merits will be numerous. If you nurture it only a little, your merits will be few. You should not wish to return [to transcendent eternity],[1] and you should not cherish the world. In going and coming, you should be natural.[2]

The Dharma Body (a term borrowed from Buddhism)[3] that Wang Zhe describes is the eternal Real Nature or Radiant Spirit that the adept recovers through self-cultivation. It is in fact the Tao itself—the eternal, universal force or principle that transcends ordinary sense perception and verbal description. Of greatest interest here is that Wang Zhe claims that the Dharma Body "penetrates" everywhere if "used." Could he be speaking of special powers that an adept can exercise by his recovery and apprehension of the Dharma Body? He also recommends "nurturing" the Tao a great deal after "acquiring" it to gain greater merit (*gong*). More concretely, he seems to be saying that one should diligently continue one's cultivation after an initial mystical apprehension has been achieved. By saying that the "merits" gained will consequently be more numerous, does he perhaps in part mean to say that the adept gains greater powers?

Quanzhen hagiography is full of miracles. People always have been and always will be fascinated by feats beyond the ordinary. In various religions throughout the world, miracles—or claims thereof—have been instrumental in bringing people to faith. China is no exception, and the rapid growth of the Quanzhen movement in northern China in the twelfth and thirteenth centuries is an excellent case in point.

Of course, the miracle stories in the Quanzhen hagiographies are probably largely a product of pious imagination and evangelistic zeal. In many cases they probably have no basis in actual events, or in the personal claims of the early Quanzhen masters. In fact, there is evidence to show that the Quanzhen masters were critical of those who placed too much emphasis on miracles. Ma Yu, for example, wrote the following poem:

> "Admonishing Those Who Speak of Nonexistent Supernatural Phenomena"
> Because of the lunatics (the Quanzhen masters) you escaped from the bondage of your home.
> Having completely escaped your familial attachments you now need to purify your mind's ground (eliminate confused thoughts).
> Stop speaking of non-existent supernatural phenomena and deceiving good people.
> Do not make light of the spirits and insult the ghosts.[4]

Hao Datong once stated:

> The Master-Father (Wang Zhe) opened below him his school of teaching hoping that each [disciple] would cultivate immortality. I now see disciples all over the place creating *karma*. They speak of strange and deceitful things such as entering dreams and sending out the Spirit.[5]

In the above passages, both Ma Yu and Hao Datong criticize disciples within their fold for speaking of miracles and other supernatural phenomena. Both masters accuse such disciples of deception and further point out that their preoccupation with such matters is detrimental to their spiritual progress. Both masters maintain that Wang Zhe, when he started the Quanzhen movement, did not intend for his followers to become obsessed with such things. One hagiographer, scholar-official Liu Zuqian (fl. 1224), echoes this same view:

> As for [Wang Zhe] sending out his Spirit and entering dreams, throwing his umbrella, tossing his cap, and other such deeds of rising

> high above or disappearing, these were are all his [acts of] expedient wisdom and are not [related to] the master's basic teachings. As for students who wish to hear the great Tao, it is [only] possible if they do not drown themselves in magical techniques.[6]

Liu Zuqian astutely observed that self-cultivation and virtuous behavior constituted the core of Quanzhen practice. To obtain magical powers and work miracles was not the objective. Nonetheless, it appears from the above passage that Liu Zuqian did not deny that Wang Zhe had performed miracles during his lifetime. He apparently just means to say that the miracles were performed as a tactic to inspire faith and piety in people. In fact, Liu Zuqian's account of Wang Zhe's life—although considerably more sober than others—does mention a few miracles.[7]

Turning our attention back to the comments of Ma Yu and Hao Datong, it appears that Quanzhen disciples may have been unusually prone to getting engrossed in the realm of the supernatural. Such is indeed not surprising in light of the strong mystical leanings of the Quanzhen masters themselves, who had striven to gain the so-called "signs of proof." As we have seen, the "signs of proof" included not only special visions and locutions (in many cases considered spiritual communications from immortal brethren) but also special physical symptoms and capacities. Once one has affirmed the veracity of such experiences and phenomena, it is probably relatively easy to entertain the notion that one can perform miracles of the kind described in the hagiographies. In fact, as we shall see, there is clear evidence that in some cases the miracle stories originated from the Quanzhen masters' own claims.

This chapter will briefly examine the simple theoretical basis for the belief in miracles in the Quanzhen tradition and then proceed to examine the extent to which the masters themselves confirmed the miraculous accounts of the hagiographies.

## How to Attain Miraculous Power

> The Tao creates Heaven and nurtures Earth. The sun, the moon, stars, demons, gods, people, and [all other] things are all born from the Tao. People only understand the greatness of Heaven and do not understand the greatness of the Tao. I, during my lifetime, abandoned my family and left my home so that I could concentrate on studying only this (the Tao).
>
> The Tao gave birth to Heaven and Earth [which] separated [and] gave birth to people. When people were first created, [their] spiritual light shined naturally, and they went about walking as

> though they were flying. The earth produced mushrooms that on their own had an excellent flavor and did not require any cooking. People all ate them. At this time they still did not cook with fire. The mushrooms were all fragrant. Their (the peoples') noses smelled the fragrance, and their mouths enjoyed the flavor. This gradually brought about the heaviness of their bodies, and their spiritual light was soon thereafter extinguished because of the deepness of their wants and desires.[8]

The above passage appears within a sermon that Qiu Chuji delivered in the presence of Genghis Khan. The claim made here is that human beings originally possessed spiritual and physical capacities far surpassing those of ordinary people in later ages. Their spirits were so powerful that they took the form of a bright light that emanated from their bodies. The strength and vitality of their bodies was so great that they moved about swiftly and easily as though they were flying. The loss of these powers is blamed on human desires, which were first stimulated by the fragrant mushrooms.

It is uncertain whether Qiu Chuji literally believed that such events transpired in primordial times. The real point of the story seems to be that there exists a power that completely transcends the ordinary, yet is present within every part of creation. Most people know of and have access to only the ordinary realm of power (the greatness of Heaven) and cannot comprehend the transcendent power (the greatness of the Tao) that lies hidden within. Thus the Taoist adept strives to access this power, and the key to this endeavor is to eliminate worldly desires that obscure this power.

Among Qiu Chuji's poems, one also can find the following short tribute to the power of the Tao:

> The Tao's power (*daoli*) and divine workings (*shen'gong*) cannot be [adequately] described.
> [The Tao] creates and completes the myriad beings and alone looms above.
> It [even] knows the lightness and heaviness of the great mountains and ocean peaks.
> It sinks to the depths and floats in empty space for 10,000 × 10,000 years.[9]

Qiu Chuji lauds the omnipotence, omniscience, and ubiquity of the Tao. The word used here to designate the Tao's divine workings is "*shen'gong*"—the "*gong*" being the same character used to denote the "merit" that a Quanzhen adept is told to accumulate through self-discipline and meditation. As we saw in the passage quoted at the beginning of this chapter, Wang Zhe taught that "merit" increases in proportion to the extent to which one has "nurtured" the Tao after having once "acquired" it. Does it follow that through much accumulation of *gong* (merit), one becomes capable of *shen'gong* (divine workings)? After all, a fundamental assumption here is that the Tao itself (the Real Nature/Radiant Spirit/Dharma Body) lies latent at the ground of one's being.

Wang Chuyi appears to have claimed that we are potentially clairvoyant because the Tao dwells within us:

> The mind is the Tao.
> The Tao is the mind.
> If the mind merges with the Tao,
> Past and present will be penetrated.[10]

The claim here is that the omniscient Tao dwells within us as "the mind." But why must the mind merge with the Tao if it is already identical to it? Presumably Wang Chuyi uses the word "mind" in two different senses. The mind that is the Tao is the Real Nature as distinct from selfish thoughts, feelings, and desires. The mind that must merge with the Tao is the individual's total mind that needs to uncover the Real Nature from the cluttered depths of its thoughts, feelings, and desires.

Liu Chuxuan, in his commentary to the *Yinfu jing*, states that the apprehension of the Tao leads to omniscience, and also to special powers in the realm of action:

> If you fathom and penetrate the Tao, Heaven and Earth will be penetrated. If Heaven and Earth are penetrated, the myriad transformations will be penetrated. If the myriad transformations are penetrated, your spirit penetrates (*shentong*).[11] *If your spirit penetrates, you will respond to circumstances with myriad changes* (emphasis added). [Thereby] you will embrace the One (the Tao) without letting go and serenely nurture your Real [Nature] and return to simplicity.[12]

The italicized sentence seems to at least imply that the omniscience obtained from apprehending the Tao also brings with it the capacity for wondrous feats. Of course, a more sober interpretation would be that enlightened wisdom enables one to spontaneously respond to any situation in the best manner—without necessarily performing any miracles. Yet it is difficult to dismiss the possibility that Liu Chuxuan has miracles at least partially in mind here, particularly in light of the fact that he employs the terms *tong* (penetrate) and *shentong* (spirit penetrates). In Chinese Buddhist literature, these words are used to refer to *siddhi*, the supernormal powers that a Buddhist saint acquires through training. Of these *siddhi*, there are said to be six (*liutong*): (1) *Siddhi* of the Divine Foot (*shenzutong*)—the ability to go anywhere instantaneously; (2) *Siddhi* of the Heavenly Eye (*tianyantong*)—the ability to see into the past and future; (3) *Siddhi* of the Heavenly Ear (*tian'ertong*)—the ability to hear sounds that ordinary people cannot; (4) *Siddhi* of the Minds of Others (*taxintong*)—the ability to read minds; (5) *Siddhi* of Past Lives (*sumingtong*)—the ability to know of one's past lives; and (6) *Siddhi* of No Outflowings (*wuloutong*)—the ability to be without the craving for existence, the craving for sensual pleasures and ignorance.[13] Taoists were certainly familiar with this usage of the word *tong* and were not averse to employing it themselves. This fact is best born out in the anonymous essay, "Lun liutong jue" (Lesson on the Six Penetrations [*Siddhi*]), found in the *neidan* anthology, *Zhuzhen neidan jiyao* (comp. ca. 1300). This essay—the actual connection to the Quanzhen movement of which is uncertain—describes six *tong* that are acquired or experienced during *neidan* meditation.[14] It should be noted, however, that these six *tong* are not identical to the Buddhist Six *Siddhis*, and to a large extent they denote "signs of proof" such as those discussed in the previous chapter.[15]

By "merging with" or "fathoming and penetrating" the Tao," one gains extraordinary abilities. But how does one actually go about this? Liu Chuxuan, in poems such as the following, indicates that the key to this lies in the elimination of desires and the purification of the mind:

> If you are free of desires like the blueness of the [cloudless] sky,
> Naturally the myriad phenomena will be clear.
> Your eternal soul will merge with the Tao.
> [When] responding to transformations, you will speak [with great wisdom] like a scripture.[16]

> If objects are eliminated [from your thoughts], the Tao's light is born.
> If the sky is blue (clear), your precious mirror will be bright.
> If your life is pure, complete and without deficiency,
> Your responses to transformations will naturally be numinous.[17]

Liu Chuxuan uses the classic metaphors of the blue sky and the bright mirror to describe the enlightened mind. This mind, purged of its desires and confusions, is said to merge with the Tao, or to emit the Tao's radiance from within. The adept, as a result, manifests extraordinary ability in his or her words and actions. Again, however, the question lingers as to whether Liu Chuxuan actually has in mind miracles as such, or simply some sort of intuitive knack for appropriate, effective words and actions. At this point it is necessary to look at some testimony from the Quanzhen masters pointing directly to specific miracles.

## Manifesting the Radiant Spirit

As we have seen in previous chapters, Quanzhen adepts strove to obtain—or, more properly speaking, to recover—the immortal life of the Real Nature/Radiant Spirit. In their meditative trances, adepts hoped to gain a vision of the immortal entity that dwelled within them. Hagiographies tell us about various extraordinary attributes and powers that the Quanzhen masters possessed in that they housed such a marvelous entity in themselves. One such attribute was the "spiritual light" (*shenguang*) that at times radiated out of their bodies.[18] When the Radiant Spirit traveled outside of the body, it was said to be visible to others. *Tixuan zhenren xianyi lu* tells of the time when Mr. Liu, the Liquor Official[19] of Cangzhou (in Hebei), invited Wang Chuyi to have a few drinks with him. After a few drinks, Wang Chuyi lay down on his side and fell asleep. While asleep inside of Mr. Liu's house, he simultaneously appeared in Mr. Liu's storehouse, where he drank massive quantities of liquor. Having witnessed this incredible miracle, Mr. Liu and his wife took faith in the Tao, became Taoist monastics, and gave everything they had to the poor.[20] Similar feats are attributed to Wang Zhe,[21] Tan Chuduan,[22] and Liu Chuxuan.[23]

The hagiographies also tell us that a Realized One could "send out the Spirit and enter dreams" (*chushen rumeng*). This, we are told by some sources, was a method that Wang Zhe used to convert Ma Yu and Sun Bu'er. One source tells us that Wang Zhe "sent out his spirit and entered their dreams with various kinds of changes and manifestations, scaring them with [scenes of] purgatory and inviting them with [scenes of] heaven."[24] Another source includes a much more elaborate account, according to which Wang Zhe—who was locked voluntarily inside of his meditation hut—appeared before Ma Yu in his sleeping quarters in the second story of his locked house. This source further reports that a person (or people?) wanted to draw a picture of this Radiant Spirit of Wang Zhe's that appeared before Ma Yu. However, this was impossible, because "his left eye turned clockwise and his right eye turned counter-clockwise, and sometimes he appeared as old, young, fat, skinny, yellow, vermillion, blue, and white with no constant form nor color."[25] Thus the text is perhaps claiming that Wang Zhe's Radiant Spirit appeared to Ma Yu not in his dreams but in waking experience, and that the Spirit was seen by others in the household. (A different source in fact claims that Wang Zhe's actual physical appearance was constantly changing.[26]) Another possibility is that he saw Wang Zhe's Radiant Spirit in his dreams but was unable to describe its appearance in a manner that could enable an artist to draw a portrait. The same text also tells of how Ma Yu had three dreams that were preindications of certain names and titles that Wang Zhe would bestow upon him.[27] While Wang Zhe himself does not appear in all of the dreams, the author most likely means to say that Wang Zhe somehow caused Ma Yu to have the dreams.

Confirmation of these specific incidents is not found in the extant writings of Wang Zhe and Ma Yu. However, Ma Yu, in his own writings, does attest to incidents where Wang Zhe supposedly somehow intentionally entered or manipulated his dreams:

> Master-Father Chongyang (Wang Zhe) resorted to a hundred different ways to persuade and convert me. However, I always would prove to have too many attachments and longings [to the world]. Suddenly one evening, I dreamed that I was standing in the middle of my central courtyard, lamenting to myself saying, "My life is like a thin ceramic bowl; if I drop it, it will shatter into a hundred pieces!" Before I had finished saying this, a bowl came falling down from midair, and I awoke crying in horror. The next day the Master (Wang Zhe) said [to me], "You were frightened last night, and [now] you have finally come to repent and understand.[28]

> The master (Ma Yu) said, "When I was in my home village (Ninghai), the Patriarch-Master (Wang Zhe) ordered his disciples to go into Laizhou to beg. For several days I hesitated. [One] night I dreamed of the master saying, "Tomorrow extend your hands [to solicit alms] for a long time and become a good fellow. Go out on the streets and put out your hands!"[29]

Thus Ma Yu affirms that Wang employed didactic dreams to guide him during different stages of his progress. The former dream, he claims, was instrumental in enabling him to shed his attachments to the worldly life by reminding him of the dire consequences (premature death, inauspicious rebirths, damnation, etc.) that await worldly people. The latter dream was meant to eliminate Ma Yu's vain pride; of course—as we saw previously (see chapter 3)—Wang Zhe also resorted to physical violence to accomplish this didactic task.

As the reader may recall from chapter 5, Yin Zhiping seems to have attributed his living teacher, Liu Chuxuan, with the ability to enter into his trance experiences. The above testimony of Ma Yu would indicate that the Quanzhen masters also shared with hagiographers the belief that a living master could enter or influence peoples' dreams and visions for didactic purposes. The premise underlying such beliefs seems to be the notion that the Realized One can send out his or her Radiant Spirit. Interestingly, one hagiography tells us that Tan Chuduan once entered a man's dreams not to instruct him but rather to cure his disease. However, I have found no direct testimony to this incident from Tan Chuduan himself.[30]

The Radiant Spirit was believed to survive the death of the ordinary physical body. Various passages in Quanzhen hagiography describe posthumous appearances and miracles of the Quanzhen masters. Such reported incidents are particularly numerous in the case of the founder, Wang Zhe. *Jinlian zhengzong ji*, for example, states:

> After the death of his exterior, (Wang Zhe) spoke of the profound and persuaded the mind of Old Man Zang under the Junyi Bridge. By the Liujiang Gorge he healed Mr. Zhang's disease by giving him medicine. At times [he was seen] dancing by the right side of the Kunming Pond, and at times [he was seen] singing and reciting [poetry] around Mt. Zhongnan. There have occurred [such incidents] that prove that he did not die.[31]
>
> Later, (in 10/15, Dading 23) a *jiao*[32] ritual was being held in Wendeng District (Shandong). Amidst five-colored clouds appeared an extremely large white tortoise with a lotus flower on its back. The Patriarch-Master was seated upon the lotus flower. After a while, he lay down on his side and left. The district magistrate, Nimang Ku, personally witnessed this and thus burned incense and reverently worshipped him. He ordered a painter to make a portrait of his true countenance. People of three regions gazed upon it in admiration.[33]

Interestingly, Ma Yu wrote a poem in praise of Wang Zhe that refers to some of the same incidents mentioned above, along with a few personal encounters with his immortalized master:

> "In Praise of True Man Chongyang's [Wang Zhe] Manifestations of His Extraordinariness"
> The True Man of Compassionate Transformations,
> Master-Father Chongyang;
> He had a penetrating understanding of all things,
> And predicted the time of his death.
> His speech was like the heart's wind,
> And his prediction came true in the southern capital.
> He went upwards ascending the mist,
> And later instructed Sir Zang.[34]
> At Qiyang Town (Shaanxi) he came down to the world wearing a cap.
> For me he once again transmitted merit (methods of cultivating Realization).

> West of the Huating city walls,
> He appeared and cured my miserable disease,
> And *qi* was distributed throughout my body.
> At Wendeng atop the clouds,
> He manifested his compassionate countenance.
> The district magistrate Nimang Hu saw him.
> After a while he again returned to the Heavenly Palace.
> Matters of truth and reality,
> Are rare amidst past and present.
> From these things [my master is] worthy of being worshipped by people.[35]

Thus not only did Ma Yu confirm the posthumous miracle stories described in the hagiographies, he also claimed to have personally met and been healed by the immortal Wang Zhe. Apparently he is referring to incidents mentioned in chapters 4 and 5. In chapter 4, we examined the incident at Huating, in which Ma Yu suffered food poisoning but refused to take medicine. While Ma Yu vowed to cure it on his own, the above poem indicates that he had a mystical encounter with Wang Zhe during his illness and credited his deceased master for his subsequent recovery. The encounter at Qiyang, mentioned in the above poem, is perhaps related to the incident that we examined in chapter 5, where Wang Zhe and He Dejin appeared before Ma Yu and told him to go to Qiyang.

Ma Yu's writings also refer to two other posthumous appearances by He Dejin.[36] In a poem extolling the deceased He Dejin, Ma Yu states that a year after his death, He Dejin, suddenly from empty space, presented him with a book of poetry illustrated with a fishing scene. He Dejin then warned Ma Yu not to "lose sight" and to refrain from being proud of his insight into what is mysterious.[37] This was probably a trance vision of the sort that occurred during meditation. However, Ma Yu also gives testimony to an incident where the deceased He Dejin appeared to a layperson in a dream:

> [The following incident occurred] after the Master-Uncle Sir He [Dejin] had ascended to the mists. In Lintong County there was a certain embroidered silk merchant named Sir Zhang, who had long been ailing from an illness that could not be cured. Suddenly one evening he saw the Master-Uncle in a dream. [The Master-Uncle] told him what the proper medicines and treatments for his illness were. When [Sir Zhang] asked him what his name was, he replied that he was Mr. He of Zhongnan. After waking up, [Sir Zhang] followed the prescription [given by He Dejin], and the illness was cured as a matter of course. On the ninth day of the ninth month of the

> *jiawu* year (October 6, 1174), Sir Zhang personally visited the grave of Sir He to burn incense and offer his thanks. He also set up a commemorative stele to be place atop his sepulchral tower. I thus presented him with this poem.[38]

Ma Yu, along with the grateful Sir Zhang, believed that the dream was a manifestation of He Dejin's compassion, wisdom, and power, and that the disease was cured as a result of it. Ma Yu's poem that follows the above passage fully confirms and extols the alleged feat of He Dejin and goes on to exhort Sir Zhang to pursue the Taoist training and attain Realization. To attain Realization, Ma Yu claims, is the best way to show his gratitude to He Dejin.[39]

Wang Zhe's alleged epiphany in Wendeng took place on 10/15, Dading 23 (November 1, 1183).[40] Ma Yu himself passed away a little over three months later, on 12/22 (February 5, 1184), which happened to be Wang Zhe's birthday, according to the Chinese lunar calendar. Three sources tell us that Ma Yu, just before dying, had visions of Wang Zhe and He Dejin (invisible to his disciples attending him), beckoning him from midair to join them among the ranks of immortals.[41] Not surprisingly, hagiographies tell us that Ma Yu manifested himself posthumously more than once.[42] For example, one source states:

> In the first month of the 24th year [of the Dading reign era] (1184), Changsheng (Liu Chuxuan) officiated a *jiao* ritual in Changyang. On the eighteenth day [of the month] (March 2) during the *si* (9–11 A.M.) and *wu* (11 A.M.–1 P.M.) [double-]hours, the *jinshi* scholar, Xu Shaozu, and others saw strange forms of auspicious clouds, phoenixes, and cranes. They flew and danced in forms that are indescribable. Chongyang (Wang Zhe), in a cloud cap and crimson garments, and Master Danyang (Ma Yu), wearing three topknots and donning a white robe, appeared upon the clouds. After a while, they left.[43]

Interestingly, Wang Chuyi, in his poetry collection, *Yunguang ji*, refers to what may be the same incident in a poem bearing the heading "Half a month after completing the Tao (passing away) [Ma Yu] suddenly manifested his true extraordinariness in mid-air." The poem reads as follows:

> Words of an immortal miraculously responded to those down below.
> Thinking about this, I realized that this must be Ma Danyang (Ma Yu).
> His flying Spirit alleviates the crises in the various counties.
> Throughout the nation let us rejoice and praise him while sitting in the place of the Tao (Taoist ritual arena).[44]

"Half a month after completing the Tao" roughly matches the date (1/18, Dading 24, although this date was actually closer to a full month after the death of Ma Yu) of the alleged incident at the Changyang *jiao* ritual. In addition, Wang Chuyi's poem seems to suggest that the incident referred to here also occurred at a communal Taoist ritual, where Ma Yu's alleged epiphany came forth in response to the prayers and piety of the faithful. Of course, there also are some significant discrepancies here from what the hagiographies report. Nothing is said about Wang Zhe appearing with Ma Yu. In fact, Ma Yu's "manifestation" appears to have taken the form of aural locutions rather than a vision. So if this poem does pertain to the same event narrated in the hagiographies, the story had become embellished considerably by the time the hagiographers got around to recording it. Whatever the case, the poem provides good evidence that the Quanzhen masters played an active and a conscious role in the deification of their Taoist brethren. In this case, it appears that witnesses reported the strange incident (apparently a disembodied voice heard at a Taoist ritual) to Wang Chuyi in the hope of receiving an explanation. Wang Chuyi then claimed that the voice belonged to the recently deceased Ma Yu, who had now become a benevolent deity that responds to prayers and relieves human suffering. Thus Wang Chuyi acted to promote the cult of Ma Yu.

Interestingly, however, there is hagiographical evidence that Ma Yu, during his lifetime, was already worshipped as a god and functioned as such. *Jinlian zhengzong ji* relates the following episode that allegedly took place when Ma Yu was still alive:

> An ox-driven cart belonging to the Seven Treasures Hermitage loaded with a large wooden pillar was passing through a steep and treacherous road. A man who was driving the cart tripped and fell onto the path of the wheels. But inside his mind, the man recited the personal name and sobriquet of Danyang (Ma Yu) and thus went completely unharmed.[45]

However, I have not found any passage in the writings of Ma Yu or any of his brethren relating to an incident such as this.

## Clairvoyance

Feats of clairvoyance described in the Quanzhen hagiographies are far too numerous to be examined comprehensively. Here we shall only examine some of the psychic feats attributed to Wang Zhe and Wang Chuyi, since the poetry collections of these two individuals contain some material that is useful for understanding the extent to which they believed or claimed themselves to be clairvoyant.

Hagiography tells us that Wang Zhe, in Dading 5 (1165), wrote a poem on the wall of the Shangqing Taiping Gong (a Taoist temple) in Zhongnan, predicting that he would die at age fifty-eight. On 4/26/Dading 7 (May 16, 1167), when he was training at Liujiang Village, he suddenly burned his hut. When people saw the flames and came to his rescue, they saw him singing and dancing joyfully in front of the burning hut. When asked why he was acting so happy, he said that it was because he knew that somebody would restore his hut in three years. In 5/Dading 7 (May 21–June 18, 1167), Wang Zhe wrote a poem on the wall of the Shangqing Gong (a Taoist temple) on Mt. Beimang, predicting that he would acquire "Ma, Tan, Liu, and Qiu" as disciples. This prophecy he fulfilled by traveling to Shandong and acquiring disciples (whom he had not previously met) with these surnames. His other prophecies were fulfilled in Dading 10 (1170). That year, Wang Zhe died in Bianjing. Ma Yu, Tan Chuduan, Liu Chuxuan, and Qiu Chuji carried his coffin back to Liujiang, where they buried him and restored the hut.[46]

Some sources tell of another prophetic act performed by Wang Zhe upon embarking on his journey form Shaanxi to Shandong. As he was going through Xianyang, he painted a picture of a triple-top-knotted Taoist monk surrounded by clouds, pine trees, and cranes. He then gave it to his friend and disciple, Shi Chuhou, saying, "Wait for me to on another day capture a horse (Ma) and return. Take [this picture] to use as a tally of identification."[47] This prophecy also was fulfilled after Wang Zhe's death, when Ma Yu—whose surname literally means "horse"—came to Shaanxi carrying Wang Zhe's coffin. Ma Yu, who was wearing his hair in three topknots in memory of Wang Zhe,[48] looked identical to the Taoist monk in the painting. According to one version of the story, Ma Yu also presented Shi Chuhou with an identical painting.[49]

So did Wang Zhe himself actually believe or claim to have such clairvoyance? Included in Wang Zhe's *Chongyang quanzhen ji*, one can indeed find his poem predicting his age at his death:

> Hai-feng, Hai-feng, an old disease will come forth,
> And his life span will not exceed fifty-eight.
> Two teachers came decisively,
> And [therefore] my Single Numinous Real Nature will truly be found
> and established.[50]

Unless this poem is a forgery interpolated into the text of the *Chongyang quanzhen ji*, it would indeed seem to indicate that Wang Zhe deemed himself capable of making such a prediction. Actually, whether this prophecy was truly fulfilled is controversial. Wang Zhe was born on 12/22/Zhenghe 2 (Northern Song dynasty, January 11, 1113) and died on 1/4/Dading 10 (Jin dynasty, January 22, 1170). According to the traditional Chinese way of reckoning age, a person is one *sui* ("year old") at the moment of birth and becomes another *sui* older every New Year's Day. By this method of reckoning, Wang Zhe was in fact already fifty-nine *sui* when he died and thus was slightly wrong—by four days—in his prediction.[51] Well aware of this problem, the author of *Qizhen nianpu* (Li Daoqian) offers an explanation:

> This year (Dading 10 [1170]) there was an intercalary fifth month, and thus the first day of spring did not come until 1/11. Thus [Wang Zhe's age at death] was only 58.[52]

His rationale here is that the New Year does not really begin until spring has officially arrived. The fact that the hagiographer is put in the position of making this explanation is actually a fairly good indication that Wang Zhe's poem is not a forgery. If forged, it probably would have been worded in a way that cast no doubt upon the accuracy of its prediction.

Also to be found in *Chongyang quanzhen ji* is the prophetic poem uttered by Wang Zhe when he burned his hut in Liujiang Village:

> The straw hut has burned completely but it does not matter.
> There will definitely be people who will want to restore it.
> Thereby they become enlightened truly ferociously.
> How can they study and acquire the flow of my wind (teaching)?[53]

According to the *Jinlian zhengzong ji*, Wang Zhe, before uttering the above poem, stated, "Three years later, there will come someone else to repair [the hut]." These words are not recorded in *Chongyang quanzhen ji*. It is possible that Wang Zhe had simply predicted that the hut would eventually be restored, without exactly specifying when.

In a prose narrative in his poetry collection, *Dongxuan jinyu ji* (1/2a–3b), Ma Yu tells us that Wang Zhe, on his deathbed, told him about his old hut at Liujiang and instructed him to bury him there and to set up a hut of mourning. Ma Yu also mentions that Wang Zhe had painted a picture for Shi Chuhou and speaks of his own first meeting with Shi Chuhou in Chang'an. However, Ma Yu does not give any description of what was depicted in the painting. He makes no mention of himself possessing an identical painting or bearing any physical resemblance to any figure depicted in the painting. He simply says that Shi Chuhou came to introduce himself. When Shi Chuhou mentioned that he himself had once been a disciple of Wang Zhe, Ma Yu recalled that Wang Zhe had indeed mentioned him in conversation and had spoken highly of him. Ma Yu then describes how he took Shi Chuhou under his wing and taught him—through skillful means—[54] to foster humility through begging (see chapter 3). Ma Yu follows up the narrative with didactic poems to Shi Chuhou that he had composed on this occasion. Also in this interesting yet puzzling narrative, Ma Yu mentions that several months before Wang Zhe first came to Shandong, he (Ma Yu) had dreamt of an immortal crane (*xianhe*) bursting its way out of the ground in his southern garden. When Wang Zhe came, he pointed to the exact same spot in the garden from which the crane had emerged in the dream and asked for permission to build his hut there. This strange occurrence also is mentioned in hagiographies, which mostly remain faithful to Ma Yu's personal testimony.[55]

Ma Yu's narrative thus gives a non-miraculous version of the events surrounding the rebuilding of the hut and his meeting with Shi Chuhou. At the same time, however, he tells the story of his dream of the cranes. In doing so he conveys a personal belief in strange psychic phenomena and provides confirmation for hagiographic accounts. Quanzhen hagiography, as we can see again from this example, was woven out of direct personal testimony from the masters, along with a great deal of pious embellishment.

Hagiographic accounts of Wang Chuyi's clairvoyant feats rival Wang Zhe's in quantity. One time, we are told, Wang Chuyi was preaching to a large group of believers late into the night. Suddenly, he wrote the word "robbers" and then shouted, "There are robbers [here]!" When the believers all went outside to look, they saw several armed robbers fleeing.[56] In Mingchang 1 (1189), when a certain Liu Zhi complained that he had no sons, Wang Chuyi wrote the words, "Four-four Respond to the Realized (One)." The next year, a son was born to Liu Zhi on the <u>four</u>teenth day of the <u>four</u>th month (May 12). When Liu Zhi, out of gratitude, asked Wang Chuyi to name his son, Wang Chuyi said, "I have already named him 'Yingzhen' (Respond to the Realized [One]). Today happens to be the day when the Realized Lord Chunyang (Lü Yan) descended into the world (was born)."[57] On the fourteenth day of the seventh month in Da'an 1 (August 15, 1209), Beijing was in the midst of a bad drought. When asked to predict when rain would fall, Wang Chuyi said that it would rain on the seventeenth day. He was correct, of course.[58] In Da'an 2 (1210), Wang Chuyi proclaimed that he saw forms of swords clashing in the sky and predicted that there would be much suffering. The Mongols invaded from the north later that same year.[59] *Tixuan zhenren xianyi lu* tells of the time when Wang Chuyi was talking and drinking with a certain Wang Zhong of Fushan (in Shandong). Wang Zhong suddenly decided to go horseback riding, despite stern warnings by Wang Chuyi. Wang Zhong fell from his horse and died, but fortunately Wang Chuyi came to the scene and resurrected him.[60]

Wang Chuyi's poetry collection, *Yunguang ji*, contains passages pertaining to the alleged prophecies of Da'an 1 and 2:

> In the seventh month of the *jisi* year of Da'an, the master (Wang Chuyi) was at the Huayang Guan (Taoist Monastery) in Beijing. There was a long drought at the time. Officials and people of the city earnestly prayed to the master saying, "The sprouts are about to whither. How can we revive them?" The master thereupon closed his eyes for a long while, after which he answered the crowd, "The empty sky will allow one foot of rain to fall tomorrow." The crowd did not believe him fully. [However,] the next day the prediction was fulfilled. The officials and people came to thank him. He [then] wrote the following poem to show to them—
>
> Auspicious breath meets vigorously with the sky of blue.
> Transforming and giving life to the many living things, the Great Tao is wonderful.
> Its light transforms in the ten directions always without night (ceaselessly).
> In one instant it rescues all, and fragrance fills the air.[61]

> In the *gengwu* year (1210), the master (Wang Chuyi) was at Jizhou (in Hebei), Yutian District. When the *jiao* ritual was over, he said to those assembled, "In the north the Tao's breath is about to turn. In the sky there are signs of gods going back and forth and swords clashing. Is it not so that living souls are about to undergo suffering?" He wrote a poem and gave it to the officials and citizens and bade farewell. Later there were occurrences in the north.
>
> (Poem by Wang Chuyi): The Radiance of the Tao's Light Made a Single Rotation.
>
> In the clouds' [military] encampments in ten directions, stars and thunder run about.
> Emperor Heaven and Empress Earth let down true forms,
> Worldly toil and fleeting elegance are but one speck of ash.[62]

The above passages appear to indicate that Wang Chuyi personally claimed to have clairvoyant powers. Regarding the drought, the text (the prose narrative in particular) seems to imply that Wang Chuyi not only predicted the rain but had caused it to rain by making a silent prayer. Of course, in both cases, the prose narrative is authored by an anonymous editor, and it is, in effect, hagiographic. The authenticity of the quotes attributed to Wang Chuyi is not beyond question. One also could challenge the premise that Wang Chuyi wrote the poems under the alleged circumstances.

*Yunguang ji* also contains yet another passage that seems to attest to a type of clairvoyance possessed by Wang Chuyi:

> In the past at the home of Zhi Erweng in Mouping District Gushuizhuang (in Shandong), he (Wang Chuyi) was expounding the teachings and greatly exposing the mechanisms of Heaven. The whole family knelt and listened. Everyone was like a deaf person (listened attentively without lending ear to anything other than what was being said by Wang Chuyi). When he saw that Mr. Zhi's remaining life span was not long, he warned him with these words:
>
> Stop engaging in the banter and frolic of the Yellow Springs (underworld).
> Inside of your body you embrace what is rare and precious.
> If you go against Heaven, 100 misfortunes will approach your body.
> If you master the Tao, myriad spirits will be influenced and moved [in your favor].[63]

The question here is how he knew (or so thought) that Zhi Erweng had little time left to live. The passage does not say that Zhi Erweng suffered from a severe illness. Rather, the implication seems to be that Wang Chuyi had a special ability to divine a person's remaining life span. This seems so, particularly in light of the fact that Wang Chuyi's poem scolds Zhi Erweng and exhorts him to live virtuously and endeavor to "master the Tao." Such a message seems a bit harsh and demanding for an invalid. Of course, there is again in this case some doubt as to whether the quotes attributed to Wang Chuyi in the prose narrative are authentic, and whether the poem was actually written under the circumstances described here. Whatever the case, Wang Chuyi's didactic point is that immoral living brings misfortune, which can be averted through self-reform.

Probably the most important witness to Wang Chuyi's psychic powers is Qiu Chuji, who wrote the following poem in his *Panxi ji*:

> "In Praise of Master Yuyang (Wang Chuyi)"
> [He is] the Realized Immortal of the old country;
> [He is] the great adept of the eastern direction.
> Pure and high, how he differs from the vulgar!
> Vibrant and excellent; he is not the same as the dust (the worldly).
> On the exterior and the interior, Heaven gave it all to him.
> Whether active or in seclusion, he is far superior to the world.
> From time to time he predicts misfortunes and blessings.
> Showing his efficacy, he silently communicates with the divine.[64]

Thus in the eyes of this most revered leader of the Quanzhen movement, Wang Chuyi's psychic feats were authentic.

## Two Physical Feats of Wang Zhe Confirmed by Qiu Chuji

Quanzhen hagiography ascribes many miraculous physical feats to the Quanzhen masters, and here again the founder, Wang Zhe, is particularly prolific. Two such miracles ascribed to Wang Zhe are as follows:

> When [Wang Zhe] reached Dengzhou, he visited the Penglai Pavilion and was gazing down onto the sea. Suddenly a gust of wind came forth, and people saw the master (Wang Zhe) get blown into the sea. While [the onlookers stood] dumbfounded, after a while [Wang Zhe] came leaping out of the water. He had only lost his hairpin and cap. A little later, [his hairpin and cap] also came flowing out from amidst the waves.
>
> Also, on his way to Ninghai, the master threw a greased umbrella into the air. The umbrella rose and mounted the wind. When it reached Wang Chuyi's hermitage on Mt. Cha, it finally came down. Thus it had traveled more than 200 *li* (about 111 km—69 miles) from where it had been thrown. Inside the handle of that umbrella was sobriquet Sanyangzi (a slip of paper on which this sobriquet was written [?]).[65]

Interestingly, a firsthand account of the above events comes from the hand of none other than Qiu Chuji. In his *Panxi ji*, there is a poem containing the following lines alluding to Wang Zhe's miracle.

> He sent out his spirit and entered dreams, and people were frightened by him [an allusion to feats mentioned above].
> He threw his umbrella and hurled his cap, and I reached the conclusion,
> That when the master resided by the eastern sea, he was like a dragon.[66]

Qiu Chuji follows this poem with a prose explanation:

> In the fourth month (April 29–May 27) of the *jichou* year of the Dading era (1169) in the summer, Danyang (Ma Yu) and I, along with several other people, followed Master Chongyang (Wang Zhe)

from Wendeng to Ninghai. As we neared Longquan the sun's force was gradually beginning to scorch. The master told us to go ahead. He was walking approximately half a *li* (about 275 meters) behind us and was carrying an umbrella. Suddenly, when I turned my head to look behind me, I saw the umbrella rising and ascending into the air. I immediately ran back to ask about it. [Wang Zhe] told me, "It caught a powerful breeze and rose up. I do not know why it is so, but it is so." At first, the umbrella rose to the northeast. As I gazed upon it, it gradually fell into the midst of the desert. I went searching for it in the direction in which it went but could not find it [the text here has five characters that are illegible due to misprint] . . . Zhuyangzi, Sir Wang (Wang Chuyi), was making his hermitage on Mt. Cha by the Eastern Sea. From the mountain to Wendeng is a hundred and ten *li*, and from Wendeng to where the umbrella arose is another seventy *li*. The umbrella rose at about the *chen* hour (8 A.M.), and at sunset it fell in front of Sir Zhuyang's hut. On its handle was written the Taoist sobriquet, "Zhuyangzi." Thus this sobriquet was bestowed upon him. The character, "*zhu*" did not yet exist but had been invented by the master. Ever since this incident, the family of Sir Di has kept this umbrella. Originally it had been borrowed [by Wang Zhe] from the house of Fan Mingshi in Ninghai. Fan later heard about this incident and went to get it back, but [Sir Di] refused to give it to him.

"Threw his cap" refers to when the master first went to Deng[zhou] and was overlooking the sea north of the city. The bamboo bark cap on his head suddenly fell into the water and drifted away. But in a little while it came back.

The pronunciation of 𨰥 is "*zhu*" (as in the character for "bamboo").[67]

On a few points, Qiu Chuji's testimony differs from the hagiographer. The sobriquet bestowed on Wang Chuyi was Zhuyangzi—not Sanyangzi—and Wang Zhe had invented the character "*zhu*" himself. While Wang Zhe was admiring the ocean near Dengzhou, only his cap went in and out of the water—rather than the master himself. Thus the hagiographic account is based loosely on firsthand testimony, and in the case of the incident at the ocean, the hagiographer has embellished the story to make it more impressive. Perhaps most interesting here is the fact that a family of lay believers treasured the umbrella as a keepsake. Fan Mingshi, the umbrella's original owner, went to the trouble of trying to get it back. This was probably because his friend, Wang Zhe, through his miraculous act, had turned this simple object into a holy relic. We can see here how the Quanzhen masters held divine status in the eyes of their believers already during the founder's lifetime. Of course, the essential unresolved questions here are whether Wang Zhe himself would have confirmed the stories, and whether Qiu Chuji was being honest in his testimony.

## Healing and Ritual Thaumaturgy

Wang Zhe, as we have already seen in chapter 4, considered it part of a Taoist monk's duty to heal diseases. He also approved of his disciples engaging in the "practice of talismans" as a means of sustenance (although he considered begging the best such means). Not surprisingly, then, the hagiographies record numerous miracles pertaining to the healing of diseases and the employment of ritual thaumaturgy (talismans and incantations).

As we have seen in chapter 4 Wang Zhe is said to have healed the rheumatism of Tan Chuduan by making him sleep cuddled up against his legs. *Jinlian zhengzong ji* tells us that when Ma Yu came down with a severe headache on Mt. Kunyu, Wang Zhe administered an incantation on some water and gave it to him to drink. The headache, which had almost killed Ma, was cured immediately.[68] (This apparently refers to the same occasion that I cited in chapter 4.)

Ma Yu also is reported to have been an expert at ritual healing. *Jinlian zhengzong ji* tells us that he once met a poor crippled man who was wailing aloud in extreme pain. When Ma Yu made him drink talisman water,[69] he was able to "go about as if he was flying." On another occasion he healed the rheumatism of a military man by laying a charm on some fruit and making him eat it.[70] Ma Yu's ritual power benefited people in many other ways. When the populace of Dongmou (in Shandong) was suffering a drought in 1182, Ma Yu prayed for rain successfully and saved the year's crops. One day, when Ma Yu saw that the water coming out of the well in front of the Golden Lotus Hall was salty and bitter, he put a charm on it and made the water sweet. He later did the same thing for a well in front of the home of a certain Mr. Han of Dengzhou.[71] Ma Yu's powers also were used to give life to plants. On one occasion he revived a dying apple tree in front of his hut in Huating (in Shaanxi), and on another occasion he revived some withering bamboo trees that had been transplanted in front of the Quanzhen Hut (located in Huang District in Shandong). On yet another occasion, he revived some small pine trees that had been planted in front of the Gold and Jade Hut (located in Huang District in Shandong).[72]

To enumerate the alleged thaumaturgic feats of the rest of Wang Zhe's disciples would be too lengthy a task. However, it should be noted that Wang Chuyi is alleged to have, on multiple occasions, performed the most impressive of such feats (i.e., resurrecting the dead). One day, while Wang Chuyi was going about begging, he saw a corpse being lowered into its grave. Wang Chuyi covered both its ears and shouted, "The Underground Ministry must not receive him!" In a little while, the corpse rose back to life and started to eat and drink as it pleased. The sons of the resurrected man offered a large sum of money to Wang Chuyi to express their gratitude, but Wang Chuyi just smiled and walked off without the money. On one occasion two wicked men invited Wang Chuyi to drink with them, all the while plotting to club him to death as soon as he got drunk. But before Wang Chuyi ever got intoxicated, the two got into an argument and clubbed each other to death. Wang Chuyi then shouted, "The Eastern Peak (the abode of the dead) must not receive them!" In a little while, the two scoundrels came back to life.[73] Another source tells us that Wang Chuyi once resurrected a woman who had suddenly fallen dead at a *jiao* ritual after eating dog meat. Wang Chuyi brought her back to life by blowing on her.[74]

Nothing quite so amazing is confirmed in the writings of the Quanzhen masters. However, it is nonetheless apparent that they indeed employed thaumaturgic techniques and certainly did so because they believed that they could be effective. In Ma Yu's *Dongxuan jinyu ji*, we do find some poems that pertain to how he revived bamboo trees:

> "Administering an Incantation on the Withered Bamboo at the Quanzhen Hut in Huang District"
> The school of Taoism is titled, "Long Life."
> My mind wishes to change and transform the shapes of what is withered and dried.
> May these several poles [of bamboo] be forever green.
> Do not allow a single leaf to not be green.[75]

The above poem seems to have been the actual incantation used by Ma Yu to revive the bamboo trees in front of the Quanzhen Hut. This poem is immediately followed by one written in celebration of his success at reviving some pine trees:

> "Rejoicing over the Life of the Pine Tree"
> I understand thoroughly the method for [bringing forth] life, and I restore life.
> If *qi* spreads through the shape and skeleton, the body will be changed.
> Outside of the windows not only is the gentleman (refers to one of the pine trees?) green,

But in front of the hut I also rejoice over the greenness of the prominent stalwart (another pine tree?).[76]

In some instances, Ma Yu seems to have called upon the divine power of his late teacher, Wang Zhe, to perform such acts:

In the sixth month I planted six pine trees in front of my hut.
But they fell over as though they had died, Ma Feng-feng (Crazy Ma).
Three times I dispersed my breath (blew on the tree?) without great force.
Six times I wished for them to revive, and had great merit.

The time was *fu* (the sixth month), which corresponded to the number [of trees],
And therefore I planted the pine trees.
Friends of the Tao calmly examined Crazy Ma (to see if he could revive the trees).
I told them that the six trees were not revived by me,
But people passed on the word that the Triple Top-knotted One (Ma Yu) has true merit.

On the third day of the sixth month I planted the pine trees.
The color of the six trees changed when they met with Fu-feng.
In praying for their revival I borrowed the force of Chongyang (Wang Zhe).
Responding to the efficacy people passed on word of the merit of the Triple Top-knotted One.[77]

Here Ma Yu affirms that he indeed employed ritual procedures to revive some pine trees. However, he also claims that he did so only through the power of Wang Zhe, and that he himself does not deserve the adulation.

Qiu Chuji tells us that this sort of life-restoring power was not the exclusive property of the Quanzhen masters. In his *Panxi ji* is included a narrative about a certain Zhan'gu, the wife of a certain Mr. Zou. Zhan'gu, who was famous for her skill in embroidery, also was an ardent believer and a patron of Taoism. She lived a frugal lifestyle personally while endowing Taoist monks with food and a hermitage. When somebody ridiculed the poor condition of the pine and bamboo trees in front of the hermitage, she pointed to a withered *qiu* tree (a species of the catalpa tree) in her yard and invoked the immortals. She said, "Now, immortal sages up above, even at the cost of my body losing all of its hair, I wish for this tree to revive. If this does not happen, I will take the responsibility." Months went by without her wish being fulfilled, and thus people ridiculed her even more. Eventually the tree died, but exactly a year after Zhan'gu had put a charm on the tree, a vermilion-colored "holy sprout" started to grow from under the dead tree. The sprout rapidly developed into the tallest tree in the vicinity. Qiu Chuji tells us that he himself heard of this incident and went to see the revived tree. He was convinced of the authenticity of the story after seeing how the tree was at least twice the height of any of the other trees around it and was like no other tree that he had ever seen. Qiu Chuji then goes on to praise Zhangu by saying, "Utmost sincerity influences objects, and brilliant virtue moves Heaven."[78]

## Wondrous Mirages

The belief that lofty human piety and virtue can move divine forces also is reflected in testimony regarding ocean mirages. Ma Yu could not bear to see any form of killing. *Jinlian zhengzong ji* tells us that on one snowy day (2/8/Dading 23 [March 3, 1183]), Ma Yu convinced all residents of Longya Village to burn their fishing boats and nets. As soon as they did this, the snow stopped falling, the sky cleared up, and beautiful mirages of towering pavilions and green mountains appeared. When he visited Zhiyang two months later, mirages again appeared over the horizon above the ocean and stayed there from sunrise until noon. Realizing that the mirages were caused by the arrival of the holy man, a certain Gentleman of Service (an honorary title for a high-ranking official), Ma—as an expression of his reverence and repentance—burned thousands of debt statements for grain that he had lent to poor people. There also was a certain Ju Bin who gathered the fishing nets in the village and burned them. Again, mirages appeared over the ocean that looked like dragons, chariots, and cranes. When two men, Guo Heng and Luan Zhou, also gathered nets and burned them, mirages of heavenly troops appeared amidst the clouds.[79]

Mirages such as these are natural phenomena that have long been known to occur off the coast of the Shantong Peninsula (in Chinese, these famous ocean mirages are known as *haishi* or "sea towns"). However, the Quanzhen hagiographies assert that in the above cases the mirages are divine responses to virtuous acts or to the arrival of a holy man. There is in fact clear evidence that Ma Yu himself made such a claim:

> The livelihood of the seamen [causes them to] not understand emptiness.
> Long amidst the big waves and great tide,
> Day after day they catch fish and bring damnation [on themselves].

Time after time they send forth their boats and turn their backs on the palaces of the immortals.
From what were they able to find it in their hearts to repent of their wrongdoings?
Meeting me and diligently persevering is better than maneuvering skillfully.
Leaping joyfully, they burned their boats and nets,
And their mercy and compassion (towards the fish in the sea) moved the gods and the dragons.
Sea towns spread across the sky and amazed the eyes of the masses.[80]

The poem then goes on to describe some of the images that appeared. This poem is followed by several similar ones dealing with the same incident.

## Conclusion

The Quanzhen masters, while fully aware and critical of the inherent dangers involved in overemphasizing miracles, clearly believed that supernormal power was attainable through their methods of self-cultivation. They believed that the power of the Tao was latent within each human being but needed to be recovered through the elimination of desires and the purification of the mind. While standards of modesty—not to mention the facts—restrained them from claiming many personal miracles, they quite enthusiastically extolled the feats of their brethren. Of course, not all of the miracles that they believed in pertained to the supernormal powers gained by those who attained the Tao. In the cases of Zhan'gu reviving the tree and the mirages, the miracle comes about due to the fact that the divine forces (the immortals, the Tao) have a propensity to respond to piety and virtuous behavior.

# Chapter 7

## Death and Dying in Early Quanzhen Taoism

How should one psychologically prepare for death? And how should one think, feel, and act at the time of death? These are important questions for Quanzhen Taoists, as they are for anybody. In this chapter we will examine how the early Quanzhen masters and their believers viewed these issues. As we have seen, the Quanzhen masters taught and practiced methods that were supposed to confer health and longevity. They also believed in the eternal life of the Real Nature/Radiant Spirit. Nonetheless, they fully admitted the mortality of the flesh. Quanzhen literature provides ample indication that a Taoist's comportment close to and during death was considered of great significance. Hagiography preserves—sometimes in considerable detail—the final words and actions of the various Quanzhen masters. While these accounts may only be partially authentic in their depictions of how their protagonists thought, felt, and acted close to and during death, they also are valuable for how they convey the expectations of those who admired the Quanzhen masters as their role models. *Yulu* ("records of sayings") sources provide us with some direct observations from the masters themselves on how to regard and deal with death.

In the following pages we shall first examine the hagiographic material and then proceed to examine the *yulu* material. In the latter portion we will depend particularly on *Panshan xiyun Wang zhenren yulu* (DT1039/TT725), the collected sayings of Wang Zhijin (1178–1263), a disciple of Hao Datong's and Qiu Chuji's, who said a great deal in regard to the issue of death and dying. In doing so he alluded to the words and deeds of the first-generation Quanzhen masters.

## Hagiography

As mentioned previously, Quanzhen founder Wang Zhe died at a certain Mr. Wang's Inn in Bianjing (present-day Kaifeng) on 1/4/Dading 10 (January 22, 1170). The hagiographies diverge on certain details yet give roughly similar accounts. Wang Zhe had been staying in Bianjing for about two months and had been subjecting his four top disciples, Ma Yu, Tan Chuduan, Liu Chuxuan, and Qiu Chuji, to unusually harsh discipline (so much so that Liu Chuxuan fled). He proclaimed to his disciples that he was about to "return"[1] or—according to other accounts—that he was about to go to his appointed meeting with the "Masters and Realized Ones" (immortal brethren).[2] He entrusted Ma Yu—who had "acquired the Tao"—with the task of mentoring the young Qiu Chuji. He also told Tan Chuduan—who "understood the Tao"—to take care of the wayward Liu Chuxuan.[3] The disciples then implored Wang Zhe to leave behind a verse as a final instruction to them. To this, he responded that he had already composed the verse for this occasion, and that it was written on the wall of the Taoist Lü's Hermitage in Luan Village, Chang'an (in Dading 6 [1166]). He recited for them the following verse:

> Master Chongyang of Difei (the Zhongnan mountains),
> [People] call [him] Lunatic Wang.
> When he comes [into the world] he nurtures the sun and moon (?).[4]
> After he leaves [the world] he will entrust himself to the west and east (roam freely).
> He makes himself a companion with the clouds and streams.
> He makes himself a neighbor with the empty void.
> His single numinous Real Nature exists.
> It is not the same as the minds of the masses.[5]

Then, after warning his disciples not to weep or mourn for him, Wang Zhe lay down on his side using his bent left elbow as a pillow, and he passed away. His disciples immediately started to wail and sob, whereupon Wang Zhe immediately opened his eyes, got up, and said, "Why are you crying?"[6] or, according to other accounts, "Why does it come to this?"[7] (i.e., why is this something worth crying about?). He then took Ma Yu aside to give him some final instructions and told him to travel westward to carry out ministry in Shaanxi (Wang Zhe's native region).[8] He then wrote one final poem, "Poem of the Unworldly True Kin." It read:

> One younger brother, one nephew, and two boys;
> Along with me, [we are] five recluses doing our cultivation.

We have joined together to become unworldly true kin.
Sloughing off the corpse that was provisionally formed in the dust,
I circle about planting and forming the radiance of clarity and stillness.
From one to another we pass on the purple numinous fungus.
Atop the mountain we together go to the Golden Flower Gathering.
I am going to Penglai (legendary island of the immortals) before [the rest of you] to pay my respects to my teachers.[9]

After writing the poem, Wang Zhe (or his mortal husk) expired again, for the last time.[10] One source states that he "had no disease."[11] As we have seen previously, the hagiographies follow the death narrative with various alleged incidents where Wang Zhe manifested his Radiant Spirit posthumously. One source even claims that Wang Zhe's corpse remained lifelike in its appearance more than a year after his death.[12]

In sum, Wang Zhe is portrayed as having been of sound mind and body on the occasion of his death. He seems to accept his death with equanimity, or perhaps even joy. He instructs his disciples not to grieve for him, and he affects puzzlement when they do. He dies, resurrects, and dies again—all peacefully and painlessly—as though he is in complete control of his own life and death. His death, to him, is a return to eternal life in the "single, numinous Real Nature" that has now been restored and set free from the karmic, samsaric personality and body in which it had been degraded and entrapped. Wang Zhe also sees his worldly death as a joyous reunion with his immortal brethen (Lü Yan et al.). It is as though Wang Zhe not only expects to die but dies voluntarily in order to keep his promise to meet with his immortal brethren. While no claim of physical immortality is made, we are told that Wang Zhe died with no disease, and that his corpse remained lifelike long after his death. These claims seem to be related to the fact that the *neidan* training regimen of the Quanzhen masters involved the body and its energies as well as the mind. An accomplished master was perhaps expected to distinguish himself—even in death—by his superior physical condition. The corpse was perhaps understood to be bestowed with unusual properties from having served as the "crucible" in which the "Golden Elixir" (Wang Zhe's Radiant Spirit) was completed (or recovered).

Of course, there is great reason to doubt whether Wang Zhe actually died free of disease. As we saw previously, Wang Zhe himself seems to have written a poem predicting that he would die at age fifty-eight *sui*, as the result of a relapse of an "old disease." Wang Zhe, when he left the Shandong Peninsula with his four top disciples, probably had intended to journey to his home region of Shaanxi. It seems quite likely that he had taken ill by the time he arrived in Bianjing—hence, the lengthy stay there. (Perhaps his unusually harsh treatment of his disciples there was due to irritability brought on by physical suffering?) While he seems to have long known that he would die roughly around the time that he actually did, he probably hoped that he could have stayed in the world a little longer in order to reunite with the handful of living brethren that he had left behind in Shaanxi.

Whatever the case, the dying Wang Zhe portrayed in the accounts represents an ideal to emulate. Wang Zhe himself at least would have wanted to die in the serene, joyful, and dignified manner in which he is portrayed. Not surprisingly, the death narratives of his successors repeat many of the same characteristics and themes.

The first to pass away among Wang Zhe's main disciples—the so-called "Seven Realized Ones"—was Sun Bu'er. According to one hagiographical source, Sun Bu'er was able to "accomplish the Tao" after six years under the tutelage of Feng Xiangu in Luoyang (see chapter 1). After this, she began to engage in preaching and acquired many disciples of her own. On the last day of the twelfth month of Dading 22 (January 25, 1183), she suddenly proclaimed to her disciples, "The Masters and Realized Ones have sent forth orders. The time for me to go to the Jasper Pond[13] has come." She then bathed and changed her robes. At the noon hour, she requested a brush and paper and wrote:

> When three thousand merits are fulfilled I transcend the Three Realms (of *samsara*).[14]
> I jump out beyond the embrace of the *yin* and *yang*.
> Hiding, appearing, moving vertically or horizontally, I have freedom.
> My drunken soul (*hun*) will no longer return to Ninghai.[15]

She then sat in a lotus position and suddenly passed away. We are told that she (her Radiant Spirit) then appeared before Ma Yu (who was then dwelling in a hut in Ninghai [Shandong]) in midair, flanked by immortal youths and jaid maidens, and announced that she was heading to Peng Island (viz. immortality) before him.[16] Other sources report that Ma Yu sang and danced in joy on this occasion,[17] much in the same manner as what is reported of the philosopher, Zhuang Zhou, on the occasion of his wife's death in the ancient Taoist classic, *Zhuangzi*.[18]

In sum, Sun Bu'er is said to have died in a very serene and dignified manner, much like her teacher, Wang Zhe. No indication is given that she was ill or suffering, yet she accepts her death as her divinely ordained destiny and rejoices in anticipation of her eternal life of freedom. Her ex-husband, Ma Yu—now her comrade in the quest for Realization—rejoices with her.

Narratives concerning Ma Yu's death particularly emphasize his intimate bond with his mentor, Wang Zhe. Curiously—and not by mere coincidence, hagiographers would maintain—Ma Yu died on Wang Zhe's birthday, 12/22, in Dading 23 (February 5, 1184) at the Youxian Guan Taoist Monastery in Laiyang (Shandong). Several days prior to this, Ma Yu picked up a brush and wrote a "Hymn for Leaving behind the Body," which contained the following words:

> Great is the ascension to Reality!
> The road enters the blue darkness.
> Unicorns follow the crimson envoy banner.
> Phoenixes pull my red carriage.
> With bells tinkling and jade pieces dangling,
> I tread on the void and pace upon the clouds.
> Rising above, I receive the True Declarations.
> Up I climb to the Jade Imperial Dwelling.[19]

As previously mentioned, three sources tell us that Ma Yu, just before dying, had visions of Wang Zhe and He Dejin (invisible to his disciples attending him) beckoning him from midair to join them among the ranks of immortals.[20] Ma Yu was looking up and gazing at the skies. When his disciple, Cao Zhen, asked him why he was doing this, he answered, "The Patriarch-Master (Wang Zhe) and Master-Uncle He [Dejin] have arrived, and [I am] about to go to the gathering of the immortals!" Yu Zhiyi, another disciple, then asked him, "[Our] school is vast and great; do you not regret [leaving it behind]?" To this, Ma Yu replied, "I must gallantly go back, to become one happy and lively immortal." Then, addressing Liu Zhenyi (another disciple), he said, "If you want to become divine immortals, you must accumulate merits and deeds. Even if you confront a thousand evils and a hundred difficulties, you must take care not to regress. If you can do so, you will get to know that my words are not deluded." Ma Yu then also made the enigmatic statement, "I can see with my eyes open, and I can also see with my eyes closed. To begin with it is not in the eyes. If all is clear within your mind, there is nothing that you cannot see!" That night, at around the second watch (11 P.M.), a thunderstorm suddenly arose. Ma Yu lay down on his side, his head pointing eastward and resting on his left elbow, and he passed away.[21] (One source states that he passed away while "seated properly."[22])

Another source differs somewhat. There we are told, through the alleged firsthand testimony of disciples Cao Zhen and Liu Zhenyi, that Ma Yu had abruptly announced his intention to "return to Reality" (*guizhen*) on the full moon (fifteenth day) of the twelfth month (January 29). Seven days later, on Wang Zhe's birthday, just as the offerings were about to be presented (at Wang

Zhe's altar?) at the first watch (around 9 P.M.), there was a sudden rumble of thunder. Wang Zhe's voice was then heard (by Ma Yu alone? by all present?) saying, "The time for you to become immortal has already arrived. You must not linger any longer!" At midnight, Ma Yu lay down on his side with his left elbow as a pillow and "transformed."[23]

The various hagiographies follow with descriptions of the miraculous posthumous epiphanies of Ma Yu's radiant spirit. *Jinlian zhengzong ji*, as it does in the case of Wang Zhe, also makes miraculous claims concerning his corpse. This source tells us that when Ma Yu was buried seven days after his death, his complexion was still very healthy. After the burial, there were many people who suspected that Ma Yu's followers might try to steal his body. Thus a little over a year after Ma Yu had died, the District Magistrate dug up the coffin to make sure that the corpse had not been stolen. When he looked inside of the coffin, he saw that "[the corpse's] appearance and visage was like that of a living person, and its limbs were soft and supple."[24]

In sum, according to the hagiographies, Ma Yu also passed away serenely and willingly, confident of his immortality and eager to reunite with his immortal brethren. He does not linger in the world; he resolutely undergoes the so-called "return" or "transformation," because it is time to do so. Before passing beyond, he leaves behind words of inspiration for his disciples, much as his teacher had done for him. None of the narratives say that he was ill or decrepit. Yet he somehow knows when his death is imminent. On the day of his death, he has visions or locutions of Wang Zhe and He Dejin beckoning him.

Of course, some skepticism is warranted as to whether he was so sound and peaceful in body and mind when he died. Also, his alleged visions or locutions might simply be hagiographic embellishments. However, as we have seen previously, Ma Yu himself had a tendency to make claims such as these, as did his fellow adepts. It is certainly also possible that the visions and/or locutions were subjectively real to him. If so, this indicates the strength of his belief in immortality and the intimacy of his bond with his deceased "otherworldly kin." The claims concerning the corpse certainly also beg for skepticism. Perhaps the most interesting information in the account is that non-believers were wary that believers might steal the body. What would have been their motive for doing such a thing? The underlying assumption would seem to be that the Quanzhen School had a strong vested interest in having the public believe that there was something extraordinary about the master's corpse.[25]

Similar claims also are made in some hagiographic accounts concerning the corpse of Qiu Chuji. On the occasion of his burial that took place a year (some say three years) after his death (in 1227; he was eighty *sui*), his disciples opened his coffin and were amazed to find the corpse still looking dignified and lifelike. For three days Taoist clerics and laypeople alike came in amazement to admire and worship him.[26] Interestingly, however, some of the same accounts state clearly that Qiu Chuji was quite ill, and they give the impression that he suffered considerably at the end of his life. Nonetheless, we are told that he was in a contented and peaceful state of mind, and that he admonished his disciples not to concern themselves with his condition.[27]

In the case of Tan Chuduan, one source—namely, *Lishi zhenxian tidao tongjian shubian*—indicates that he suffered a rather gruesome physical condition at the end of his life. There we are told that in Dading 21 (1181), while staying at the Chunyang Grotto[28] at Huayin (the famous Western Peak Mt. Hua in eastern Shaanxi), Tan Chuduan developed boils on his head and neck. He asked those present whether they thought he was about to die. An awkward silence ensued, after which he proclaimed, "I will not die yet. When [the boils] form on my feet, I will die." He later relocated to a hut next to the Chaoyuan Gong Taoist Monastery in Luoyang. In Dading 25 (1185), he had a dream in which he encountered his ascended brethren, Wang Zhe and Ma Yu, who informed him that it was time for him to become an immortal. When he woke up, he told his disciples to start making arrangements for his funeral. Boils had formed on his feet. He then wrote a poem, lay down on his side, and passed away.[29] Strangely, one source differs completely, claiming that he died "with no illness."[30]

Thus while hagiographers seem to consistently portray the protagonists as being of sound and peaceful mind at death, not all of them see the need to make claims of total physical well-being.

Perhaps most intriguing of all are the death narratives regarding Li Lingyang and Wang Zhijin.

Li Lingyang, the reader may recall, was one of the monks with whom Wang Zhe had lived and trained in Liujiang Village (from 1163 to 1167) prior to his departure to Shandong. After Wang Zhe's death, Li Lingyang formed a solid bond with Wang Zhe's disciples from Shandong—particularly with Qiu Chuji, whose company he shared at the Liujiang Zuting (Patriarchal Garden) Monastery[31] during the late years of his life. In 2/Dading 28 (February 29–March 29, 1188), Qiu Chuji was summoned to the capital (Beijing) by the Jurchen Emperor, who was eager to benefit from his ritual services and wisdom. Upon departure, he entrusted the care of the Liujiang Monastery to Li Lingyang. Li Lingyang responded by requesting that Qiu Chuji return the following spring to serve as his chief mourner. Approximately a year went by, whereupon one day Li Lingyang, who was not ill, suddenly stopped eating. After ten days his disciples became very worried and asked him why he was fasting. Li Lingyang replied, "You must not worry. I am simply waiting for my chief mourner." He then sent out messengers to beckon Qiu Chuji, who had left the capital the previous fall and was on his way home but had gotten waylaid in nearby Qindu Township by friendly local Taoists. Qiu Chuji, upon receiving word, hurried to see his elderly friend. Almost as soon as Qiu Chuji arrived, Li Lingyang presented him with a poem and passed away.[32]

Wang Zhijin, as mentioned earlier, was a prominent disciple of Hao Datong, and later Qiu Chuji. We are told that one day during the summer (sixth lunar month; July 7–August 5) of Zhongtong 4 (1263), he stopped eating and speaking. He would sit all day in his abbot's quarters with his eyes closed, his mind concentrated, and his finger pointing into empty space. After bathing and retiring for the night, he would go into a sleep so deep that one could scarcely even hear him breathe or detect any movement in his body. His disciples became very worried and attended him constantly, but he would reprimand them, saying, "You all just go mind your own business!" After seventeen days had gone by in this manner, Wang Zhijin casually lay down with his elbow tucked under his head and peacefully passed away. He had reached the ripe old age of eighty-six *sui*.[33]

As we have seen, Quanzhen hagiographies almost invariably tell us that the protagonist anticipated his or her death and accepted it happily. Li Lingyang and Wang Zhijin, it would appear, induced their deaths through starvation. One can conceive of several different reasons they may have done this, and all might hold true simultaneously. They may have been ill at the time (although this is expressly denied in the case of Li Lingyang), and it would appear that both men were quite elderly.[34] Perhaps they had simply grown weary of living in their bodies. Another possibility is that they had somehow—perhaps through "communications" with immortal brethren (?)—come to regard a specific date as the appointed time for undergoing the great transformation. The fast may have constituted in their minds a final exercise—or a sacred ritual purification of sorts—necessary for completing the full recovery and liberation of the immortal Real Nature/Radiant Spirit. This implication seems particularly strong in the case of Wang Zhijin, who, while fasting diligently, carried out some special sort of meditation exercise.

Intriguing here are parallels with other ascetic traditions in Asia. One is reminded of the practice of *sallekhana*, the self-starvation unto death carried out by Mahavira and various other Jain saints in India.[35] One also is reminded of Kûkai (a.k.a. Kôbô Daishi, 774–835), the revered founder of Japanese Shingon Buddhism, who shunned all "human food" as he entered into his "eternal meditation."[36] Allegedly, he still sits in this "meditation" inside of a special stone structure on Mt. Kôya (public viewing is strictly prohibited). Kûkai's alleged feat inspired many imitators in Japan over the centuries whose bodies are preserved as mummies known as *sokushin butsu* ("Buddhas immediately in the body"). In these cases, voluntary starvation and dehydration seem to be an instrumental factor in bringing about the mummification.[37]

This practice, or something similar, in fact, has existed from even earlier in China—primarily within Buddhist circles—and has continued into modern times.[38]

In light of this, it is interesting that in the Quanzhen tradition, we have stories about monks who fasted unto death, as well as monks whose corpses showed a remarkable capacity to resist decay. Unfortunately (one might say?), there does not appear to be any single Quanzhen hagiographic narrative that combines both of these suggestive elements. Nonetheless, one cannot rule out the possibility that some Quanzhen adepts may have fasted to death in part with the intention of producing a non-perishable corpse. (Hachiya conjectures that Ma Yu's corpse may very well have resisted decay extraordinarily well, since his years of training had made him extremely thin. The condition of Ma Yu's body at death, Hachiya speculates, probably resembled that of a *sokushin butsu*.[39])

Taoist hagiography records at least two different cases in the Song period (both in Hunan Province in the south) where a Taoist adept left behind a mummified corpse to be admired by the living. Both stories appear to bear some connection to the Zhong-Lü *neidan* tradition and involve some of the same legendary immortals extolled by the early Quanzhen School.

Zhao He (a.k.a. Zhao Xiangu [immortal girl]) was a female adept who is said to have encountered and been given a peach by Lü Yan when lost in the wilderness at age twelve. For the rest of her life, she ate only fruits and water and lived in a bamboo tower with her elder brother and his wife. There she was visited frequently by Lü Yan. After describing a number of strange incidents and miracles performed by her, our source concludes the story by saying:

> She bathed, donned her cap and garments, sat properly, and transformed (passed away). Today her *real body* (emphasis added) still exists atop the tower.[40]

Lan Fang was a Taoist who was briefly accommodated as a palace guest by Northern Song Emperor Renzong (r. 1023–1063) but lived out most of his 172 years (!) in the Zhaoxian Guan Monastery on the Southern Peak Mt. Heng (near Hengyang, Hunan Province). We are told that a certain Li Guan went to visit him. On the way, Li Guan encountered a metal wares merchant who gave him a letter to deliver to Lan Fang. The letter, read, "After ten months of pregnancy, how does one send it out?" Upon reading the letter, Lan Fang asked Li Guan if the man he had encountered had a white mole between his eyebrows. When Li Guan affirmed that such was indeed the case, Lan Fang proclaimed that the man was in fact the immortal Liu Haichan (Liu Cao). When Li Guan, out of lively curiosity, repeated to Lan Fang the question that Liu Haichan had posed in the letter, Lan Fang clapped his hands and laughed loudly. The sound of thunder rumbled from his head, and from there emerged a luminous replica of Lan Fang's physical form. After the luminous Spirit had ascended to the sky, the mortal body of Lan Fang was found dead. Our source then concludes the story with the statement, "a *flesh body molded statue* (emphasis added) exists there."[41]

As has been discussed by Joseph Needham, "real body" (*zhenshen*) and "flesh body" (*roushen*) are terms used in Chinese Buddhist literature to refer to the self-mummified bodies of saintly people (mostly Buddhist). The standard practice in China in these cases was for devotees to complete the desiccation of the corpse (already accomplished in part by the deceased master's austerities) by drying it over a charcoal fire and smoking it with incense. Finally the body would either be lacquered over or used as the base of a statue of dried clay or plaster. The latter option appears to have been employed in the case of Lan Fang.[42] Whether or not such a procedure was ever carried out within Quanzhen circles is a matter that needs to be further looked into in the future.

## Collected Sayings

> The Patriarch-Master (Wang Zhe) said, "The way of non-action (*wuwei*) is to first abandon your family, and then abandon your body. Illness thus causes *him* to be ill. Death thus causes *him* to die. Relentlessly unto your death embrace the Tao and pass away. Entrust yourself to and obey the decision of Heaven." This is a great saying.[43]

The above passage is found in an epistle that Qiu Chuji wrote to his Taoist friends in the "western counties." It preserves statements by Wang Zhe that remained vividly in the memory of his most celebrated disciple. Wang Zhe here teaches complete emotional detachment from one's very own body. The body that suffers illness and death is "he," not "I." While thus detaching from this suffering, impermanent "he," one is to embrace the eternal Tao (the true, universal "I") and obediently accept death when it comes.

We can thus see that the accepting attitude toward death attributed to the Quanzhen masters in the hagiographies is consistent with the teachings of the founder. Here Wang Zhe comes across sounding much like the Buddha who speaks in the texts of the Pali Canon, who teaches complete renunciation of all things—including one's own person—that partake in impermanence and suffering and that are "not self" (*anatman*).[44]

Somber sentiments of this kind were apparently also echoed by Ma Yu and were later elucidated upon by Wang Zhijin:

> Someone asked, "[I have heard that in] the past Master-Father Danyang (Ma Yu) completed the way quickly because he understood death. What does this mean?"
>
> [Wang Zhijin] answered, "A person who cultivates and practices should look on his/her body as though it were a death row convict bound and being dragged into the marketplace [for a public execution]. With each step it gets nearer to its death. If you keep death on your mind, the various affairs can be cut off and abandoned. Even if there are things and appearances such as music and attractive women, or you are surrounded by boisterousness, your eyes will see nothing, and your ears will hear nothing. All of your thoughts will be forgotten. If this body is abandoned [by you] in such a way, how much more will other things?[45]

In other words, Ma Yu made rapid progress in his self-cultivation, because he remained constantly in frank awareness of the mortality of his flesh rather than live in cowardly, uneasy denial. This, Wang Zhijin attests, leads to detachment from one's mortal body and subsequently to detachment from all impermanent worldly things. The underlying logic here is that one can certainly renounce all other objects, once one has renounced that which is dearest to him or her.

Seemingly lacking in the above insights of the masters is any presumption that they can avoid the kinds of physical agony that ordinary people undergo close to and during death. This constitutes a major divergence from the attitude frequently conveyed by hagiographers. The most lengthy and thorough sermon on how to face up to illness and death comes from Wang Zhijin. In it, he is frank in acknowledging that even diligent and worthy Taoist adepts can and will suffer illness and death. This is everyone's inevitable destiny. However, he also conveys the belief that a disciplined lifestyle can go a long way toward preventing disease, and that mental equanimity can mitigate the severity of suffering and maybe even heal the illness:

> The master, because one of the men of the Tao was ill, proclaimed to everybody [as follows]: "When a practitioner is moderate in his eating and drinking, constant in his movement and stillness, peaceful in his mind and spirit, and does not act foolishly in any particular way and yet still happens to get ill, this is due to Heaven[-ordained] destiny. Dare he not accept it?
>
> Perhaps it is due to the progression of his/her natural destiny (lit., "cycles and numbers"), or maybe it is due to causes from past lives that he/she has this demon of disease.
>
> "First you must be fully aware that each of these four great elements (earth, water, fire, and wind) [that make up the body] are

provisional. Sickness, in other words, makes *them* (the four provisional elements) sick. Death, in other words, makes *them* dead. Gracefully bear it with your mind and will, following along with their transformations. If your mind is not on the illness, a heavy illness will become light, and a light illness will heal by itself. Your own nature will be peaceful and harmonious, and the dirty and evil energy will scatter. Thus you will have returned the [karmic] debt [that caused] the disease, and will have burst through a crucial barrier and juncture [in your progress].

"If you do not understand [how to employ] this [state of] mind, you will certainly not be at ease. There will only be the suffering of illness, and your mind will be crazed and disorderly. You will cry out endlessly, yelling out in your aches and pains. You will resent heaven and earth, or perhaps resent other people for not lending you support or seeking out a physician. [Perhaps] you will be angry at other people for not preparing you medicine, or blame them for not visiting you. All the while you will only give rise to ignorance and darkness. [As for] what the karma [-creating] mind perceives; there is no aspect of it that is good.

"Do you not know that your life and death already has a predetermined number (of years)? Even if you fret [over death], how can you avoid it? Your mind then becomes disorderly beyond what is appropriate and cannot give peace to itself. Also, do you not know that the mind is the master of the body? If the master is not at ease, the whole body will become disorderly. Have you not heard, as a man of old once said, 'For the mind to be turbulent and the will to be disorderly is the gate to hell'?[46] Thus you will beckon disasters beyond what was allotted to you. If your mind is in such a state a light illness will become heavy, and a heavy illness will lead to death. This is because your nature has become muddled and disordered.

"If you are unrestrained in various matters, you will suffer illness beyond your [normal] share. In this case the disease has been created by you yourself. What you create, you must receive. Who else do you have to blame? Those who exercise the ground of their minds must not be like this. Each of you please keep this in mind."[47]

Wang Zhijin himself seems somewhat unsure of what principle is at work in ordaining a person's allotted life span. Certainly he acknowledges the law of karma and the role that it plays in the process. However, he also seems to think that there are other natural laws ("cycles and numbers") at work. Whatever the case, he maintains that illness and death are inevitable and must be faced and accepted bravely. Wang Zhijin apparently draws on the teachings of

Wang Zhe in pointing out that the elements comprising the body are "provisional" (*jia*), that is, they are impermanent and lacking in inherent self-nature. It is "they" who get sick and die, not "I" (the immortal Real Nature/Radiant Spirit that is identified with the Tao or the Dharma Body).

However, the expectation clearly is that a disciplined lifestyle ought to confer good health. Furthermore, Wang Zhijin claims that by maintaining peace of mind during serious illness, the misery will decrease, and it is even possible that the illness might be cured. On the other hand, there is no use being distraught and resentful. This, Wang Zhijin states, will only compound the misery, worsen the disease, and lead to unhappy circumstances in the afterlife.

What if the physical agony is acute to the point where death seems desirable, yet does not readily occur? This situation also is addressed eloquently by Wang Zhijin:

> The master, because there was an ill person who had reached the extreme [in the severity of his illness] but was unable to leave (die), proclaimed to everybody [as follows]: "A person who engages in training first must be fully aware that the myriad causes are empty and illusory. Next, you must fully be aware that this body is a mound of dust and dirt. If you are pure and detached from the affairs of ordinary days, you will definitely be free at the time of your going.
>
> "In the past in Shandong there was an abbot who at the time of his end [of his worldly existence] and his passing and transformation [into eternal life], lingered about unable to escape and leave [the world]. He sent a person to inquire of Realized Man Changchun (Qiu Chuji). The Realized Man said, 'In past days he has only concerned himself with external stimuli, objects and surroundings. He has never cultivated and refined himself. This is why he lingers about and cannot escape.' He thus sent on to him [through his messenger] the words, 'Your body is not your possession. Your [Real] Nature is originally the empty space. If a single thought is not formed, your whole body can be abandoned.' When the abbot heard these words, it was as though his mind had a realization. He thus told his brethren, 'Because I was confused by external stimuli, I had gained no merit on my mind's ground. Upon going I was indecisive. I now encourage all of you to each pursue your practice to cultivate and refine your body and mind, and bring relief to this great matter of life and death.' After saying this, he finally came to an end.
>
> "Also, there was once a man of the Tao who was facing death but could not be decisive [at relinquishing his life]. He inquired of his brethren, 'How can I be able to leave?' There were some who said [in

reply], 'Contemplate about (or visualize?) the Masters and Realized Ones.' That person (the ailing man of the Tao) contemplated [about the Masters and Realized Ones] for several days, but was still unable to go [to his death]. There was [also] someone who said, 'Contemplate the void emptiness.' That person again was unable to leave [after following the advice]. There was then an old Immortal (a senior Taoist monk) who heard about this and came to see him. That person (the ailing man of the Tao) told him about what he had contemplated and about how he had still been unable to leave. The old Immortal rebuked him, saying, 'At the time you came, what was there? After you leave, what is there to think about? Peacefully await your destiny. When the time comes, then go!' The ailing man heard these words, bowed his head in gratitude, and died.

"In sum, in regard to people who cultivate and practice, all external stimuli are [things for] expedient use before one's eyes. Your own original Real [Nature] must be fully trained. If you can pass through things and affairs pure and detached, how can you not be pure and detached when you are about to go [to your death]? If you are attached to and defiled by things and affairs, how can you be pure and detached when you are about to go [to your death]? It is urgent that you cultivate and refine [yourself]. Birth and death are difficult to prevent. When the day arrives, how can you be saved from external stimuli? I ask each of you to think about this."[48]

The underlying assumption here is that physical death is inevitable, and that every Taoist adept has a proper time for which to leave the world behind. One should then "decisively" undergo the great transformation and liberation. Wang Zhijin perceived the monk's severe illness as a sure sign that his time had come and attributed his plight to his woeful attachment to his body and to the world. In the first of the anecdotes, we find out that Qiu Chuji also had once counseled a monk in the same predicament. Qiu Chuji emancipated him by reminding him that his body is not "his," and that his "Real Nature is the empty space (*xukong*, the ineffable, eternal, universal Tao/Dharma Body)." This insight bred the detachment that made liberation possible. In the second anecdote, we have an interesting situation where concerned brethren recommended that the ailing monk try out various contemplation techniques to help induce his liberation. After none of these worked, the ailing monk was helped out of his misery by an elderly monk, who simply enjoined him to renounce all attachments and peacefully accept death.

Thus in Wang Zhijin's mind, the key to a quick, decisive liberation was having the proper insight and state of mind. Curiously, however, as the reader may recall, hagiography gives the impression that Wang Zhijin induced his death through fasting and perhaps employed some special contemplation method during his final days. If such was the case (which is uncertain), then one might perhaps say that his actions were slightly contradictory to what he advised in his sermon. But until the moment of death comes, does anybody truly know what it will be like, or how he or she will face up to it?

## Conclusion

A good Quanzhen adept was expected to face death with equanimity. Ideally, death was supposed to be a joyful occasion, an emancipation from worldly travails, and a transition into everlasting divine existence. Hagiographies further insist that the Quanzhen masters predicted their deaths with uncanny accuracy, proclaimed or wrote words of inspiration on the day of death, suffered little or no illness, and manifested their immortal Spirits on numerous occasions after death. We also are told that the corpses of some of them remained lifelike long thereafter.

The reality attested to by the masters is somewhat different. They knew that they, too, in spite of their superior control of mind over body, were subject to much misery at life's end. However, they possessed insights on how to prepare for and face up to such adversity. Most importantly, they believed that one needed to foster emotional detachment from the body and the world.

# Chapter 8

## The Compassion of the Early Quanzhen Masters

"Building Virtue"
[People of] the school of the Tao have no friends and have nobody who is not a friend (their love is impartial).
They pity [living things], pity other people, and pity themselves.
Their hearts give rise to mercy and compassion, and they practice great virtue.
Their minds have no [selfish] emotions and thoughts, and [thus] they manifest their spirit [of compassionate virtue].
[Their] surroundings [in the midst of] action they sweep away from time to time (they are not distracted and confused by worldly influences).
Their gardens and pavilions of non-leakage (their superior state of mental and physical discipline) are renewed from day to day.
Secretly they accumulate deeds and merits, and their merits and deeds are sufficient.
Accompanied by the clouds, they leave to return and greet the Masters and the Realized Ones.[1]

While self-cultivation in the Quanzhen tradition had much to do with subduing the emotions, there was one type of emotion that was encouraged and exalted. That emotion was compassion. Compassion was to be directed toward everybody, without preference or discrimination. As described in the above poem by Ma Yu, compassion inspires virtuous deeds. These "deeds" (*xing*), combined with the "merit" (*gong*) accumulated through self-discipline and meditation, bring about the ultimate recovery of eternal life.

Universal and unlimited compassion was considered a defining trait of a Realized Being, both before and after physical death. Ma Yu had the following words of praise for his deceased master, Wang Zhe:

> "In Praise of Chongyang (Wang Zhe), the Realized Man of Compassionate Transformations and Marvelous Deeds"
> Wearing a cloud cap and a mist vest with crimson silk hems,
> His body entered the circular light and departed for Purple Purity.
> The Realized Man of Marvelous Deeds fulfills his original vows,
> Rescuing those in danger, relieving those who suffer, and bringing salvation to sentient beings.[2]

What Ma Yu seems to be saying here is that Wang Zhe, even after his death, will intervene in human affairs out of his feelings of compassion. Based on such a premise, Wang Zhe and his disciples were deified and worshipped in the hope that they would exhibit the qualities described here. Naturally, Wang Zhe's putative predecessors also were regarded as divine beings dedicated to helping others. One hagiographic source has the following to say about Zhongli Quan and Lü Yan:

> From antiquity, divine immortals that have attained the Tao have been extremely numerous. But the names of Zhong[li Quan] and Lü [Yan] alone are renowned throughout the world. Why is it that even woodcutting boys, boy servants, women, and girls all know about them? It is probably because their hearts of mercy and compassion came in contact with [living] things and benefited the living, without having any place where they did not reach.[3]

This compassion was seen not only as an attribute of the Quanzhen patriarchs but as an attribute of the "Most High" (Taishang), as can be seen in the following words of Liu Chuxuan:

> Heaven and Earth are square and round, and [they] create the myriad [living] things. They do not favor and give life to [only] those that they love. They do not harm and bring extinction to those that they hate. The Most High spreads out its virtue and saves the myriad souls. It does not love and cherish the noble, and does not cut off the lowly. Heaven and Earth give birth to the myriad [living] things and spread out the air equally (for all living things to breathe).

> The Most High saves the myriad souls and spreads out its virtue equally.[4]

By "Most High," Liu Chuxuan most certainly means the Tao, and perhaps he also has in mind the highest deities of the Taoist pantheon (the Three Pure Ones [Sanqing]) that personify it. The possibility that he has such personal deities in mind is strongly suggested by how he emphasizes the "Most High's" capacity to save the myriad souls. Liu Chuxuan probably means in part by this the power to rescue people from purgatory and bad rebirths. If so, this is the very capacity of the Taoist trinity (particularly Yuanshi Tianzun) most emphasized in the mythology of the Taoist Lingbao movement of the fifth century, as well as the liturgies and rites for the dead that are based on it (rites that the Quanzhen masters themselves performed).[5] Whatever the case, Liu Chuxuan extols a benevolent and just quality that he sees in Nature (Heaven and Earth) and the supreme divine force that both pervades and transcends it.

Among the early Quanzhen masters, Qiu Chuji was perhaps the one most responsible for turning the Quanzhen movement into northern China's predominant Taoist school. He also is probably the one most admired to this day. Qin Zhi'an (1188–1244; see chapter 1), in his editorial comments that follow Qiu Chuji's hagiography in *Jinlian zhengzong ji*, records a conversation that supposedly took place between three men. The topic of the conversation was the accomplishments of Qiu Chuji. Each man took turns describing what he considered Qiu Chuji's greatest accomplishment. The first man cited his seven years of arduous training at the Panxi Gorge, his successful completion of "the great medicine of the golden [internal] elixir," and the tremendous miraculous powers that he gained as a result. The second man disagreed and said that Qiu Chuji was to be most praised for his great success in evangelism as well as his construction and restoration of temples. Finally, the third man stated:

> What you two gentlemen have talked about looks at only his small accomplishments and fails to see his great accomplishment. . . .
>
> I think that [his greatest accomplishment] took place when the powerful Mongolian troops came south. When they watered their horses, the Yellow River almost dried up. When they shot their whistling arrows, Mt. Hua almost collapsed. Even jade and stones were burned together. The wise and the foolish were slaughtered indiscriminately. Corpses piled up to form mountains so high that they almost scraped the Big Dipper. The sea of blood overflowed as though it was about to cover the heavens. Their wrath was like thunder, and they were merciless like tigers.

> Fortunately our Changchun, the venerable immortal Qiu [Chuji], responded to the imperial summons [of Genghis Khan] and rose [to go on his journey to see him]. When they had their first meeting, the dragon's expression gradually began to soften (Genghis Khan began to mellow). After they had their second meeting, his [Genghis Khan] heavenly will was changed. [Genghis Khan] ordered that those who obey orders not be executed and that the lives be spared of those who surrendered their cities. By disbanding their troops, [the Chinese] could bail out their soldiers that had been taken as prisoners and thereby submit. In the four hundred districts half the people acquired a secure livelihood (rather than the entire nation getting slaughtered). Several tens of thousand *li* [of land][6] quickly received the Emperor's gifts (gained the privilege of being under his rule).
>
> [What Qiu Chuji did] was what is referred to by expressions such as "stretching out the arms to hold back a crumbling mountain" or "lying sideways to blockade an overflowing river." He rescued living souls out of the midst of an execution cauldron. He snatched living [people] away from under the execution sword and saw. [The lives that he saved were] no fewer than hundreds, thousands, tens of thousands, or even hundreds of thousands. [The people whose lives he saved] were more numerous than the kernels of grain numbering tens and thousands of billions.
>
> [Because he had] this kind of hidden merit he corresponded above with the will of Heaven. He was definitely able to return to the blue skies and fly in broad daylight. Aside from this [great hidden merit obtained from saving all those lives], what use did he have for the Cinnabar Sand of Nine Cycles and Jade Liquid of Seven Returnings?[7]

Thus we are told here that Qiu Chuji saved innumerable lives by persuading Genghis Khan to adopt a more benign approach in his conquest of China. This saving of lives was what Qiu Chuji was (and still is) most admired for. Here it is suggested that "deeds" hereby accumulated were so great that he could have attained the highest level of immortality by this achievement alone.

Whether or not Qiu Chuji's persuasion of Genghis Khan actually was so effective is a question that cannot be properly resolved here. However, the humanitarian spirit conveyed in the above passage was certainly very much apparent in the teachings and the lives of the Quanzhen masters. Their writings frequently convey a deep sympathy for the plight of fellow sentient beings. Such is particularly the case with the poetry of Qiu Chuji. In the following poem, he expresses his feelings about the misfortunes of his people tormented by war:

> In the *dingwei* year of the Cheng'an reign era (1197), after the winter solstice when we were troubled by heavy snow, there was an uprising in the north [so I wrote this poem]:
> [From] the time before winter [till] the time after winter (throughout the winter) the snow falls heavily.
> When the warm breath of spring dissipates, the myriad objects wither.
> Horses departing from the fortresses are scared of the treacherous mountain paths.
> People defending the borders suffer in the coldness of their iron garments (armor).
> While I despair over the suffering of the souls at the northern border by the sea,
> I am glad that the gentlemen and commoners of Shandong are safe.
> If you daily spend 300,000 in state funds [on warfare],
> How can lives not wither and die?[8]

Here we have a poignant protest, directed at rulers who drain the nation's resources on wars, at the expense the people's welfare. Qiu Chuji sympathizes with those forced to participate in war (on top of the difficulties imposed by a harsh winter followed by drought conditions) and rejoices in the safety of those spared from war's ravages.

Northern China also was rife with other agonies, such as poverty, homelessness, natural disasters, and epidemics. The Quanzhen masters experienced these difficulties with the people and felt for them. In the following poem, Qiu Chuji bemoans the plight of the people during a severe drought and pleads their case to the divine forces:

> "Pitying [Living] Things" (Qiu Chuji's comments): Two verses. I wrote this because in this particular year a drought and an epidemic coincided:
> The sky is blue as it overlooks the soil below.
> Why does it not relieve the suffering of the myriad souls?
> The myriad souls day and night together weaken and decline.
> Drinking air and swallowing their voices they die without speech.
> Facing Heaven they loudly cry out, but Heaven does not respond.
> If a single miniscule [living] object vainly belabors its body,
> How can the great thousand realms of the universe revert to the state of primordial chaos,

And avoid causing the creator (the Tao) to give life to the vital spirits (living things)?

Oh! Heaven and Earth vastly separated [from each other],
And created the sentient beings numbering in the thousands, hundreds, and hundreds of thousands.
The violent and the wicked attack each other relentlessly.
The suffering that they receive as they transmigrate [through *samsara*], what limits does it know?
Emperor Heaven and Empress Earth each have their gods.
[But upon] seeing death [the gods] do not rescue; do you know the reason for this?
On the soil below [people] have sad hearts and still have no good fortune.
Laboring fruitlessly day and night they taste only sourness and bitterness.[9]

In stark contrast to Liu Chuxuan, who affirms the benevolence and justice of Nature and "The Most High," Qiu Chuji protests against the callous cruelty of Nature and the gods. His anguish over the world's plight reaches the point where he yearns nostalgically for the state of primordial chaos. While one can perhaps glimpse in the poem some recognition that people have brought on their misfortunes through their own wickedness, the main sentiment conveyed is that they have suffered too much. In this time of desperation, Qiu Chuji put sermonizing aside and pleaded on behalf of his fellow living creatures.

Qiu Chuji, however, also at times could rebuke his fellow human beings for their callousness and cruelty:

When a dog gets sick, there is no one who will cook porridge for it.
When a donkey falls to the ground because of the cold, its four limbs become rigid (it dies without any attention or help).
This is because people do not know how to cultivate hidden virtue (benevolent acts).
Changing shells (transmigrating through various incarnations), how can they avoid misfortunes?[10]

Qiu Chuji recognized an epidemic of indifference in the society in which he lived. Indifference to the well-being of another living thing, even a lowly beast, was to him an ugly manifestation of the ignorance that causes the endless suffering of the world. While rebuking people for their callousness that allows a lonely dog or a donkey to die, Qiu Chuji also is apparently offering the reminder that cruel, wicked people are liable to be reborn as dogs or donkeys themselves.

The early Quanzhen School, as part of its solution to this epidemic of indifference, involved itself with the feeding of the poor. It appears that at times it carried out projects to gather donations of rice and to feed porridge to the destitute. These projects were referred to as "winter porridge" (*sandongzhou*), or "gatherings for administering to the needs of the poor" (*shepinhui*). Ma Yu wrote a series of poems exhorting laymen to participate in or to donate to a winter porridge project overseen by him:

> Pity the poor and feed them porridge without seeking anything in return.
> If you establish your virtue [secretly] like a thief, you will enhance your cultivation of [your] Real [Nature] . . .
> [Let us] pity those who are hungry and together feed them winter porridge.
> I bow to you gentlemen, wishing only for a slight amount of merciful rice [donations] from the wealthy households,
> In order to rescue those who are poor.
> I would deeply appreciate your consent! . . .
> Winter porridge should [be administered] for a long time year after year.
> If you do so with a pitying heart you will firmly sow seeds in your field of merit for your present and later incarnations and you will have no lack of wisdom.
> Even if you give only a small amount of rice, you will acquire limitless blessings.
> If you accumulate deeds and your merit is complete,
> You will definitely in the future show [good] results and ascend the blue sky as an immortal. . . .
> Those who beg on the streets while freezing and starving will be overjoyed by your [deeds of] commiseration and compassion.
> Feed them as if they were immortals (generously and with deep respect), worrying only that a sage may be hidden among them.
> You must be diligent and devoted [in your service to the poor].
> [To administer winter porridge] is better than performing a *jiao* ritual (a large-scale Taoist ritual) with a thousand altars.
> You will plant your causes [for salvation] even more [than you would with any other activity], and your [required quota of] blessed deeds will be completed.
> You will definitely hereby in the future walk upon azure lotuses and go to visit the divine court of the highest gods . . .

[If you contribute] one and a half handfuls of merciful and compassionate rice,
The merit and deeds [that you will accumulate] will not be slight.
[Contributing rice for the poor] is greatly superior to reading the scriptures.
[Those who act out of] commiseration reach the Jade Capital and are recorded among the names of the immortals.
Swords of wind and arrows of snow are the miseries of winter.
You must pity the poor.
On their bodies they have no clothes, and in their mouths they have no food.
They always feel hunger and are extremely lonely and miserable.
People must willingly cultivate their meritorious virtue.
They must give rise to compassion in order to rescue those who are drowning and to help those who are in danger.[11]

Ma Yu's plea is an urgent and earnest one that appeals to his audience's desire for salvation as well as their compassion. Ma Yu reminds them that the accumulation of good deeds is essential for the highest salvation and assures them that cooperation with his winter porridge project would be meritorious indeed. While thus exhorting them, he also reminds them to give generously without any desire for recognition or reward. Also, he tells them that they must treat the poor respectfully, because "a sage may be hidden among them."

Ma Yu here is alluding to a recurring theme in Taoist hagiography, where immortals are said to disguise themselves as beggars or vagrants in order to test the character of people.[12] In such stories, people who are able to recognize the disguised holy man or who simply treat him kindly and respectfully, regardless of his loathsomeness, receive blessed results. Those who mistreat him suffer unfortunate results. Such stories seem to have been well known among people at the time. Ma Yu apparently utilized this popular belief to make people help and respect the destitute.

A good example of an immortal/beggar legend—which Ma Yu and his audience may have been familiar with—is found in *Chunyang dijun shenhua miaotong ji*. The story takes place in Bianjing (Kaifeng) at the end of the Latter Zhou dynasty (951–959), and it pertains to one of the many marvelous deeds of the immortal, Lü Yan. Lü Yan, we are told, would frequently disguise himself as a beggar in tattered clothing, his body covered with filth and bloody sores. Every day he would go into the Shi family's tea shop and beg for tea. Nobody wanted to go near him except the Shi family's young daughter. This little girl never shunned him. She always gave him the best tea in the shop, even though her parents scolded her every time. This had been going on daily for about a month when one day, after receiving his tea from the girl as usual, Lü Yan beckoned her to come and drink the tea left over in his cup. The girl, repulsed by the filthiness of the tea that had come into contact with the beggar's lips, emptied the cup's contents onto the ground. As soon as she did this, a wonderful aroma rose from the ground, so—regretting her actions—she quickly licked what she could from the inside of the cup. When she did this, her spirit and *qi* felt energetic. Lü Yan then revealed his identity by saying, "I am Mr. Lü; [I am] not a beggar. I regret that you were not able to drink all of my leftovers. But anyway, do you wish for wealth, noble status, or longevity?" The little girl then answered, "I am but the daughter of a lowly family, and do not know what you mean by 'noble status.' I would like to have wealth and a full life span." The girl went on to marry an official, to become the nanny for a future empress, and to live to the age of 135.[13]

The above story exalts the virtue of undiscriminating kindness. In Bianjing, the only person able to treat the loathsome beggar kindly was the little girl, who was amply rewarded with extraordinary longevity. If she had been able to drink the entire contents of the cup, she perhaps might have gained immortality. Thus the small amount of squeamishness (a symptom of pride) that she had in her seems to have prevented her from gaining the highest benefits. Of course, as we have seen, the Quanzhen masters frequently engaged in begging. Their purpose for doing this was to support themselves and to foster humility in themselves. But perhaps it had a didactic purpose as well, as a means of evoking the latent kindness in peoples' hearts.

In any organized religion there exists the danger that naive faith might be exploited. This danger is particularly strong in a movement such as the early Quanzhen School, which incorporates beliefs in supernatural beings, miraculous phenomena, and ritual healing. Wang Zhe, much to his credit, recognized this danger and addressed it:

> How can those who are hateful and vicious possibly understand the profound truth? [They] envy the wise and resent the talented, bringing about misfortunes. [They] covet life and fear death, thus committing sins. [They] write talismans and sell their techniques and thus deceive people. [They] administer medicines and heal diseases [in order to] receive heavy remuneration . . .
>
> I do not approve of preaching to people with confusing words. Also, I disapprove of attracting others by means of dishonest methods. I sternly tell you superior stalwarts of the Quanzhen [School] to help and persuade the confused people in the world to each and everyone understand the words of the Lunatic (Wang Zhe) so that all people will together ascend to the orthodox teaching.[14]

The Quanzhen masters drew a line between properly and improperly motivated healing and preaching. Healing was properly motivated if it was done for the purpose of helping the patient, not for the remuneration. Preaching had to be done honestly in a way conducive to moral and spiritual growth.

Of course, because their ministry was directed at all people, and people vary in their capacity to understand, the Quanzhen masters had to be versatile and skillful in their preaching methods. One hagiographic source has the following to tell us about Qiu Chuji:

> In bringing salvation to his disciples, he always examined their capabilities. The superior ones he guided with [teachings about] the Tao. Those who were next in ability he educated on the principles of merit and deeds. Those of even lesser ability he brought to goodness by [speaking of] punishments and blessings.[15]

Only the most capable could be guided in the subtleties of the Tao itself. Well-intentioned yet less accomplished disciples needed to be frequently exhorted toward diligence and perseverance in accumulating merit and deeds. Ignorant people had to be persuaded toward repentance and goodness by chastisement and encouragement. Good examples of this last method can be found in the poetry of the Quanzhen masters.

Wang Zhe, in the following poem, warns his readers that a sinful life can lead to reincarnation in a subhuman form:

> The appearance of the donkey is an ugly form.
> Its very long ears and snout are disproportionately big.
> Furthermore, its four legs are light and swift,
> [Yet] its skin is rough, and its back is hunched,
> [To the point where] it has no place to hold a load.
> It pulls carts and carriages and is furthermore ridden on.
> It also drags the stone grinders of various families.
>
> Exposed to whippings and exposed to beatings, its flesh is tattered and its skin is broken.
> I asked, "For what reason did you receive punishment severe as this?"
> Suddenly it shed tears and spoke to me saying,
> "It is because I strayed from the path and had not paid the debt for my deceitfulness."[16]

Qiu Chuji, in the following poem, gives a graphic description of purgatory:

The demons and gods wield their whips and clubs.
Kneeling and despairing, [sinners] open their eyes to reflect upon their arbitrary desires, thoughts, and crafty plots (in order to repent of them).
At their head is held a *karma* mirror.
High above, the names of the families that they have murdered are posted.
Pulling out their tongues and gouging out their hearts, [the demons] make [the sinners] pay for [past] pleasures.
[This punishment] is nothing like the fragrant aromas and delectable flavors [that they enjoyed] in previous days.
Along the three paths[17] they are exposed to a hundred poisons and to execution by slow slicing.[18]

We can thus see that the Quanzhen masters included the "fire and brimstone" method among their evangelistic tactics. The ordinary layperson was in such a way warned to refrain from evil. It should be noted, however, that Wang Zhe also had some positive advice for laypeople. The following poem is addressed to people who wish to follow the Tao and gain its blessings but are not ready to abandon the secular world:

"[If You] do not yet Want to Escape the Household":
If you do not yet wish to cultivate [as a monk or nun],
You should first [at least] understand [how to live in a manner that is] auspicious and good.
To create blessings while in the household you certainly must
Worship morning and evening and constantly burn fine incense.
Gradually decrease your sexual activity (translation tentative).
Attentively look after the sustenance of your father and mother.
Capture the monkey and horse (control the disorderly mind).
[Take to heart] the ancient phrase, "The soft and weak triumph over the strong and obstinate."

Obey your superiors.
In all the hundred affairs,
Put others first and yourself last.
Carefully discern the warmth and coldness (degree of intimacy) [in your relationships with people].
Be friendly with your six categories of relatives.
Be amicable toward your friends.
[As for the] offerings to your ancestors at the holy clan temple,
Frequently carry them out.

Keep them (ancestors) in your thoughts.
When festive occasions arrive,
You should joyfully visit [your kin] and drink.
Together with everybody sing "The Fragrance That Fills the Garden"
("Manting fang," a tune to which lyric poems were commonly set).[19]

In the first stanza, Wang Zhe enjoins the layperson to accumulate religious merit and to cultivate mind and body to the extent that such is possible for him or her. This is achieved by carrying out daily worship (presumably of the Tao, Taoist gods, and immortals), caring for one's parents, maintaining mental composure, and being mild in one's conduct and demeanor. If the tentative translation of the fifth line is correct, then Wang Zhe also is recommending here that a layperson try to decrease his or her sexual activity. In the second stanza, Wang Zhe enjoins deference, prudence, and congeniality in all social relationships and recommends frequent, cheerful participation in ancestor worship and the celebrations connected to it.

More ideally, of course, the Quanzhen masters desired that people would enter the monastic life and pursue the path of Realization. Ma Yu lamented the indifference of people toward the task of cultivating the immortal Real Nature:

"Lamenting That People Only Know How to Eat Food and Defecate, without Ever Assigning Their Minds to Their Nature and Life":
The grain cart enters, and the manure cart exits.
They take turns coming and going.
When will it come to an end?
Even if [people can] cause their life to span over a hundred years,
This is only 36,000 days.[20]

Ma Yu bemoans the fact that people thoughtlessly go about their living their lives, heedless of the dire problem of their own mortality. Ironically, one must note, this description of the ignorant, worldly person strangely resembles Wang Zhe's description of proper cultivation in which one eats when hungry, sleeps when tired, does not meditate, and does not study the Tao (see chapter 2). Of course, the those criticized here by Ma Yu are those whose minds are not clear and pure, and whose lifestyles are filled with selfish, sinful conduct. When they die, they are likely to go to purgatory and then get reborn in a subhuman form. Life in a human body is a precious opportunity earned through accumulating much good karma in previous lives; it is an opportunity to escape *samsara* once and for all. However, this opportunity is a short one that gets wasted all too often.

To jar people from their complacent indifference, the Quanzhen masters liked to remind them of their mortality. To do this, they often employed the image of a skeleton, as Wang Zhe did when trying to persuade Ma Yu to become his disciple.

"I Drew a Picture of a Skeleton to Warn Ma Yu":
Lamentable is the sad plight of people!
I now need to draw a picture of a skeleton.
During his life he was only able to greedily commit evil deeds.
He did not cease until he ended up like this.

When you become a person you should be aware of the torrents of dusty labor.
The true mind of purity and clarity is your true treasure.
Seize the pearl from the mouth of the black dragon.
Thereby make it run into the cavern of Kunlun.[21]

Wang Zhe, as both the heading and contents of the poem indicate, drew a picture of a skeleton to go along with the poem. One wonders whether—and how frequently—he may have used this technique in preaching to the general lay listener; it seems particularly appropriate for communicating with those less cultured and literate. We do have clear evidence that Tan Chuduan employed the same tactic. The following poem by him was written to go along with a picture that he had drawn:

The skeleton, the skeleton, its countenance is ugly.
[This is] simply because he loved flowers (sex) and liquor during his lifetime.
Endearing himself to fine furs and plump horses, he took enjoyment in his mind.
His blood, flesh, and skin gradually declined and rotted, gradually declined and rotted.
Yet he coveted and sought, coveting wealth.
A leaking jar will not hold [water].
If lust and desire are limitless, the body will have its limit.
Eventually he caused himself to today become a skeleton, become a skeleton.
You must heed [the following fact].
To obtain the human body with its seven treasures,
Is not easy to do.
You must understand,

Your life is like [one who] hangs from a silk thread (its demise is imminent).
Be indifferent [to worldly things] and do not go chasing after [objects] of human desire.
Therefore I hereby draw this picture and present it to you.
Will you be enlightened today, or not?[22]

Tan Chuduan thus eloquently laments the demise of the worldly man who squandered his golden opportunity for liberation and eternal life. This man neglected the task of self-cultivation and chose to pursue worldly things. All too soon he ended up a skeleton.

Some people who came into contact with the Quanzhen masters were already suffering from diseases and had come to them in hope of healing. Such people did not need to be reminded of the grim realities of existence. The Quanzhen masters needed to take a gentler, more sensitive approach in exhorting them.

The following poem by Ma Yu was probably written for a believer who came seeking medical advice, and was perhaps ailing:

"Healing Diseases"
If *qi* does not flow [properly], and your legs and knees are ailing,
Mica ointment should be applied and spread and should always be kept available.
If you want to cure tetanus, what could be better than finely ground flower stamen rock?

To heal diseases of the heart-mind [you should use] the Pure Heart Powder.
To heal your nature [you should] avoid the (poisonous) wolfsbane plant.
The pill inside the principle is the Lingbao Elixir.
Imbibe it in large quantities, and exchange it with your skeleton.[23]

Ma Yu starts out first by prescribing medicines for specific ailments that his believer/patient was perhaps suffering from. Interestingly, however, after giving advice on healing the physical body, he uses medicinal metaphors to prescribe the spiritual cultivation that leads to eternal life. The "Pure Heart Powder" probably refers to the cultivation of mental clarity and purity. The "wolfsbane plane" is most likely a metaphor for ignorance and the deluded thoughts and desires engendered by it. The "Lingbao Elixir" probably refers to the Real Nature/Radiant Spirit. To "imbibe" this and "exchange it with your skeleton" most likely means to shed the mortal body and proceed to eternal life in the Radiant Spirit. Thus in two stanzas Ma Yu gives practical medical advice, endorses mental discipline, and offers hope for the life beyond.

Wang Chuyi also wrote poems of a similar nature:

Wang Yasi, because of an Illness, Sought My Instructions:
Lengthily and intricately nurture your harmony.
Serenely cultivate your mind, and depart from the river of desire.
Increase and lengthen your Spirit in the valley, always without leaking.
Make flow your blood vessels and forever have no illnesses.
The way in which the Quanzhen [School] expounds the Tao is to forget about birth and extinction.
See your [Real] Nature and communicate with the holy, and get rid of obstructive demons.
For many *kalpas*, probably because your meritorious virtue is proper,
Ten thousand gods will carry you out of the world of suffering (*suopo*).[24,25]

The Wife of the Provincial Judge who was Ailing from an Illness Came Seeking Healing:
Heaven gives birth, and Heaven nurtures; cultivate in accordance with Heaven.
Do not speak of the dusty world and the worldly skeleton.
The four provisional elements (that make up the body) are unable to visit the Phoenix Palace (the realm of the immortals).
How can the Three Corpses go to Yingzhou (one of the legendary islands of the immortals)?
Understand Reality, illuminate the inside (of yourself), and forget [about making] new [worldly] contacts.
Reach the origin and with a heart like ashes eliminate old worries.
In formless true emptiness transcend to the other shore.
Ride leisurely upon the great divine boat of freedom.[26]

In the first poem, Wang Chuyi emphasizes the physical benefits of self-cultivation. He maintains that by cultivating inner serenity, one can strengthen the vital principle (the Real Nature, the Real *qi*, the "Spirit in the Valley"). This not only cures one's current ailment but also prevents future diseases. Only at the end of the poem does Wang Chuyi speak of the final reward that is the eternal life of the Real Nature/Radiant Spirit. It would appear that the patient in this case was not suffering a terminal illness, thus Wang Chuyi anticipated his full recovery and provided him with guidelines to follow for the rest of his life. In the second poem, it appears that the illness was critical. Wang Chuyi consoles his patient with the hope of eternal life and enjoins her not to fret or despair over the inevitable and irrelevant demise of the "four provisional elements" (mortal body). Such was the bedside manner of Wang Chuyi.

In the early Quanzhen School, compassion was extolled as a definitive trait of a Realized Being, both before and after his or her worldly death. The Quanzhen masters aspired to foster this compassion. Evidence in their poetry indicates that they felt genuine agony at the sight of the suffering of others. This feeling translated into acts of charity, preaching, and healing. In preaching, they displayed discretion and sensitivity toward the situations, needs, and abilities of their audience. They chastised evil people in the hope of helping them evade hell and other bad rebirths. The worldly they encouraged to reject the world to gain eternal life and thus never to be born and die again. The ill they provided with well-chosen words of comfort and advice. Self-absorbed ascetics they were not.

# Chapter 9

## Rituals in Early Quanzhen Taoism

"Conducting the Yellow Register *Jiao* Ritual at the Xiuzhen Guan [Taoist Temple] in Dengzhou"
. . . In the fourth year of the Cheng'an reign era (1199), during the winter in the tenth month (October 22–November 19),
We held the Yellow Register [*jiao* ritual] on a grand scale and performed the Golden Liturgy.
The Red Book and the Jade Letters exist from the time preceding Heaven (the prior realm before creation).
The White Tablets and True Talismans have been vanquishing the wicked since times of yore.
Triple-tiered ornate jade altars gleam with precious brilliance.
Nine liquor vessels and divine lanterns capture the stars.
The majestic peak to which we expended our (paper?) money[1] is Mt. Fengdu.[2]
[Try as one may to] ascend to immortality over its many peaks, it cannot be climbed.
For four nights we reverently lined up our incense fire and sacrifices.
For nine mornings we awaited and listened (for the gods' response?), circumambulating by pacing the void (*buxu*).[3]
1,000 gates and 10,000 doors (all households and families) gave rise to rejoicing.
Six streets and three marketplaces together lined up their contributions.
Golden flowers and silver torches together shined and glimmered.

On the surface and in the interior, the light's brilliance naturally penetrated.
Suddenly we heard joyous auspicious signs manifested outside in the sky.
There was an extraordinary [manifestation] that spiraled in a lonesome manner.
The Jade Emperor (Yudi) passed on his proclamation and carried out great redemption.
Immortal Youths descended to Nanchang[4] mounted on cranes.
The imprisoned *hun* souls and stagnant *po* souls all rose up [from purgatory] and were delivered.
White[-haired] old timers and yellow[-haired] youths were all reverent and faithful.
To the furthest limits of the heavens a better thing [than this] has never been heard of.
We have completely subdued [the harmful forces of (?)] the regions of Shandong and Hebei.[5]

The above poem by Qiu Chuji describes the ongoings at a Yellow Register (*huanglu*) *jiao* festival. The Yellow Register *jiao*[6] was carried out extensively by the Quanzhen School. The primary aim of the Yellow Register *jiao* was (and is) to deliver the souls of the dead out of purgatory. The act of delivering damned souls also was thought to greatly benefit the living, since the distraught souls of the dead were believed to cause many of the misfortunes and illnesses that afflict the living. To perform a task as important as this, no ordinary effort could suffice. It required the skills of a Taoist ritual master versed in the liturgies and equipped with the proper *lu* (registers of the names, titles, and physical descriptions of the gods to be called upon) and *fu* (talismans). The ritual would go on for several days and nights. The full participation, reverence, and support of the entire community would be essential. As a result, in the case of the poem just quoted, the Jade Emperor is said to have been moved to extend his pardon to the damned souls, and the entire area of Shandong and Hebei gained immunity from the potential hazards wrought by the unhappy dead. (The poem also indicates that some sort of wondrous, auspicious omen manifested itself in the sky, but it gives only a vague description of it.) The Yellow Register *jiao* that Qiu Chuji describes must have been performed on a grand scale indeed.

As we shall see, the early Quanzhen masters—including the founder, Wang Zhe—were involved in ritual activities of the kind traditionally carried out within the Taoist religious tradition. They did not categorically disdain such rituals as superstition, nor did they attempt to exclude them from their religious system. However, the Quanzhen masters held both negative and positive attitudes toward rituals. On the negative side, they saw ritual involvement as a potential distraction from the task of self-cultivation and showed a definite disdain toward certain kinds of ritual conduct. But on the positive side, the Quanzhen masters saw it as their humanitarian duty to exercise their ritual skills and powers. They clearly believed in the efficacy of liturgies, prayers, incantations, and talismans if employed properly with the proper state of mind. One also can plausibly speculate that their growing reputation as ritual masters was based on their even greater reputation as ascetics and masters of meditation. Because they cultivated clarity and purity of mind and observed what was tantamount to ritual taboos (celibacy, vegetarianism, etc.) on a permanent basis, their prayers were considered extra powerful.

## Attitudes Toward Rituals

Wang Zhe regarded the performance of rituals an integral part of the life and activity of a Taoist master. This is apparent from the following poem, which extols the merit of the rites for the deliverance of damned souls:

> [As for] the True Ritual Register of the Chaotic Origin of the Great Unity (*Taiyi hunyuan zhen falu*),
> Carry it out with a clear mind with sharp precision.
> First capture those worms and corpses within yourself.
> The smoke from the incense penetrates into the upper realm,
> And the mighty power is secretly administered.
> Rescuing and delivering lost *hun* souls erases old karma.
> Those presently existing (the living?) vastly acquire great blessings.
> Demons will be startled, and gods will be scared, afraid of getting captured and pursued.
> Your deeds and merit alone will stand out,
> And on another day colorful clouds will follow you.[7]

Wang Zhe here alludes to a certain True Ritual Register of the Three Origins of the Great Unity and asserts that by employing it one can administer mighty power that can rescue damned souls, benefit the living, and dominate spirits and demons. (This ritual register may in fact bear some relationship to the Ritual Register of the Three Origins of the Great Unity [*Taiyi sanyuan falu*], employed by the contemporaneous Taiyi School of Taoism; see chapter 1.) Doing so, however, requires that one maintain a clear mind and first conquer one's own inner demons ("corpses and worms").[8] Through his ritual performance, the Taoist master benefits himself as much as others, since he thereby erases old karma and accumulates merits and deeds. Self-cultivation and ritual activity in this way facilitate each other. This premise seems to have been widely understood and accepted, which is probably why Wang Zhe's main disciples—so highly esteemed as ascetics and meditation masters—eventually would come into high demand for their ritual services.

Wang Zhe was an enthusiastic participant in Taoist rituals. *Chongyang quanzhen ji* includes the following poem written by Wang Zhe to invite the Taoist believers in Jingyang (in Shaanxi) to participate in a *jiao* hosted by a certain Mr. Lü:

> In the past [Mr. Lü] started to embrace [his faith in the Tao],
> And this morning he is holding a *jiao*.
> [At this *jiao*] more than anywhere else there is a special kind of purity and joy.
> Windy companions and misty friends have all arrived.
> We all devote our sincere hearts,
> And only wait in hope for our old acquaintances of Jingyang to join us in clearing and cleansing (preritual purification and bathing?).
> With our vision spread out, we devotedly invite and beg you gentlemen and superior stalwarts.
> We all wish for you to come to the altar of the immortals.
>
> When we gather together to worship the Great Tao,
> We do not need *jian* (a type of incense wood) and *ru* (frankincense).
> And what need do we have for garoo wood or sandalwood?
> We take our heart's incense and burn it, and the throngs of sages come to observe and inspect.
> We attain the completion of our merit and our deeds.
> [Their] (gods and immortals?) returning and responding is all a matter of cultivating Reality at the edges of the clouds.
> This evening we shall together rejoice, and one by one ride on phoenixes.[9]

This poem was undoubtedly written prior to Wang Zhe's journey to Shandong in 1167. Wang Zhe appears to have been an active member of a circle of Taoists who gathered for joint worship and prayer. Wang Zhe extols the gathering as an occasion for believers to join in worship and cultivate themselves in a mutually supportive, uplifting atmosphere.

The efficacious power of the scriptures, liturgies, and talismans was clearly affirmed by Wang Zhe:

In the outer courtyard,
Submitting a jade message.
Feathered robed ones (Taoist priests) line up in a procession.
When the medicine spoon has been allowed they (we?) present new writs.[10]
In unison they recite the words in the writ,
And burn the message [as an offering].
When the flames rise up, clouds and rain will arrive.
The earth gods will pass [the message] on without confusion,
Lengthily and continuously until it reaches the Lord of Heaven.
Passed on from mouth to mouth are the words in response,
Declaring that the Sages of the Tao have been made aware.

On a white tablet is written,
The golden lessons and registers.
Recorded there are the lost *hun* souls of other surnames.
The ghosts are startled, and the spirits are scared and [are thus made to] reflect [upon their transgressions].
You thus receive posthumous recommendation;
Which recommends you for receiving entry into the gate of life.

When the gates are opened up, the mysterious wonders are carried out.
The people are together in harmony with the Heavenly Worthy.
The single point of light is never again obscured.
The sun radiates, and the moon shines,
As the fire and water come out from [Mt.] Kunlun.[11]

The first of the two poems describes the writing of various memorials to be burnt and sent up to the highest deities. It is unclear whether Wang Zhe himself was among the ranks of those priests participating. However, he does clearly convey his belief that the prayers do reach the attention of the gods, and that rain for the crops is thus quickly and effectively brought about. The second poem describes ritual procedures of "posthumous recommendation" for the salvation of the lost souls of the dead. The priest administering the rites in this case seems most likely to be Wang Zhe himself—at least this is what seems to be implied by the use of the second-person pronoun to refer to the souls being delivered. Whatever the case, there can be no doubt that Wang Zhe believed in the efficacy of these ritual procedures.

Wang Zhe sincerely believed that the talismans he wrote were capable of alleviating the sufferings of people and preventing disasters. He also believed that people who received these benefits could be brought to faith as a result:

"Begging for Ink at the Place of Jingzhao Superintendent of Schools Lai Yanzhong"
. . . [I] write miraculous talismans and precious seals,
Rescuing those who suffer and eliminating disasters.
I wish to cause each and every household to honor the Tao,
And [cause] each and every person to be enlightened.
Thereby they will all avoid *samsara* and accomplish their merit and deeds.
With a secret road ahead of them, they will together go and celebrate at Penglai (legendary island of the immortals).[12]

Provided that I have understood the above poem correctly, Wang Zhe here is begging an official to give him some ink so he can continue to write talismans that he can employ for the benefit of other people.

The following poems seem to indicate that Wang Zhe taught Ma Yu special methods of reciting scriptures and writing talismans and memorials to be presented to the gods and immortals in a ritual context:

"Presented to Danyang (Ma Yu) [from Wang Zhe]"
[If you] strive continuously without interruption you will become a divine immortal.
Atop the mountain the wind is pure, and the moon is truly round.
If your mouth recites the true scriptures there will be nothing that will not respond.
In your mind uphold the marvelous lessons and diligently present [offerings and messages (?)].
When [presenting] the Jade Message Slabs, you should obey the Tao.
Wearing a golden cap on your head, you naturally unite with Heaven.
Generally in all things I simply wish,
To make you hereby obtain good causes [for future good fortune].

Danyang's (Ma Yu) verse in response:
The *tuan* commentary that distinguishes the trigram emblems is the Crazy Immortal (Wang Zhe).[13]
Fufeng (Ma Yu)[14] below the mountain is incomplete in his fruits.
When the oral lessons are transmitted, I must nurture my [Real] Nature.

To scare off my mind's demons with a shout is better than swinging my fists.
Holding the ivory brush in hand I write the talismans and message slabs.
The sun shines on the silver toad (the moon), illuminating the grotto heavens.
The Great Tao is formless, returning to non-duality.
When the One is penetrated [by me], I attain good causes.[15]

It would appear that Wang Zhe was coaching Ma Yu in the ritual procedures of preparing and employing ritual memorials and talismans.

Thus so far we have seen that Wang Zhe knew and trusted various ritual methods. He approved of ritual activities because they benefited people in need, strengthened the solidarity and faith of Taoists, and facilitated the adept's own spiritual progress.

However, there also is evidence that Wang Zhe disdained certain types of rituals:

"The District Magistrate[16] Invited Me to Worship Lost Souls. I did not Go Along."
The Master-[Buddhist] Monk (*shiseng*) rings the cymbals and praises the lost souls.
There is only Windy (Crazy) Wang who is alone sober.
If this (my body) was a skeleton, I would go along to the worship,
[But] by not going along to the worship, I eliminate my skeleton shape.[17]

Unfortunately, the reason Wang Zhe gives (in the poem's last two lines) for declining the invitation is not very clear. One can only surmise that there was something about the ritual being performed by the Buddhist monks that he disapproved of. Perhaps he considered it beneath his dignity as a Taoist adept to venerate the ghost of an ordinary deceased person. Taoist masters, although they deliver dead souls through the power of the Tao, should not venerate them; perhaps such was Wang Zhe's attitude. The deceased person in question here, as Hachiya points out,[18] may have been Wang Zhe's own older brother, since the poem directly preceding this poem in the text is one that Wang Zhe wrote on the occasion of his brother's death. If so, it would seem as though he somehow disapproved of the common Chinese familial/ancestral religion. Yet evidence previously cited attests to the contrary. Wang Zhe seems to have encouraged laypeople to make frequent offerings to their ancestors (see chapter 8). Perhaps, as a man who had resolutely rejected the secular world, he held himself to different standards.

The writings of Ma Yu contain even more evidence of ritual activity than the writings of Wang Zhe. It is clear that Ma Yu believed in the power of prayer:

> "Praying for Rain in Chang'an (present-day Xi'an) on the Twenty-Fourth Day of the Eighth Month of the *Gengzi* Year (September 15, 1180)"
> [I], Barefoot Crazy Ma pray for rain,
> My heart's incense wafts up to the headquarters of the immortals.
> How long will we have to wait before the moisture is sufficient to plough?
> Five times five, not beyond the twenty-fifth [day].
>
> The sprouts are on the verge of withering,
> And all the people are in despair.
> [I] burn up my heart's incense, and auspicious breath floats.
> Again I pray to the Three Realized Ones that in all of the lower realm,
> A torrential stream will bring forth a good fall harvest.[19]
>
> "A Response to [Our] Prayers"
> The heavens were extremely high (clear, without clouds or precipitation).
> [So we feared] that our sprouts would dry up.
> The immortals responded to our prayers,
> And we had downpours for three mornings.[20]

The first of the above two poems indicates that Ma Yu prayed to the "Three Realized Ones" for rain to relieve a severe drought and expresses confidence that the prayers will be answered. The second poem pertains to another similar occasion and states that the Taoist deities indeed answered Ma Yu's prayer with abundant rain. The identities of the Three Realized Ones (*sanzhen*) named as the objects of worship are unclear. They are perhaps the Three Pure Ones (Yuanshi Tianzun, Taishang Daojun, and Taishang Laojun) who have prevailed at the summit of the Taoist pantheon since about the fifth century. However, Ma Yu may actually be referring to a group of three immortals more exclusive to the Quanzhen tradition. The most likely candidates in such a case would be Zhongli Quan, Lü Yan, and Wang Zhe, although Liu Cao or He Dejin also could be possibilities.

In some poems we find evidence that Ma Yu, during public *jiao* rituals, would sometimes pray for the salvation of the dead in solitude in his meditation hut while deferring to others the performance of the sublime and elegant altar rites.

"Adding Support (*jiachi*)[21] at the *Jiao* at the Home of the Gentleman of Service Ma"[22]
When enlightenment arrives one enjoys the Tao and follows one's pleasure.
For food at the *jiao* one must ask for just one bowl of noodles.
Fortunately I have met up with yellow caps (Taoist priests) administering their rites.
To help their pure *jiao* I diligently expiate disasters.
I add my support by purifying myself and residing in a hut,
[In order to] give posthumous recommendation for lost souls to ascend to the Jade Terrace.[23]

The wording of the poem seems to suggest that Ma Yu just happened to find a *jiao* ritual being administered by "yellow caps"—apparently these were qualified Taoist priests who were not connected to the Quanzhen movement. Ma Yu volunteered to help them out by performing prayers privately in a meditation hut. He clearly appears to have been confident in his own ability to expiate disasters and deliver the souls of the dead from purgatory. Ma Yu also makes mention of his austere diet (one bowl of noodles) and how he "purifies" himself. Of course, his whole life was one of austerity and purity; this, theoretically, made his prayers extra powerful.

Confident though he was in his own power of prayer, Ma Yu appears to have been quite reluctant to administer the *jiao* rites at the altar. This reluctance was due to certain misgivings about the example he might set for his disciples. Ma Yu also claimed that he lacked mastery and experience in the ritual procedures:

Friends of the Tao of Zhiyang have come to Wendeng . . .
The local official sent a letter inviting me to be in charge of a *jiao* and rescue the lost souls.
To rescue lost souls is a good thing indeed.
However, there are a few small matters that I need to consider.
I only fear that my successors will emulate me,
Frequently going to *zhai*[24] and going to *jiao* without cultivating the Tao.
If one does not cultivate the Tao, how can one attain immortality?
How can they thus attain immortality?
. . . Why do friends of the Tao seek for posthumous recommendation?
Earnestly they implore to me to rescue the *yin* convicts (prisoners in purgatory).
As for rescuing the *yin* convicts, how should I do this?

I am a non-active gentleman of clarity and purity.
Never before have I gone to a *jiao* with the [Primordial] Heavenly Worthy.
I do not know how to ascend the altar and administer the rites.
To administer the rites [you should] invite the yellow caps,
[Who will] purify themselves, ascend the altar, and perform inner visualization.
I shall add my support while dwelling in a hut (*huandu*).
I will silently pray to my original master, the Heavenly Immortal Official.
The Heavenly Immortal Official is [none other than] Chongyang (Wang Zhe).
Letting out a sigh (of pity), he gives rise to mercy and carries out his compassionate transformations.
The 1,000-layered shackles and chains of purgatory are unlocked,
And all of the lost souls are cleared of their guilt.
Cleared of their guilt, [the lost souls], and the lonely *hun* souls (wandering ghosts),
Together travel to the Purple Mansion and enter the Gate of the Immortals.
In the homestead of no night (eternal daylight), they attain true joy.
In the grotto of eternal spring they receive the golden liquor barrel.[25]

The occasion described here occurred in either 1182 or 1183, during Ma Yu's final days of ministry in Shandong, after his banishment from Shaanxi (see chapter 1). From his reaction to the invitation from the Taoist friends of Zhiyang, it would seem as though this was the first time Ma Yu had been asked to administer *jiao* rites. Such may not have been the case, however; on 6/17/Dading 21(August 26, 1181), we are told by one source that he "did" (*zuo*) a Yellow Register *jiao* at Liujiang (Shaanxi).[26] The same source also indicates that in the fourth month of Dading 23 (April 24–May 22, 1183), he went to preach in Zhiyang, and that he "did" a *jiao* in Wendeng on 10/15 (November 1) of the same year—and it was at this *jiao* that the Radiant Spirit of the deceased Wang Zhe is said to have appeared in the sky, mounted on a white tortoise (see chapter 6).[27] In both cases, the wording of the text leaves open the possibility—or even implies—that Ma Yu himself administered the altar rites. Whatever the case, in the above poem, Ma Yu reacts to the invitation with feelings of both gratitude and misgiving. He is worried that his disciples, by following his example, might overengage in ritual activity to the detriment of their own personal training. Thus he modestly proposes to relegate himself to the task of silent, secluded prayer in a meditation hut. Most interestingly, he declares that he will pray to his late master, Wang Zhe. He thus once again claims posthumous divine status for his beloved master. Furthermore, he ascribes to him a power normally attributed to Taoism's highest deities, namely, the power to save the dead from purgatory. In claiming to be incapable of performing the proper ritual procedures before the Primordial Heavenly Worthy, he is perhaps truthfully admitting to his lack of sufficient training in ritual procedures. Then again, in polite interaction in China, it is a standard practice to speak in this sort of self-deprecating manner.

Ma Yu perhaps feared that the success, fame, and wealth that might be gained from such activities would have a distracting, corruptive effect. Thus in some of his poems he strongly asserts that self-cultivation and compassionate action are far more important than ritual worship:

> If a son of good nature embraces his good nature,
> He does not need incense, and he does not need *zhai* rituals.
> He receives from above the envelopment of the clouds (receives divine protection),
> And completely avoids disasters.
> Internally cultivating his extraordinary womb (the Real *qi* in his Elixir Field),
> He forgets his plans, cuts off his worries and gets rid of his dust.
> He gives birth to a miraculous child that has great talents (the immortal and omnipotent Radiant Spirit).[28]

> [Feeding the street beggars] is better than holding a *jiao* with 1,000 altars. . . .
> The merciful and compassionate blessings of helping the poor and rescuing those who suffer;
> The meritorious virtue [attained by it] is limitless!
> It is superior to that of burning *jian* and garoo wood.[29]

Ma Yu's younger brethren, Liu Chuxuan, Qiu Chuji, and Wang Chuyi, all performed *jiao* rituals at the imperial court. Presumably they suffered no lack of confidence in their own mastery of the altar rites. However, they also shared a wary attitude similar to Ma Yu's. Their writings show that they were fully cautious of the possible drawbacks of overemphasizing rituals, and that they recognized higher priorities. Liu Chuxuan's attitude can be glimpsed at from the following poems:

Praying for rain, I go from village to village.
If the people are good, Heaven sends down its blessings.
Non-killing brings about miraculous blessings,
As the incense, lanterns, tea and fruit are maintained (the proper sacrifices continue to be made).[30]

As the *jiao* draws near, people listen to,
[My instructions to] refrain from [eating] meats and spices and keep the body still (abstain from sex).
Altruistically and selflessly they acquire a bit of merit and deeds.
If they go against the rules of Heaven,
They will have annual disasters and monthly illnesses.
Respond to objects while forgetting the dust (worldly matters),
Your small soul is like a mirror.
Commander gods secretly observe you.
Rectifying your heart with every thought,
Get rid of [feelings of] hatred, and eliminate [feelings] of affection,
And purely understand equality.
If you want to avoid rebirth,
Take refuge in the sacred sages.[31]

We can see that Liu Chuxuan emphasized the internal, moral element that gave the rituals their fundamental significance. These poems stress purity in action (observance of dietary and sexual injunctions) and thought as the essential factor that makes rituals efficacious and bestows blessings upon the participants. Liu Chuxuan reminds ritual participants that their conduct is always under the scrutiny of the gods, and that morality and piety should be maintained always—not only during the *jiao*.

The fact that morality and self-cultivation were a higher priority than ritual in Liu Chuxuan's mind is clear from the following statements:

It is better for the myriad [living] things to be free of misfortunes (due to good daily conduct) than it is to hold a *jiao*.[32]

It is better to rid one's mind of hate and affection than it is to perform a large *jiao*.[33]

It is better to complete your Nature and Life than it is to repeatedly perform the *jiao*.[34-2]

In other words, if people could stay out of trouble by living morally, they would never find themselves in a position where they had to beg for divine help.

But in reality, people misbehave, and people suffer. Qiu Chuji and Wang Chuyi were clearly eager to aid the suffering masses with their ritual skills and powers as often as possible. Qiu Chuji, for example, wrote:

"Going to the Northern Sea *jiao* at Weizhou"
The *yin* wind of the northern extreme blows across the sea.
The scenery of the sea and the mountains is desolate.
Snow has piled up on the north side of the mountains, and coldness has enveloped the land.
The layers of ice on the sea have frozen [and piled up high enough to] reach Heaven.
The swans have already migrated 1,000 *li* away.
The water dragons are in deep sleep at the bottom of the nine-layered pools.
The man of the Tao preserves his incompetence, so why must he lend an ear (pay attention to these arduous conditions)?
Sternly he braves the ice and frost and goes to the *jiao* feast.[35]

The mountains and rivers have been stabilized, and shields and lances are no longer wielded.
In a time of Great Peace, there are truces in the eight directions.
We carry out *zhai* and *jiao* rituals frequently in order to answer to these responses (give thanks to the gods for the peace that has arrived).
To the vacuous emptiness and to Heaven and Earth, we give thanks for their abundant blessings and their secret mercy and compassion.[36]

Wang Chuyi similarly wrote:

The flooding of the Yellow River came in contact with the various directions (extended over a large area).
At every place, all living souls were injured.
Therefore, I went to see the Chaoyuan,[37] and we discussed matters together.
[We decided to] quickly perform the Yellow Register and pray for high and clear skies.[38]

Amidst the violent waves of the sea of suffering, I escaped the danger and difficulty.
Having completed my Real [Nature], I spread out an incense altar at every place I go.

I climb mountains and cross rivers, never turning down a request.
I rescue the living and the dead, and this vow (to save everybody) is vast.[39]

The good man of the Real One;
Only his virtue is his assistance.
He widely performs his mercy and compassion,
Delivering the dead and rescuing those who suffer.[40]

By the time Qiu Chuji and Wang Chuyi had become the leading figures of the Quanzhen movement, there no longer seems to have been much hesitation involved in performing public rituals. In fact, the attitude conveyed in the above poems is that a Taoist master would be balking from his or her duty if he or she ever turned down a *jiao* invitation.

## The Quanzhen Masters As Ritual Purists

When the master (Ma Yu) returned to the [eastern] coast, every household was diligently observing the abstentions and ordinances and had affiliated themselves with the five congregations which had been established by the Patriarch-Master (Wang Zhe). When the teachers and children (*shitong*)[41] heard that Master Ma was in Deng Prefecture, they gathered a group of a hundred and some people and said to the master, "The disciples have each already bathed, remained celibate, and avoided meats, spices, and liquor for seven days. I wish for you to join our pure gathering in order to pray for blessings and erase future karma."

The master said, "I am pleased about your being pure and immaculate for seven days. Furthermore, I say you will have blessings. The disciples of Crazy Ma are all pure and immaculate throughout their lifetimes, eliminating their wants and desires and avoiding meats, spices, and liquor. Their blessings are even greater." Those assembled all bowed to him and exclaimed, "The Teaching of Clarity and Purity (the Quanzhen School) is truly beyond comprehension and discussion (profound and marvelous)!" From this time on, every household within the three prefectures received his teaching. Gradually, people in the ten directions heard his wind (teachings) and were brought to faith. The revival of the Great Teaching (Quanzhen Taoism) [in Shandong] began from the master.[42]

The above passage shows how it was common practice to undergo a period of purification and abstention prior to engaging in ritual worship. In order to enhance the efficacy of their "Pure Gathering," the people in Deng Prefecture—apparently lay members of the Jade Flower Congregation—invited Ma Yu to participate. They were extremely impressed and delighted to hear that Ma Yu and his disciples lived austerely on a permanent basis. This was apparently because they believed in a direct correlation between one's purity and the efficacy of one's prayers.[43]

While the Quanzhen masters were probably not great innovators in the area of ritual, they were ardent ritual purists interested in ensuring the proper performance of rituals. They asked that all participants (clergy and laity) observe proper conduct and be sincere in their devotion. The clergy who administered special ritual services needed to be properly trained and properly motivated. They were not supposed to desire any financial profit.

First of all, the Quanzhen masters stressed that one must understand what causes good and bad fortune. Liu Chuxuan, in his commentary to the *Yinfu jing*, criticized popular religious rituals as follows:

> Worldly people only know of earth deities and *yin* gods and thus think of them as gods. They take gods carved from wood and molded from mud to be [real] gods. The foolish do not understand that whenever one creates a single portion of sin and transgression, Heaven will send down a single portion of misfortune and suffering. [Thus they] murder pigs and sheep and vastly burn [paper] coins and horses (presumably paper effigies) in order to pray and worship. [Only] when they have illnesses do they seek comfort [from the gods], and [only] when they have misfortune do they seek for blessings [from the gods]. . . .
>
> [Worldly people] do not know that up in Heaven the ultimate gods of the *yang* Tao each take their direction and position to secretly observe the goodness and badness among people. If people of the world create goodness for three years, before 1,000 days go by, [Heaven] will send down auspicious blessings. If people create evil for 1,000 days, within three years [Heaven] will send down disasters.
>
> Worldly people do not understand that among the myriad [living] things, that which is the most numinous and the most penetrating is their own primal Spirit, which has the capacity to penetrate Heaven and abound through Earth with brilliant radiance. [As for the] wise sages of old, all of them understood the Tao, cultivated Reality, and went from ordinariness into sacredness.[44]

The gist of the critique is that popular ritual not only worships false or inferior deities but is pervaded by an amoral religiosity of convenience that seeks—only in times of need—to gain divine help through material offerings and prayers. Liu Chuxuan asserts that people can much better secure their well-being through moral everyday behavior, since the true Taoist gods observe human conduct at all times and hand out blessings and punishments in accordance to virtue; they are not impressed by bloody sacrifices and empty displays of piety. Naturally, then, the key to the success of a Taoist ritual lies in the purity and discipline of the participants:

If you want to move Heaven and Earth,
Be pure and still[45] and eat bland food.
In the several days preceding the *jiao*,
While you go about your daily activities,
There will be divine officials secretly watching over you day and night.[46]

Before and during a *jiao* it is vital that the participants restrain their desires.
Also, they must distance themselves from meats and spices.
If they act arbitrarily, their life spans will be short.
Divine officials are secretly watching, and the punishment and blessings are not small.
Near [the time of] the *jiao* in visiting the Realized [Beings] do not yell.[47]

At the time of the *jiao*, all of you gentlemen must restrain your conduct.
[If you do so,] your purity will move Heaven, and the blessings which result will not be slight.
Water will refresh the precious fields, and the farmers will all rejoice.
In the fall the pearls of the grain fields will mature,
And long bean sprouts will be born.

If you wish to repay Heaven's blessings,
You must venerate the Tao's virtue.
Accord with your fate, know what is sufficient,
And do not compete with each other.
At dawn gaze [up with reverence at the immortals], burn incense, and eat bland meals.
Without hate and with a fair mind,
Speak [with wisdom] like an immortality scripture.[48]

The basic idea here is that by getting large groups of people to undergo intense purification before and during the *jiao*, the gods can be moved, and the crops can be saved. A *jiao* is a time when the gods, attracted to the festivities by the prayers and sacrifices, observe every action of every person with greater attention than usual. Thus blessings or misfortunes result more readily from good or bad conduct. This seems to be what Liu means when he says, "the punishments and blessings are not small." As we can see, generous drought-relieving rains were expected as an immediate response to the ritual purification and abstention.

Qiu Chuji conveys the same basic principle eloquently in the two following poems:

> I composed [the following poem] because of a drought:
> The Great Tao of the Profound Origin controls *yin* and *yang*.
> [It] creates and transforms *qian* (Heaven) and *kun* (Earth), and all things flourish.
> If the high and the low were each able to be content with their lot,
> They would be able to avoid misfortune.
> As for now, why are there so many disasters and obstacles?
> It must be because the hearts of people are corrupt and reckless.
> They eat good food, wear elegant clothes, and for equipment use what is lavish.
> Depraved scoundrels and shady fellows are ruled by wickedness and lust.
> The mingling and clashing of *yin* and *yang* has been passed down from antiquity.
> Blessings and misfortunes give birth to each other in accordance with nature.
> People are continuously unable to be frugal day after day,
> And their complacency directly brought about the year of drought. . . .
> One time [I] took a group with me to pray for rain.
> Sliced meat decorated their plates, and they drank while choking themselves.
> Out of carelessness, they inflicted this harm on living things.
> How can their loud shouts suffice to move the gods and deities?
> How sad is their vulgar behavior, with reckless [attachment to] music and sex!
> Each of them is putting themselves on the brink of danger and overturning their bodies.
> How can I get the hearts of people to be like my heart,
> And thus avoid the disasters that are imminent?[49]

Qiu Chuji's opinion is that misfortunes are created by the doings of the victims themselves. If people could be unselfish and content with what was given to them by the Tao, then there would be no misfortunes, and life would be one big blessing. But people, in their selfishness, want more, and they indulge their desires in a self-destructive manner. To alleviate their plight, they need to do two things: beg for divine mercy and reform their ways. Qiu Chuji laments how people only do the former and neglect doing the latter. And in pleading to the gods, they only aggravate their plight by pleading in the wrong manner. Worst of all is their use of blood sacrifices. Qiu Chuji's solution to the problem is to diligently carry out ritual abstention and prayer, making an effort to be righteous and venerating the holy sages (immortals of past and present) daily. The immortals are much more likely to be pleased by self-discipline and reverence than by lavish sacrifices and material adornments. We also can observe in Qiu Chuji's words a definite disdain for the clamor of popular rituals.

Because piety and self-discipline were so essential to the success of a *jiao*, the feasts that customarily took place near or at the end of the festival could cause problems. Qiu Chuji strongly recommended that the food served not be sumptuous:

> "Written to *Jiao* Participants a when a certain Mr. Qiang Suffered from Choking"
> In setting up a *zhai* feast, you must exercise restraint.
> You must refrain from excessively lining up food for the guests.
> Even though [the *jiao*] is supposed to bring about blessings and seek grace,
> You are on the contrary summoning disasters and causing misfortunes.
>
> The elderly Mr. Qiang, did you see what happened to him?
> There is none of this [excessive indulgence] that does not have an effect on the body.
> His great mistake just now was to indulge in the hundred-flavored delicacies,
> With his eyes staring and while swallowing his drool.[50]

Here Qiu Chuji points to the unfortunate—although fortunately not fatal—choking of an elderly believer to demonstrate the principle that self-indulgence inevitably causes misfortune. He further points to the irony of the fact that such a misfortune had occurred at an event intended to bring blessings. He may even be implying here that the choking was direct divine punishment for letting the mind be distracted with culinary pleasures.

Ma Yu also on occasion remonstrated against ritual indiscretions involving food and feasting. For example, we find the following poem:

"While I was adding my support (*jiachi*) at the Shrine of the Purple Extreme, I heard the voices of pigs being slaughtered. Therefore I wrote this poem":
When the Taoist throngs of Laizhou hold the Yellow Register [*jiao*],
All of them are solemn and sincere, and none of them are not devoted.
They invited me to add my support by silently reciting a scripture to save the lost souls.

Why are they butchering and decapitating in the neighboring houses?
Without thinking of what lies ahead in the future, they slaughter and kill living things,
Causing pigs to cry out in painful agony.
I cannot bear to hear it! It saddens me more than anything else does![51]

It is unclear whether or not the pigs were being slaughtered to be eaten at the *jiao* feast. If they were, the reason for Ma Yu's disgust is obvious. But even if such was not the case, the cruel slaughter occurring in such close proximity to the holy gathering was undoubtedly considered by Ma Yu extremely harmful to the efficacy of the ritual and the well-being of the community.

After many days of rigorous self-restraint, it is inevitable that one would look forward to the large feast that would follow. *Dongxuan jinyu ju* includes a poem that Ma Yu wrote to the "high merit" (*gaogong*) priest at a *jiao* festival. Apparently, during the prayers, the high merit priest had stolen a glance at the food that had been spread out. In the poem, Ma says, "While rectifying our thoughts during the leap month during the winter inside the hut, how dare you think of the lavish spread!"[52]

It is hard to tell what the relationship between Ma Yu and this high merit priest was in terms of status. However, the fact that Ma had the audacity to reprimand a high merit priest in this fashion seems to be a reflection of how the Quanzhen masters saw it as their duty to make sure that rituals were being performed properly.

It is only natural that they demanded even more from the clergy than from the laity. Thus they demanded that monks and priests perform and participate in rituals with the proper attitudes and motives and warned them not to concern themselves with remuneration. Liu Chuxuan, for example, wrote:

When the elderly monk, Leng Qi, ascended (passed away), his family held several *zhai* rituals. At the ritual arena, I sincerely urged the men of the Tao to not demand a scripture reading fee [by writing the following poem]:

Read the scriptures for no money, and just eat the food at the *zhai.*
A feather-robed person (Taoist master) himself wishes [to be at (?)] the place of the Tao (ritual arena) and is fond of reading [the scriptures].[53]

The talismans and registers of the Most High have 24 levels.
The Tao stores the essential marvels, and the precious altar is always open.
The heavenly plane passes on [the secrets] and instructs those with [an] aptitude for immortality.
The Realized Ones cultivate their Nature (spirit) and Life (*qi*), and the pretenders nurture their physical bodies.
The confused sink into the six paths of existence,[54] and the enlightened leave and do not come [back (?)] (are not reincarnated?).
Amidst empty space, the wise sages save the world with a pitying heart.
Purify the *hun* souls and cleanse the *po* souls, embracing and preserving the immortal embryo.
Rationally and clearly with 10,000 wise insights,
[Engage in] the utterly serene true *zhai.*
From time to time sublimely and marvelously move about the Three Tai Stars.
Doing nothing, in a natural manner, be peacefully righteous without going against [the Tao].
The Rectifying Rites of the Celestial Heart do not love the money of people.[55]

The above poems say that a Taoist master must offer his ritual services willingly, out of his own desire to benefit living things. If he is properly motivated, then the satisfaction of helping people ought to be sufficient reward. Liu Chuxuan's statement, "The Rectifying Rites of the Celestial Heart do not love the money of people," is interesting, since the Rectifying Rites of the Celestial Heart (*Tianxin zhengfa*) is the name of an influential tradition of Taoist ritual that emerged in the tenth century.[56] It would appear that Liu Chuxuan, as well as perhaps his Quanzhen brethren, was versed in the methods of this particular tradition. Within the extant material from this Celestial Heart tradition, one can indeed find exhortations to the effect that Taoist masters must be generous and not demand exorbitant fees when performing *zhai* and *jiao* rituals. If the rite is performed for a poor family, then the ritual master must provide all of the necessary paraphernalia and offerings for them.

(However, the rich clients who are not generous in compensating the ritual master will suffer unfortunate consequences.[57])

## Final Remarks

During his audience with Genghis Khan (as recorded in *Xuanfeng qinghui lu*), Qiu Chuji made comments that reflect a genuine pride in the history and heritage of the Taoist religion:

> China has been blessed with peace for a long time. Heaven above has frequently sent down scriptures and teachings to encourage people to do good deeds. North of the great [Yellow] River, Xichuan (Sichuan), and left of the [Yangzi] River (Jiangsu and Zhejiang), all these regions have [seen such an occurrence]. During the Eastern Han, Gan Ji received the *Taiping jing* in 157 volumes, all of which contained methods of cultivating the self and governing the nation.[58] People of the Tao in China who recited it and practiced [its methods] were able to gain blessings and accomplish the Tao. Also, on the seventh day of the first month of the first year of the Yongshou reign era (155 C.E.) of Emperor Heng (*sic*, Huan), the Most High [Lord Lao] descended upon Linqiong in Shu (Sichuan) and transmitted the Southern Bushel and Northern Bushel scriptures along with over 1,000 volumes of the 24 levels of Ritual Registers to the Heavenly Master, Zhang Daoling.[59] During the Jin period (265–419), Wang Zuan met the Most High Lord of the Tao, who was riding his Dharma chariot in midair. [The Most High Lord of the Tao] gave him several dozen (lit. "several tens") scriptures.[60] During the original (Northern) Wei period, the Heavenly Master, Kou Qianzhi, while residing on Mt. Song (Henan), received over sixty volumes of scriptures from the place of the Most High and others.[61] These are all techniques for governing the mind, cultivating the Tao, praying for blessings, averting calamities, exorcising demons, and healing diseases.[62]

It is apparent here that Qiu Chuji accepted the authenticity of various scriptural revelations touted by Taoists over the centuries. Whether or not Qiu Chuji and his followers actually possessed and employed the above-mentioned texts, of course, is uncertain. Interestingly, the previously cited poem by Liu Chuxuan mentions twenty-four levels of talismans and registers of the Most High Lord Lao that are perhaps equivalent to the "24 levels of Ritual Registers" mentioned by Qiu Chuji. As we also have seen (chapter 1), Tan

Chuduan is said to have recited the Northern Bushel Scripture and experienced a divine vision during his illness prior to his conversion and healing by Wang Zhe. Quanzhen hagiography perhaps mentions this because the Northern Bushel Scripture was revered and recited within the Quanzhen tradition. (It is perhaps also significant to recall here that Yin Zhiping, when confined to his home by his disapproving father, bowed in prayer 1,000 times nightly toward the Pole Star; see chapter 5.)

As was mentioned in chapter 1, some modern scholars have viewed the early Quanzhen masters as reformers who set out to purge Taoism of its magico-religious elements and—in great part by drawing from Buddhism and Confucianism—to create a more rational Taoism geared toward mental and moral self-cultivation. Taoist rituals are among these magico-religious elements that the early Quanzhen masters supposedly deemphasized or disapproved of. It has further been asserted that the "reforms" of the Quanzhen masters represented a reaction against the extreme state of decadence that the Taoist religion had fallen into by the final years of the Northern Song period (960–1127). The most infamous figure of this period was Lin Lingsu, a Taoist ritual master from Wenzhou (Zhejiang Province), who won the favor of Emperor Huizong (r. 1101–1127) through flattery, declaring him a worldly incarnation of a supreme celestial deity called the "Great Imperial Lord of Long Life (Changsheng Da Dijun)." The emperor proceeded to lavishly expend the nation's resources on the performance of Taoist rituals and the building of Taoist temples. His excessive dabbling in Taoism has been widely blamed for the decline of the Song and the eventual loss of the empire's northern half to the Jurchen invaders.[63]

Of course, the Quanzhen masters were very different from Lin Lingsu and the like. The Quanzhen masters lived and preached among the masses, and their primary concern lay in the areas of self-discipline, meditation, and evangelism. However, the evidence examined in this chapter shows that they did engage in Taoist rituals and believed strongly in their efficacy (if properly performed). If this aspect of their activity has gained less renown, then it is probably because they made no claim to being experts and innovators in this area. None of their extant writings are ritual liturgies or manuals. In this facet of their religion, they were content to draw on the rich heritage that preceded them. Their pride and esteem for this heritage are apparent in the words uttered to Genghis Khan by Qiu Chuji. In fact, Qiu Chuji seems to have even admired Lin Lingsu and Huizong.[64] Qiu Chuji also told Genghis Khan the following story:

> The prior emperor of Song (Huizong) of times past was originally a celestial man. There was a divine immortal named Lin Lingsu who took him on a spiritual journey up to Heaven and entered [with him]

> into the palace where he had lived [during his days as a celestial man]. [Huizong] wrote on a placard [a poem saying in effect], "In the Divine Empyrean one neither hungers nor thirsts, nor does one suffer from cold or heat. One roams carefree without affairs, freely, in blissful joy. I wish to live here forever and never return to the company of humans." Lin Lingsu persuaded him, saying, "A heavenly decree for your Highness exists in the human world. If the merit quota for the Son of Heaven has not yet been fulfilled, [your Highness] cannot dwell here [in this heavenly palace]." They then came [back] down to the human world.[65]

There is nothing condemnatory in Qiu Chuji's attitude toward the infamous duo. Lin Lingsu, as far as he was concerned, was a sagely Taoist master—a "divine immortal"—with the power to lead souls in a journey to the celestial realms. Huizong was truly a "Son of Heaven."

Thus while to some extent it is valid to claim that early Quanzhen Taoism represented a departure from the elegant, extravagant Taoism patronized by the Northern Song emperors, this was not due to any conscious endeavor to renounce or reform it. The Quanzhen masters never tried to eliminate or significantly change Taoist rituals, aside from attempting to reinforce the standards of discipline, purity, and piety that they deemed essential for their effectiveness.

# Chapter 10

## Conclusion

The preceding chapters have examined the doctrines and practices of the early Quanzhen masters in detail. Hopefully some misconceptions have been cleared up, while fresh insights have emerged.

The core of this multifaceted religious system lies in the cultivation of the clarity and purity of mind that occurs not only within seated meditation but also throughout all daily activities. The early Quanzhen masters were unanimous in making this the greatest point of emphasis. Through mental purity and clarity, one was to recover one's Real Nature that is endowed with a spontaneous propensity for wisdom and compassion. Joyous peace of mind, physical health, and virtuous actions were thought to come about as natural results of this rigorous path of cultivation. In this core affirmation of the Quanzhen masters, there would seem to be little discrepancy with a rationalistic and naturalistic worldview.

However, further examination also reveals a belief in the eternal life of the Real Nature/Radiant Spirit that transcends the cycle of reincarnation and comes to bear divine attributes and miraculous powers both before and after the death of the physical body. The Real Nature is equated to the single, universal Tao (sometimes also referred to by the Buddhist term, *Dharma Body*). However, the Quanzhen masters clearly perceived their ascended brethren as retaining individual, divine personalities, despite supposedly being identical or in union with the Tao. Unfortunately, I have not found passages where this seeming inconsistency is consciously addressed and rationalized. (One conceivable means of doing this might have been through a doctrine resembling the Buddhist theory of the Buddha's Three Bodies—various medieval Taoist variations of this scheme are in fact enumerated and discussed in the seventh-century Taoist catechism, *Daojiao yishu*.)[1]

However, the greatest problem in this book has been the attempt to properly understand the attitudes of the Quanzhen masters regarding *neidan* practice, particularly in its more physiological, longevity-oriented aspects. In spite of their occasionally stated disdain for complex and bothersome longevity practices, they appear to have been very well versed in Taoist physiological theories and methods, which they incorporated out of their understanding of the inextricable link between Nature and Life, or spirit and *qi*. Unfortunately, the two texts (*Chongyang zhenren jinguan yusuo jue* and *Dadan zhizhi*) that describe *neidan* theories and methods in greatest detail are somewhat problematic in their authorship, despite being attributed to Wang Zhe and Qiu Chuji, respectively. Furthermore, the theories and methods in these two manuals—despite their similarities—are neither identical nor mutually coherent. It is difficult to identify a specific comprehensive *neidan* regimen that was transmitted exclusively and uniformly within the early Quanzhen movement, if indeed there was such a regimen.

The Real Nature, when manifested, is thoroughly compassionate. Furthermore, the recovery of the Real Nature in part requires the accumulation of virtuous actions. Based on these convictions, the Quanzhen masters engaged energetically not only in evangelism and charity but also in healing and ritual. Doing so entailed the use of incantations, talismans, and liturgies developed by their Taoist forebears. Unscientific as these things may seem to some modern sensibilities, the Quanzhen masters held no disdain for them, provided they were not employed in bad faith or for selfish gain.

Almost 800 years have elapsed since Wang Zhe and the Seven Realized Ones passed away. During that span, the Quanzhen School and the *neidan* tradition as a whole have undergone many developments. Numerous new *neidan* manuals and anthologies appeared during the late Yuan, Ming (1368–1661), and Qing (1662–1911) periods, which, on the whole, manifested an even greater tendency toward "Three Teachings" syncretism and an improvement in thoroughness and clarity of exposition. Numerous new factions formed around famous *neidan* masters. The Quanzhen School itself divided into several subsects, each of which claimed provenance from a different one of the Seven Realized Ones. Of these Quanzhen subsects, the Longmen (Dragon Gate) Sect—which claims provenance from Qiu Chuji—rose to prominence in the seventeenth century under the charismatic leadership of Wang Changyue (d. 1680). This event constituted a great revival in the prestige and influence of Quanzhen Taoism as a whole, which had dwindled severely during the Ming period.[2]

The social strife and upheaval of the dawning of the modern age severely sapped the vigor of the Quanzhen School yet again. Like all other religions in mainland China, Taoism went on to suffer heavy persecution during the first thirty years of Communist rule—particularly during the Cultural Revolution of 1966–1976. Most temples, monasteries, and icons were destroyed. All Taoist clergy were defrocked, although some secretly continued to pursue their religious vocations. Some of the leading figures among them committed suicide or died in prison after suffering extreme condemnation and harassment as alleged "rightists" or "counterrevolutionaries."[3]

However, after the Cultural Revolution ended, the People's Republic of China embarked cautiously on a policy of religious freedom. In 1980, Taoism was allowed to reorganize itself as a religion. Many of the defrocked clergy returned to the religious life, including some of the leading monks once condemned as "rightists." Many temples and monasteries have since been rebuilt or restored, with fresh new icons. The number of Taoist monks and nuns today is said to be approaching 10,000 (with perhaps one-third being female). The China Taoism Association (Zhongguo Daojiao Xiehui) is the government-sanctioned clerical body that administrates the affairs of both the Quanzhen and Zhengyi[4] Taoist schools. It has its headquarters at the Baiyun Guan (White Cloud Monastery) in Beijing—the traditional headquarters of the Quanzhen Longmen Sect and the burial place of the great Qiu Chuji. This monastery also houses the national Taoist seminary. Bright, promising young monks, nuns, and priests[5] from all around the country are selected and sent to study here.[6]

Within the ranks of today's Quanzhen clergy are those of a scholarly bent who are actively engaged in researching the history, teachings, and practices of their school, as well as the Taoist tradition as a whole. The China Taoism Association frequently publishes its work in its official magazine, *Zhongguo daojiao*, as well as in various short monographs. Probably the most erudite and well known among today's Quanzhen scholar-monks are Ren Farong of the Louguan monastery and Min Zhiting of the Baiyun Guan (the chairman of the China Taoism Association since 1998).

Min Zhiting—who was once condemned as a "rightist" during the Cultural Revolution—has published *Daojiao yifan* (1986; revised edition, 1990), a richly informative handbook for Quanzhen clergy that sets forth fundamental precepts, liturgies, and guidelines for moral and spiritual cultivation. In one particularly interesting section (pp. 268–75), he exhorts his modern brethren on the ideals and standards of conduct that they must uphold. In his view, a Taoist in his or her words and actions, must not cause detriment to others nor seek to advance his or her selfish interests. All Taoists should passionately love and serve their country and their religion and set a worthy example for others. While Taoism is essentially nonviolent and opposed to unjust warfare, Taoists must be willing to support and courageously participate in a just struggle. Min Zhiting then points to numerous historical exemplars.

As Taoists who helped bring glory and well-being to the Chinese nation and people, Min Zhiting cites Zhang Liang, Chen Ping, Zeng Can,[7] Zhuge Liang,[8] Wei Zheng,[9] Sun Simiao,[10] Qiu Chuji, and Liu Bowen.[11] He then extols the deeds of Taoists who bravely served just causes during the crises of the first half of the twentieth century. The Taoists of Mt. Mao (Jiangsu Province, near Nanjing) aided in the resistance against the invading Japanese army. The Taoists of Mt. Luofu (Guangdong Province, near Guangzhou), Mt. Hua (eastern Shaanxi Province), and Mt. Wudang (western Hubei Province) aided the Red Army in its struggles against the Guomindang. As a more specific example, Min Zhiting cites Xu Benshan, a Wudang monk martyred in 1932 at the hands of the Guomindang, for hiding and providing comfort to over 200 injured Communist soldiers.

Although he professes and enjoins complete loyalty to the present Communist regime and its socialist principles, Min Zhiting also candidly mentions the atrocities suffered by his religion during the "ten-year calamity" (in his own words) that was the Cultural Revolution. In doing so, he extols the courage and perseverance of Taoist monks and nuns who weathered the abuse and protected—to the best of their abilities—the scriptural and artistic treasures of their religion. Some monks refused orders to abandon their vocation and monastery. As a result, the "insurrectionists" (i.e., the Red Guards) made them wear hats bearing the words "bovine ghosts and snake spirits," and they subjected them to public harassment. Min Zhiting also praises the Baiyun Guan's Chen Luqing for risking his life to hide and protect the priceless treasures of the great monastery.

Min Zhiting thus exhorts his contemporary brethren to cherish and perpetuate the legacy of their forebears. They must obey the laws of the land and set a good moral example for the entire Chinese people. They should assist the government in preventing evil people from misusing religion to engage in destructive, counterrevolutionary activities. In dealing with foreign visitors, they must conduct themselves with modesty and dignity, without coveting their money and material possessions, otherwise, they will bring disgrace to their religion and their country. Min Zhiting then exhorts all Taoists to maintain their solidarity. They must not bring forth criticism, ridicule, and schism between the two major factions—the Quanzhen School and the nonmonastic, more ritualistically oriented Zhengyi School. While the two schools differ in their emphases (self-cultivation vs. ritual), there is and only can be one Taoism.

After thus discussing the desired norms for outward conduct, Min Zhiting moves on to the topic of self-cultivation (pp. 280–303). Here he simply presents numerous quotes from various venerable Taoist texts, including the *Daode jing*, the *Zhuangzi*, and the "records of sayings" of Ma Yu, Tan Chuduan, Liu Chuxuan, Hao Datong, Qiu Chuji, Wang Zhijin, Yin Zhiping, and

Dong Qingqi (an early nineteenth-century Quanzhen master). Interestingly, therefore, he relies on much of the same material examined in this book. This is a clear reflection of how Quanzhen monks and nuns today in their self-discipline and meditation continue to be inspired by the teachings and examples set forth by the early Quanzhen masters.

However, it must be duly noted that under present circumstances, the integrity of Quanzhen Taoism is compromised in various ways. The China Taoism Association—though staffed by sincerely religious clerics—in part functions as an organ through which the government can monitor Taoists and maintain their compliance to its own principles and agenda. In its publications and seminary curriculum, the China Taoism Association is constantly required to expound views that are staunchly patriotic and pro-government (Min Zhiting's book cited above is a good example of this). To outwardly plead for greater liberties or to question any government policies is out of the question.

The lifestyle of mendicancy is now virtually nonexistent among the Taoist clergy and would draw harsh criticism for being "parasitic."[12] To accumulate "true deeds" is now more difficult, since the government discourages religious activity (such as preaching and rituals) outside of approved, designated locations. While the Communist government—at least for now—does not require Taoists to abandon their belief in the supernatural, it is pressuring them to avoid or curtail activities that it deems particularly unsavory. These include spirit possession, spirit writing, divination, and ritual healing; in other words, it appears that the government frowns upon practices that endeavor to bring supernatural beings and forces into one's realm of experience in any sort of direct or dramatic way.[13]

Of course, the early Quanzhen masters did not engage in spirit possession and spirit writing; only one of them (Hao Datong) is known to have been an expert at divination. However, ritual healing was for them an important means of accumulating "true deeds." Furthermore, their cultivation of mystical experience—to which they bear such vivid testimony—would probably also draw suspicion and disapproval from the authorities today. Most of the contemporary Quanzhen monks and nuns that I have spoken to—with occasional exceptions—tend to be reticent on matters pertaining to mystical experience or miracles. While this may be due largely to their discretion or modesty, it also may reflect some modification in the belief system imposed by the government on the China Taoism Association.

# Notes

## Chapter 1

1. Although the Quanzhen temples in northern China are, as a general rule, monastic establishments, the same is not always true in the southern provinces. There, particularly in Guangdong and Hong Kong, one can find temples staffed by Taoist clergy who affiliate themselves with the Quanzhen School but are householders. An excellent study of non-monastic Quanzhen Taoism in Hong Kong and Guangdong Province is Bartholomew Tsui, *Taoist Tradition and Change: The Story of the Complete Perfection Sect in Hong Kong* (Hong Kong: Christian Study Centre on Chinese Religion and Culture, 1991). The largest non-monastic Quanzhen organization (to my knowledge) is the Ching Chung Taoist Church (Qingsong Guan), with temples in Hong Kong (New Territories and Kowloon), Singapore, Australia, Vancouver, and San Francisco.

While most of the Quanzhen organizations outside of China are predominantly Chinese in their membership, there is at least one highly notable exception. The British Taoist Association (BTA) is a group of six British Taoist priests who were instructed and ordained by a Quanzhen monk (Feng Xingzhao of Leigutai monastery, Shaanxi) in China in 1995. This group publishes a magazine called *The Dragon's Mouth*.

2. Since at least the Han dynasty (206 B.C.E–220 C.E.), some seekers of immortality in China have practiced sexual yogic methods. These methods have survived and continue to be practiced to this day among certain segments of the Taoist religion. It is possible that this also has been the case historically and presently, even within monastic circles. However, at present, I have no clear evidence of this. If sexual yogic methods are at all practiced in Taoist monasteries, it is perhaps only among a limited circle of high initiates.

3. The meditation method is called "internal alchemy," because the psychophysical procedures and phenomena that unfold in the mind and body of the practitioner are said to be analogous to the procedures and chemical reactions that take place in laboratory alchemy (*waidan*, "external alchemy"). *Neidan* texts draw heavily on the abstruse terminology employed in the more ancient *waidan* materials. The best and most comprehensive study of Chinese alchemy (external and internal) in English is Joseph Needham, *Science and Civilization in China*, vol. 5, nos. 2, 4, and 5 (Cambridge: Cambridge University Press, 1974, 1981, 1983). A good history and introduction to

the art of *neidan* is Isabelle Robinet, *Introduction à l'alchimie intérieure taoïste: De l'unite et de la multiplicite* (Paris: Le Cerf, 1995).

4. *Samsara* is a Sanskrit term denoting the cycle of reincarnation that is governed by the principle of *karma* (actions that have consequences that determine one's lot in future lives).

5. I can recall conversations with two different people who claimed to have such experiences. One was a priest at the Ching Chung Taoist Temple in San Francisco, and the other was a monk at a monastery on Mt. Hua (Shaanxi Province) in China.

6. This is a procedure in which a medium rapidly writes characters (which are typically illegible to the common observer and need to be interpreted by a reader) that are believed to convey the will and insights of a deity. The characters are written with various implements on various types of surfaces, but a peach wood stick and a tray of sand are typically used. Numerous contemporary religious groups in Taiwan, Hong Kong, and overseas Chinese communities—only some of whom describe themselves as "Taoist"—practice spirit writing. For a good study of the history of spirit writing and its role in contemporary popular sects, see David Jordan and Daniel Overmyer, *The Flying Phoenix: Aspects of Chinese Sectarianism in Taiwan* (Princeton: Princeton University Press, 1986).

7. In the late nineteenth century, Chen Minggui (1824–1881), a scholar-official turned Quanzhen priest, wrote a book, *Changchun daojiao yuanliu* (Taipei: Guangwen Shuju, 1975). In it (pp. 2, 173–74), he emphasized that Qiu Chuji (arguably the most famous Quanzhen master) excluded all practice of laboratory alchemy and talismanic ritual and denied that the flesh could be made immortal. (Qiu Chuji actually did engage in talismanic ritual, otherwise, this observation is accurate.) Thus Chen Minggui asserted that Qiu Chuji is completely different from the infamous Taoist quack alchemists and magicians who appear in the standard histories. Chen Minggui's work inspired academics in the mid-twentieth century to advance the notion that the early Quanzhen School was a rationalistic, syncretistic "New Taoism." The two influential monographs representing this view—written, respectively, in Chinese and Japanese—are Chen Yuan, *Nansong chu hebei xindaojiao kao* (A Study of New Taoism North of the Yellow River in the Southern Song [Beijing: Furen Daxue, 1941]) and Kubo Noritada, *Chûgoku no shûkyô kaikaku: Zenshin kyô no seiritsu* (The Chinese Reformation: The Founding of the Quanzhen School [Kyoto: Hôzôkan, 1967]). See also Yao Congwu, "Jin-Yuan quanzhen jiao de minzu sixiang yu jiushi sixiang," *Dongbei shi Luncong* 2 (1959): 175–204; Chen Junmin, "Quanzhen daojio sixiang yuanliu kaolüe," *Zhongguo zhexue* (1984): 168. For a lengthier critique of the views expounded in these works, see Stephen Eskildsen, "The Beliefs and Practices of Early Ch'üan-chen Taoism" (master's thesis, University of British Columbia, 1989), 23–35. Similar critiques are found in Bartholomew Tsui, *Taoist Tradition and Change: The Story of the Complete Perfection Sect in Hong Kong*, 19–34; Yao Tao-chung, "Ch'üan-chen: A New Taoist Sect in North China during the Twelfth and Thirteenth Centuries" (Ph.D. diss., University of Arizona, 1980), 220–40.

8. See note 4 above.

9. See, for example, Chen Bing's chapters on Quanzhen Taoism in the two recent comprehensive histories of Taoist religion (both entitled *Zhongguo daojiao shi*—edited, respectively, by Ren Jiyu [Shanghai: Shanghai Renmin Chubanshe, 1990] and Qing Xitai [Chengdu: Sichuan Renmin Chubanshe, 1996 (4 vols.)]). Other noteworthy works that have substantially improved our understanding of Quanzhen doctrine and practice include Yao Tao-chung, "Ch'üan-chen: A New Taoist Sect in North China during the Twelfth and Thirteenth Centuries"; Hachiya Kunio, *Kindai dôkyô no kenkyû: Ô Chôyô to Ba Tan-yô* (Tokyo: Kyûko Shoin, 1992); Vincent Goossaert, "La creation du taoïsme moderne: L'ordre Quanzhen" (Ph.D. diss., Ecole Pratique des Hautes Etudes, 1997); Zhang Guangbao, *Jin-Yuan Quanzhen dao neidan xinxing xue* (Beijing: Sanlian Shudian, 1995).

10. Instances of applying the terminology and metaphysics of laboratory alchemy to meditation can occasionally be identified in texts as early as the fourth century (certain Shangqing texts). However, this was not particularly common until the tenth century onward, when we see the appearance of *neidan*-oriented commentaries to the *Zhouyi cantongqi*, as well as *neidan* classics such as the *Wuzhen pian* and *Zhong-Lü chuandao ji*.

Another noteworthy development in Taoism in the early second millennium was the emergence of numerous new forms of therapeutic ritual. An excellent recent study of this phenomenon is Edward L. Davis, *Society and the Supernatural in Song China* (Honolulu: University of Hawaii Press, 2001).

11. This is not to say that the internal alchemists were the first within the Taoist religion to reject or deemphasize physical immortality. Already in the Lingbao scriptures of the fifth century C.E. one can see a tendency to emphasize the immortality of the Spirit (*shen*) while describing the body as a temporary dwelling that is "empty" (lacking inherent existence). However, the possibility of heavenly ascension in an immortal flesh is affirmed elsewhere in the Lingbao corpus (see Eskildsen, *Asceticism in Early Taoist Religion* [Albany: State University of New York Press, 1998], 121–28). Some early Tang (i.e., seventh-century) Taoist writings—which bear heavy influence from Buddhist Madhyamika philosophy—set forth insights on how to recover the birthless, deathless (i.e., eternal) Real Nature, which also is referred to as the "Tao Nature," "Dharma Nature," or "Dharma Body." These writings say little or nothing on how to nurture and perpetuate the flesh; rather, they enjoin total detachment from the body and all other "empty" things and concepts. (Good examples are the writings of Cheng Xuanying, Li Rong and Wang Xuanlan, and Meng Anpai. See Qing Xitai, ed., *Zhongguo daojiao shi*, vol. 4, pp. 171–222, 259–77 [this part of the book is written by Li Gang].) The views expressed in these writings do not appear to have held full sway over the Taoist tradition of the time, since many other works of the Tang still strongly maintain a belief in physical immortality and an emphasis on macrobiotics. However, their influence on the Quanzhen and larger *neidan* tradition is unmistakable. *Neidan* texts ingeniously fuse speculations on the Real Nature and its recovery with intricate physiological theories. It should, however, be mentioned that some of the earlier *neidan* works hold fast to the goal of physical immortality. A good example is *Chen xiansheng neidan jue* of the eleventh century (see Eskildsen, "*Neidan* Master Chen Pu's Nine Stages of Transformation," *Monumenta Serica* 49 [2001]: 1–31).

12. The sobriquet (*daohao*) is a title given to a Taoist disciple by his or her master. It also was customary for a master to give new personal names (*ming*) to his or her disciples. Thus all of the personal names and sobriquets enumerated here were not their original names given by their parents. Quanzhen writings, when referring to the masters in the third person, generally refer to them by their sobriquets. As much as possible, this book will refer to each personage by his or her personal name.

13. The Taoist Canon (*Zhengtong daozang*, compiled in 1444) contains no works by Sun Bu'er. There do exist various later works that are ascribed to her, some of which have become familiar to Western readers through the work of Thomas Cleary (*Immortal Sisters: Secret Teachings of Taoist Women* [Boston: Shambhala, 1989]). Sun Bu'er's stature as a Taoist Mistress-Immortal appears indeed to have grown substantially in the minds of Taoists during the Ming and Qing periods. The popular novel, *Qizhen zhuan* (author and date unknown), which depicts the adventures of Wang Zhe and the Seven Realized Ones, portrays Sun Bu'er much more prominently and heroically than do the hagiographies of the Jin and Yuan periods (the works relied on in this book). For example, the *Qizhen zhuan* depicts her as having been wiser and more devout than her husband, Ma Yu, and it credits her with helping him gain the resolve to abandon the world and to follow Wang Zhe. The earlier hagiographies contrarily tell us that she tried to prevent her husband from entering the religious life, and that she became a disciple of Wang Zhe a full year after her husband did. The *Qizhen zhuan* has been translated into English by Eva Wong (*Seven Taoist Masters: A Folk Novel of China* [Boston: Shambhala, 1990]), so perhaps some readers familiar with this work will be disappointed with the scant attention given to Sun Bu'er here.

14. This denotes the twenty-second day of the twelfth lunar month of the second year of the Zhenghe reign era (of the Northern Song dynasty).

15. We are told that his mother became pregnant after seeing a "strange dream" and gave birth after a pregnancy of twenty-four months and eighteen days. From his childhood, Wang Zhe stood out among his peers and grew up to be a large man of impressive countenance and demeanor. He had large eyes, beautiful whiskers, a resounding voice, and great muscular strength. He was hearty and noble minded by temperament and possessed a sharp intellect. Once, during a severe famine, bandits ransacked the Wang family estate. Government officials combed the surrounding villages and soon recovered the stolen goods and arrested the bandit chief. However, Wang Zhe compassionately pleaded for the bandit's release, on the grounds that the burglary was committed out of desperation due to the famine conditions (see Wanyan Shou, "Zhongnan shan shenxian Chongyangzi Wang zhenren Quanzhen jiaozu bei," in *Daojia jinshi lüe*, comp. Chen Yuan et al. [Beijing: Wenwu Chubanshe, 1988], pp. 450–51; Liu Zuqian, "Zhongnan shan Chongyang zushi xianji ji," in *Daojia jinshi lüe*, pp. 460–61).

16. See Shen Qingyai, Wu Tingxi et al. *Shaanxi tongzhi Xu tongzhi* (Taipei: Huawen Shuju, 1933), 28/51b.

17. It is not known how many sons and daughters Wang Zhe had. In one poem he does refer to son (s) (*Chongyang quanzhen ji* [DT1144/TT793-795], 9/12a). (The DT number indicates the number under which the text is catalogued in Ren Jiyu, ed., *Daozang tiyao* [Beijing: Zhongguo Shehui Kexue Chubanshe, 1991]. The TT number indicates the fascicle of the Taoist Canon [1962 Shanghai photo reprint edition] in which the text is found.) One source tells us that upon renouncing the secular world, Wang Zhe entrusted his young daughter to the family to which she had been betrothed, remarking, "I have raised a member of another family" ("Zhongnan shan shenxian Chongyangzi Wang zhenren Quanzhen jiaozu bei," in *Daojia jinshi lüe*, p. 450).

18. There are six principal hagiographic sources on Wang Zhe: (1) "Zhongnan shan shenxian Chongyangzi Wang zhenren Quanzhen jiaozu bei," in *Daojia jinshi lüe*, pp. 450–53; (2) "Zhongnan shan Chongyang zushi xianji ji," in *Daojia jinshi lüe*, pp. 460–61; (3) Qin Zhi'an, *Jinlian zhengzong ji* (DT172/TT75-76); (4) Liu Zhixuan and Xie Xichan, *Jinlian zhengzong xianyuan xiangchuan* (DT173/TT76); (5) Zhao Daoyi, *Lishi zhenxian tidao tongjian xupian* (DT296/TT149); (6) Li Daoqian, *Qizhen nianpu* (DT174/TT76). By far the most thorough and illuminating study of Wang Zhe's life by a modern scholar is found in Hachiya, *Kindai dôkyô no kenkyû: ô Chôyô to Ba Tan-yô*, 23–151.

19. The wearing of such warm clothing in the middle of summer is to be seen as a hint that they were accomplished Taoists who fostered in themselves an extraordinary capacity to withstand extreme heat or cold.

20. "Zhongnan shan shenxian Chongyangzi Wang zhenren Quanzhen jiaozu bei" and "Zhongnan shan Chongyang zushi xianji ji."

21. *Jinlian zhengzong ji*, *Jinlian zhengzong xianyuan xiangzhuan*, *Lishi zhenxian tidao tongjian xupian*, and *Qizhen nianpu*.

22. See Yu Yingmao, "Huxian Qinduzhen chongxiu Zhidao guan bei," in *Daojia jinshi lüe*, 478–79.

23. Lü Yan (sobriquet, Chunyang; style name, Dongbin) is probably the most revered Taoist immortal from the Song period onward. While his historicity is uncertain, hagiographical records indicate that he was born at the end of the eighth century. Various internal alchemical writings are supposed to have come through his hands, and hagiographies are full of his miraculous feats. He also is an important deity among popular spirit-writing cults. *Chunyang dijun shenhua miaotong ji* (DT304/TT159), an early fourteenth-century text compiled by a Quanzhen monk, Miao Shanshi, records in detail his conversion and tutelage under Zhongli Quan, and it presents over 100 stories of his subsequent miracles and exploits. Accounts of his life also are given in Zhao Daoyi, *Lishi zhenxian tidao tongjian* (DT295/TT139–148), *Jinlian zhengzong ji*, and *Jinlian zhengzong xianyuan xiangzhuan*. Also see Farzeen Baldrian-Hussein, "Lü Tung-pin in Northern Sung Literature," *Cahiers d'Extreme Asie* 5 (1989–1990): 133–69; Paul Katz, *Images of the Immortal: The Cult of Lü Dongbin at the Palace of Eternal Joy* (Honolulu: University of Hawaii Press, 1999), 52–93.

Zhongli Quan (sobriquet, Zhengyang; style name, Yunfang) is said to have been the teacher of Lü Yan. Although he almost certainly is a fictional character, he is said to have been a government official and military general during the end of the Han dynasty and the beginning of the Western Jin dynasty (i.e., third century A.D.). Accounts of his life are found in *Lishi zhenxian tidao tongjian*, *Jinlian zhengzong ji*, and *Jinlian zhengzong xianyuan xiangzhuan*.

24. *Lishi zhenxian tidao tongjian xupian*, 1/2b. In another source (*Qizhen nianpu* 5b), Wang Zhe is quoted as saying, "In the future I will make the teachings of the four seas into one house!" Since the first character of *haitang* means "sea," it appears that Wang Zhe chose this specific type of tree to symbolize the seas of the north, south, east, and west.

25. The personal name (*ming*) of Li Lingyang is unknown. "Lingyang" was his sobriquet.

26. Liu Cao (style name, Haichan) is said to have been a wealthy government official under the Khitan Liao dynasty (937–1135) before undergoing a religious conversion at the hands of Zhongli Quan. Accounts of his life are found in *Lishi zhenxian tidao tongjian*, *Jinlian zhengzong ji*, and *Jinlian zhengzong xianyuan xiangzhuan*.

27. *Lishi zhenxian tidao tongjian xupian*, 1/2b-3a.

28. "Zhongnan shan zhenxian Chongyangzi Wang zhenren Quanzhen jiaozu bei," in *Daojia jinshi lüe*, 451.

29. *Qizhen nianpu*, 6b–7a.

30. See Pierre Marsone, "The Accounts of the Foundation of the Quanzhen Movement: A Hagiographic Treatment of History," *Journal of Chinese Religions* 29 (2001): 97–101.

31. *Chongyang quanzhen ji*, 1/4a, 2/22b.

32. *Chongyang quanzhen ji*, 2/20b, 24b.

33. See Hachiya, *Kindai dôkyô no kenkyû*, 150–51. Some of Wang Zhe's poems refer specifically to the *Diamond Sutra* (*Chongyang quanzhen ji*, 1/12b) and *Heart Sutra* (*Chongyang quanzhen ji*, 5/3a-b, 12/5a). He also is known to have recommended the recitation of the *Heart Sutra* to his followers.

34. See Hachiya, *Kindai dôkyô no kenkyû*, 134. The passage in question (by Wang Zhe) reads, "Gentlemen, if you truly want to cultivate yourselves, just eat when hungry and close your eyes when sleepy" (*Chongyang quanzhen ji*, 10/20b). The cognate statement by Dazhu Huihai that Hachiya seems to have in mind is found in Daoyuan's *Jingde chuandeng lu*, in *Taishô zôkyô*, no. 2076, a Song period compilation recording the lives, deeds, and sayings of eminent Chan masters. The passage in question reads, "There was a certain Vinaya Master Yuan who came and asked, 'In cultivating the Way, do you also employ any sort of practice?' The Master (Dazhu Huihai) said, 'I do employ a practice.' [Vinaya Master Yuan] said, 'What sort of practice do you employ?' The Master said, 'When I get hungry I eat, and when I get tired I sleep.' [Vinaya Master Yuan] said, 'All people are like this. Are they not carrying out the same practice that you do?' The Master said, 'They are not the same.' [Vinaya Master Yuan] said, 'How are they not the same?' The Master said, 'When they eat, they cannot bring themselves to eating [because of] their hundred forms of attachments. When they sleep, they

cannot bring themselves to sleeping [because of their] thousand forms of calculation. Thus they are not the same [as me].' The Vinaya Master shut his mouth" (vol. 51, p. 247).

35. See Hu Qide, "Wang Chongyang chuang Quanzhen jiao de beijing fenxi," *Taiwan zongjiao xuehui tongxun* 8 (May 2001): 28–29. According to Hu, Yuanwu Keqin's influence on Wang Zhe is apparent in four areas: (1) The emphasis put on employing poems to help enlighten others; (2) the emphasis on ministry to laity organized in congregations; (3) the emphasis on eliminating all thoughts and discriminations from the mind (Yuanwu Keqin used the term *quanzhen* to denote the state in which this is achieved); (4) specific jargon and phrases employed in discourses. Yuanwu Keqin was the compiler of the influential *Biyan lu* (Blue Cliff Record).

36. *Qi*, in its most common general usage, refers to steam, air, or gas of some form. (The character's radical derives from a pictograph depicting rising steam.) It also can refer to an invisible force or energy. In the context of *neidan* practice (and early methods of Taoist meditation), *qi* refers alternately to the air breathed by the adept or to the currents of energy that run through his or her body—two things that appear to be conceived of as mutually transmutable.

In its broadest sense, *qi* refers to the basic material that constitutes the universe. The idea is that before the creation of the world, there existed only an undifferentiated mass of *qi* that eventually condensed and differentiated itself into various forms and consistencies. Thus essentially all that exists is *qi* in its varying degrees of turbidity (*yin*) and rarefaction (*yang*). Spirit (*shen*) is *qi* of a most rarefied form.

37. See Hachiya, *Kindai dôkyô no kenkyû*, 184–87.

38. This text is found in the internal alchemical anthology, *Xiuzhen shishu* (DT262/TT122–131), in *juan* nos. 14–16. It was putatively authored by Zhongli Quan, compiled by Lü Yan, and transmitted by the ninth-century internal alchemist, Shi Jianwu. It takes the format of a conversation between the master, Zhongli Quan, and his disciple, Lü Yan.

39. The full title is *Bichuan Zhengyang zhenren lingbao bifa*. It was putatively authored by Zhongli Quan and transmitted by Lü Yan. Farzeen Baldrian-Hussein has translated this important text into French and analyzed it in depth (see *Procedes secrets du joyaux magique: Traite d'alchimie taoiste du Xie siecle* [Paris: Les deux oceans, 1984]).

40. Putatively authored by ninth-century internal alchemist Shi Jianwu. However, allusions to Liu Cao, a tenth- or eleventh-century figure, suggest that this ascription is spurious.

41. Liu Chuxuan wrote commentaries to both the *Yinfu jing* and *Huangting neijing jing*. Liu Tongwei, a lesser-known disciple of Wang Zhe, wrote a commentary to the *Qingjing jing*. These commentaries are found in the Taoist Canon. The *Yinfu jing* is a text of unknown origin that came to be emphasized within Taoist circles during the Tang dynasty. Its cryptic statements pertain primarily to the relationships between human conduct and natural phenomena and their bearing upon matters of governing the state and nurturing life. The *Qingjing jing* is a Tang period text that discusses how one must purify the mind and eliminate desires. The *Huanging neijing jing* is a text of

the fourth century or earlier. It gives an intricate description of the human inner anatomy and the gods dwelling in it, while providing various directions on meditation and self-discipline aimed at longevity and immortality.

42. See Hachiya, *Kindai dôkyô no kenkyû*, 149–50.

43. The nineteenth *juan* of the *Daoshu* (DT1008/TT641–648), a large Taoist anthology compiled in 1136 by Zeng Zao, contains a short treatise by Jin Daocheng entitled "Chongzhen pian." The beginning part of the treatise is nearly identical to a portion in the *Jin zhenren yulu*, suggesting that the two texts come from a common author.

44. The most important example is Zhang Boduan (984–1082), author of the *neidan* classic *Wuzhen pian*. A scholar and military official by vocation, he expressly denied the necessity of physically severing attachments from society and family, since one ought to be able to maintain spiritual detachment regardless of external circumstances. See Ren Jiyu, *Zhongguo daojiao shi*, 495–504 (by Chen Bing).

45. See Marsone, "The Accounts of the Foundation of the Quanzhen Movement, 100.

46. The term *corpse liberation* (*shijie*) is used in Taoist texts to refer to ways in which Taoist adepts were thought to attain immortality in spite of the apparent fact that they had died. In some cases, the idea conveyed is that the adept had in fact faked his or her death, leaving behind a magically created semblance of a corpse. In other cases, the corpse is indeed thought to be real, but a miraculous transformation or resurrection is thought to occur after burial. (See Eskildsen, *Asceticism*, 93; Stephen Bokenkamp, *Early Daoist Scriptures* [Berkeley: University of California Press, 1997], 359, 411; Livia Kohn, ed., *The Taoist Experience: An Anthology* [Albany: State University of New York Press, 1993], 120, 217, 304, 331–32.)

47. See *Lishi zhenxian tidao tongjian xupian*, 3/8a–b; Li Daoqian, *Zhongnan shan zuting xianzhen neizhuan* (DT949/TT604), 1/1a–2b; *Jinlian zhengzong ji*, 2/10a–12a.

48. *Zhongnan shan zuting xianzhen neizhuan*, 1/3a.

49. The Zhongnan mountains are in fact said to be where Laozi wrote the *Daode jing* and transmitted it to his disciple, Yin Xi (which allegedly would have occurred ca. sixth century B.C.E.). It is possible that a temple existed there as early as the third century C.E. The Quanzhen School, under the leadership of Yin Zhiping, restored the temple and claimed it for its own in 1236. Louguan is today one of the largest active Quanzhen monasteries. See Wang Shiwei, *Louguan dao yuanliu kao* (Xi'an: Shaanxi Renmin Chubanshe, 1993).

50. See *Qizhen nianpu*, 9a; *Zhongnan shan zuting xianzhen neizhuan*, 1/2a.

51. After this initiation, Liu Tongwei did not follow Wang Zhe eastward but instead went westward to the Zhongnan mountains to pursue his self-training. See *Zhongnan shan zuting xianzhen neizhuan*, 1/4a–b.

52. *Jinlian zhengzong ji*, 2/4b–5a.

53. Both Kubo Noritada and Hachiya Kunio have pointed out that the "Realized Man Xiao" alluded to here would have been the school's second patriarch, Xiao Daoxi, who was only ten years old at the time. This—along with the fact that only one source bothers to mention the episode—compromises the credibility of the alleged incident, since it is hard to imagine Wang Zhe trying to interact with a mere child in such a way. Hachiya has brought to attention the fact that in one poem (*Chongyang quanzhen ji*, 12/9b–10a) Wang Zhe alludes to a ritual text with a title strikingly similar to a text employed by the Taiyi School. This issue will be returned to in chapter 10. See Kubo *Chûgoku no shukyo kaikaku*, 116–18; Hachiya, *Kindai dôkyô no kenkyû*, 75–76.

54. The asterisk denotes that it was in the intercalary month inserted into the lunar year to harmonize it with the solar year. Dading 7 had two "seventh months," the latter of which was the intercalary month.

55. *Jinlian zhengzong xianyuan xiangzhuan*, 23b–24a.

56. Hachiya is inclined to think that Qiu Chuji did not join the group until they had moved to Mt. Kunyu. His reasoning is based on the fact that Wang Zhe does not mention Qiu Chuji in the poems datable to a period when he stayed at the Hut of Complete Realization (see Hachiya, *Kindai*, 97). However, three different sources (*Qizhen nianpu*, 7a, *Jinlian zhengzong xianyuan xiangzhuan*, 20b, 32a, and *Lishi zhenxian tidao tongjian xupian*, 2/20a) agree that Qiu Chuji did indeed join prior to the move to Mt. Kunyu.

57. On 10/1, the day he began his confinement, he gave Ma Yu a single pear. On 10/11, he sliced a pear in two pieces, for Ma Yu and Sun Bu'er to share. Every ten days thereafter, he continued to give a sliced pear to the couple, each time increasing the number of slices by one. The total number of pear slices by the 100th day came to a total of fifty-five. Also, on the sixth, sixteenth, and twenty-sixth days of each month, Wang Zhe gave Ma Yu and Sun Bu'er six chestnuts and six taros each. While the symbolism here is not clear in its entirety (particularly the numerology), it was apparently a pun, the meaning of which points to the impermanence of all human bonds, along with the need for husband and wife to sever their attachment. "Chestnut, taro, divide pear" is pronounced "*li yu fen li*," which, if written with different characters, means "Suddenly meet [only to be] divided and separated." See Hachiya, *Kindai*, 86–87.

58. *Qizhen nianpu* (7b) claims that he ate about once every five days. According to "Zhongnan shan shenxian Chongyangzi Wang zhenren Quanzhen jiaozu bei" (*Daojia jinshi lüe*, p. 451), he "sometimes ate and sometimes did not eat." "Zhongnan shan Chongyang zushi xianji ji" (*Daojia jinshi lüe*, p. 461) says that he sometimes went several days consecutively without eating. *Lishi zhenxian tidao tongjian xupian* (1/4a) states that he ate once a day. *Jinlian zhengzong ji* (3/5a) makes the most seemingly far-fetched claim, stating that Wang Zhe never ate during the entire 100-day period.

59. The most vivid accounts of these alleged events are given in "Zhongnan shan shenxian Chongyangzi Wang zhenren Quanzhen jiaozu bei," in *Daojia jinshi lüe*, p. 451, and *Lishi zhenxian tidao tongjian xupian*, 1/4a–b.

60. See "Zhongnan shan shenxian Chongyangzi Wang zhenren Quanzhen jiaozu bei," in *Daojia jinshi lüe*, p. 451.

61. Wang Zhe had previously visited Hao Sheng at his fortune-telling shop in Ninghai. We are told that Wang Zhe entered the shop and, without saying a word, sat down with his back facing Hao. Hao said, "Please turn your head around sir," to which Wang Zhe replied, "Why don't you turn your head around?" Intrigued, Hao followed Wang Zhe to the Chaoyuan Guan Taoist Temple, where Wang Zhe bestowed him with two edifying poems. However, Hao chose to not yet become a disciple at this point, since he had an elderly mother to care for. See *Jinlian zhengzong xianyuan xiangzhuan*, 39b–40a. When Hao became his disciple, Wang Zhe changed his personal name to Lin and gave him the sobriquet, Tianran. In 1170, Hao is said to have encountered a "divine man" (*shenren*) who changed his personal name to Datong and his sobriquet to Guangning—the names by which he is best known to posterity. See Florian Reiter, "The Soothsayer, Hao Ta-t'ung, (1140–1212) and His Encounter with Ch'üan-chen Taoism," *Oriens Extremus*, no. 28, part 2 (1981): 198–205.

62. *Jinlian zhengzong xianyuan xiangzhuan*, 36a–b.

63. *Qizhen nianpu*, 8a–b.

64. *Lishi zhenxian tidao tongjian xupian* (1/6a) states, "In Laizhou [Wang Zhe] established the Equality Congregation. Hereby wind moved far and near, and over a thousand people participated in the congregation." See Hachiya, *Kindai*, 132.

65. This is the standard term (of Buddhist origin) used to refer to the act of becoming a monk or nun.

66. *Qinghe zhenren beiyou yulu* (DT1298/TT1017), 2/22b.

67. *Jinlian zhengzong ji*, 3/4a–b.

68. See Hachiya *Kindai*, 210.

69. The Taoist Canon includes several scriptures that include the term *beidou* in their titles. The one that appears most likely to correspond to the *Beidou jing* in question here is *Taishang xuanling beidou benming yansheng zhengjing* (DT617/TT341). This text describes a ritual directed toward astral deities that purports to expiate one's transgressions and prolong one's life span. This text is said to have been revealed to the first Heavenly Master, Zhang Daoling (putative founder of the Heavenly Masters School—one of the two earliest known Taoist religious organizations), by Taishang Laojun (the deified Laozi) in 155. However, the text's actual authorship is likely the tenth century or later. The Taoist Canon also contains three commentaries (DT744-746/TT527-529) to this text, which range between the Song and Ming periods in their dates. See Ren Jiyu, *Daozang tiyao*, 449.

70. See Wanyan Shou, "Changzhenzi Tan zhenren xianji beiming," in *Daojia jinshi lüe*, p. 454; *Lishi zhenxian tidao tongjian xupian*, 2/1b.

71. "Seven *sui*" means his age was "seven" according to the traditional Chinese method of reckoning a person's age. According to this method, a person is "one" at the moment of birth and gains a year in age every New Year.

72. *Jinlian zhengzong ji*, 5/1a. Donghua Dijun ("The August Lord of the Eastern Flower") is said to have been a man named Wang Xuanfu, who was born and gained immortality a long time ago (nobody knows exactly when). During the Han dynasty,

he is said to have transmitted the Tao to Zhongli Quan in the Zhongnan mountains (see *Jinlian zhengzong ji*, 1/1a–b; *Jinlian zhengzong xianyuan xiangzhuan*, 13a–b). The induction of this figure into the Quanzhen patriarchy seems to have taken place after the first generation of masters had passed on. However, it must have taken place before 1241, when *Jinlian zhengzong ji* (which includes an entry on him) was written. The movement's decision to glorify this relatively obscure figure may indeed have been inspired by Wang Chuyi's testimony of his personal encounters with him.

73. *Lishi zhenxian tidao tongjian xupian*, 3/1b–2a; Yao Sui, "Yuyang tixuan guangdu zhenren Wang zongshi daoxing bei bing xu," in *Daojia jinshi lüe*, p. 718. *Jinlian zhengzong ji* (5/1a–b) combines the two incidents. There the old man on the boulder reveals that his name is Xuanting Gongzhu, and he then disappears.

74. *Lishi zhenxian tidao tongjian xupian*, 3/1b–2a; *Qizhen nianpu*, 7b.

75. His elder brother, Junyan, attained the glorious jinshi degree and served as magistrate of Changyi County. (See Xu Yan, "Guangning tongxuan Taigu zhenren Hao zongshi daoxing bei," in *Daojia jinshi lüe*, p. 672.)

76. *Jinlian zhengzong ji*, 5/6a, states that "his hands never let go of [the books of] Huang (Yellow Emperor), Lao (*Laozi*), Zhuang (*Zhuangzi*), and Lie (*Liezi*)."

77. *Lishi zhenxian tidao tongjian xupian*, 3/6a.

78. See *Jinlian zhengzong ji*, 4/7a; *Lishi zhenxian tidao tongjian xupian*, 2/10a; Chen Shike, "Changchun zhenren benxing bei," in *Daojia jinshi lüe*, p. 457.

79. "Zhongnan shan shenxian Chongyangzi Wang zhenren Quanzhen jiaozu bei," in *Daojia jinshi lüe*, 451.

80. *Qinghe zhenren beiyou yulu*, 2/5b–6a.

81. Ibid., 3/11a.

82. Wang Zhe taught that one should read books only to glean their essential teachings—after which the books should be abandoned. He also warned that reading books hinders one's progress if it is done to memorize phrases and facts that can be flaunted before others. (See *Chongyang lijiao shiwu lun* [DT1221/TT989], 1b–2a.)

Ma Yu warned that extensive reading only makes the mind confused. He went so far as to state that it is best to not read at all, although it is fine to occasionally study the *Daode jing* with Heshanggong's commentary, or the *Yinfu jing* with Jinlingzi's (Tang Chun) commentary. (See *Danyang zhenren yulu* [DT1047/TT728], 10a.)

83. The poetry collections of the Quanzhen masters contain numerous poems addressed to Taoist nuns.

84. We are told that he "made her burn a pledge document before the Tao (i.e., at an altar devoted to some Taoist deity, the identity of which is unclear)." He then bestowed upon her the personal name, Bu'er, and the sobriquet, Qingjing, and he presented her with a poem. (See Zhao Daoyi, *Lishi zhenxian tidao tongjian houji* (DT295/TT139-148), 6/17a.)

85. *Lishi zhenxian tidao tongjian houji*, 6/17b.

86. Ibid., 6/15b–19a.

87. Both the Taiyi and Dadao schools appear to have been monastic movements like the Quanzhen School. (The leaders of the Taiyi School all took the surname, Xiao, upon succession, but the position was not hereditary.) The Taiyi School began in Ji County in present-day Henan Province and spread into Shandong and Hebei. This school was best known for its performance of talismanic ritual and healing, employing the "Ritual Register of the Three Origins of the Great Unity" (*Taiyi sanyuan falu*). However, there also is some evidence that its clergy practiced some sort of meditation to cultivate inner serenity.

The Dadao School began in Yanshan County in Shandong and at its height had spread into Henan and Shaanxi. This school required its monks to support themselves by growing their own food rather than resort to begging (in this respect differing greatly from the Quanzhen School). The main emphasis was on the cultivation of outward simplicity and inner serenity through self-discipline and meditation. The monks of this school also prayed on behalf of other people and healed their diseases. However, in doing so, they simply "prayed silently into empty space" and did not use talismans, registers, and liturgies such as those used by other Taoists.

Unfortunately, not much more can be said about the doctrinal content of the two schools. No works composed by either school survive in the Taoist Canon. One must rely on the standard history, *Yuan shi*, and on various stone monuments (the contents of which are preserved in *Daojia jinshi lüe*, pp. 818–65). A good, thorough discussion of both movements is found in Qing Xitai, *Zhongguo duojiao shi*, vol. 3, pp. 2–29 (by Chen Bing).

88. See Vincent Goossaert, "Entre quatre murs: Un ermite taoïste du XIIe siècle et la question de la modernite," *T'oung Pao* 85 (1999): 391–418.

89. Liu Biangong began his lifelong self-confinement when he was only fourteen *sui*. While in mourning for the death of his father, he encountered a "strange person" and received secret teachings. He then devoted himself to a life of near-constant meditation in a tiny, meagerly furnished chamber (called a *huandu*) near his family home. He never spoke, he wore a single cloth robe throughout the year, and he maintained a strict, bland vegetarian diet. He also never married. After his death, one of his brothers discovered from among his belongings a short treatise on how to maintain clarity and purity of mind in meditation and in all daily activities (see Zhang Xiaochun "Gaoshang chushi xiuzhen ji," in *Daojia jinshi lüe*, pp. 1007–1009). His lifestyle and teachings indeed bear a rather striking resemblance to the Quanzhen masters.

90. The term *huandu*, in its literal sense, refers to a small square hut measuring four *du* on each side (one *du* equals one *zhang*, which, during the Song and Yuan periods, was equal to 3.027 meters). The oldest occurrences of the term are found in the *Zhuangzi* and the *Li ji*, where the *huandu* serves as the dwelling of a wise, virtuous hermit. Tao Hongjing's (456–536) *Zhen'gao* (DT1007/TT637-640), one of the representative texts of the prominent medieval Shangqing School, describes a type of meditation hut that it calls a *huandu* (18/6b–7a). See Goossaert, "*La creation*," 172.

91. *Danyang zhenren yulu*, 8b.

92. See Hachiya, *Kindai*, 120–22, 197. The poems cited as evidence by Hachiya are found in *Chongyang quanzhen ji*, 9/6a–b, 10/18a.

93. "Zhongnan shan zhenxian Chongyangzi Wang zhenren Quanzhen jiaozu bei," in *Daojia jinshi lüe*, p. 452.

94. "Zhongnan shan Chongyang zushi xianji bei," in *Daojia jinshi lüe*, p. 460.

95. *Chongyang quanzhen ji*, 9/11b–12b.

96. See John King Fairbank, *China: A New History* (Cambridge: Belknap Press of Harvard University Press, 1992), 108–27; Kubo Noritada, *Chugoku*, 40–53, 181–82.

97. *Qizhen nianpu*, 9a–b.

98. A temple stands there even today, although the tomb of Wang Zhe was desecrated during the Cultural Revolution. When I visited there in 1990, the temple was in the early stages of renovation and a single Taoist monk resided there. I have been told that the temple has since been further renovated, and that more monks now live there.

99. See *Lishi zhenxian tidao tongjian xupian*, 1/18b–19a; Wang Liyong, "Quanzhen di'erdai Danyang baoyi wuwei zhenren Ma zongshi daoxing bei," in *Daojia jinshi lüe*, p. 640.

100. *Qizhen nianpu*, 13a.

101. *Qizhen nianpu*, 13a–b, 15a.

102. There is no proper reign era year that can be assigned here, since the Mongols had just conquered northern China and had not yet begun to institute reign eras in the Chinese fashion.

103. See Kubo Noritada, *Chugoku*, 183–88; Qing Xitai, *Zhongguo*, vol. 3, pp. 183–87 (by Zeng Zhaonan). A comprehensive, firsthand account of the journey is given in *Changchun zhenren xiyou ji* (DT1417/TT1056; Record of the Westward Journey of Realized Man Changchun) by Li Zhichang (1193–1256), another prominent disciple who eventually succeeded Yin Zhiping as leader of the Quanzhen School. Arthur Waley translated most of this work and published it in English under the title, *The Travels of an Alchemist: The Journey of the Taoist Ch'ang-ch'un from China to the Hindukush at the Summons of Chingiz Khan* (London: George Routeledge and Sons, 1931).

104. See Goossaert, "The Invention of an Order: Collective Identity in thirteenth-Century Quanzhen Taoism," *Journal of Chinese Religions* 29 (2001): 117.

105. See Qing Xitai, *Zhongguo*, vol. 3, pp. 212–16 (by Zeng Zhaonan). The original *Xuandu baozang* was compiled in 1190 under the sponsorship of the Jin (Jurchen) government. It was destroyed accidentally by fire in 1202.

106. On these debates, see Kenneth Ch'en, *Buddhism in China: A Historical Survey* (Princeton: Princeton University Press, 1964), 184–86.

107. The temples in question were probably, for the most part, not taken by force. The Buddhists probably had deserted them during the Mongol conquest.

108. See Qing Xitai, *Zhongguo*, vol. 3, pp. 216–26 (by Zeng Zhaonan). The primary source giving most of the information we have on these events is Xiang Mai, *Zhiyuan bianwei lu* (*Taishô zôkyô* 2116: 48), a Buddhist polemical work.

109. See *Jinlian zhengzong xianyuan xiangzhuan*, 3b–9a.

## Chapter 2

1. An ancient Indian term denoting very lengthy periods of time—typically a period long enough for a world to undergo creation, to flourish to decline, and to destruct.

2. *Chongyang quanzhen ji*, 1/16b–17a.

3. Ibid., 1/8a.

4. "*Gong'an*" would literally translate into something like "public announcement(s)." These are generally phrases or passages from Chan "records of sayings" that a master assigns to a student to contemplate. They are generally of a puzzling, enigmatic nature, incomprehensible by ordinary logic. Contemplating the *gong'an* is supposed to frustrate and exhaust the conceptual, dualistic thinking capacities of the disciple, eventually allowing intuitive wisdom (*prajna*) to burst through in a sudden enlightenment experience. The Linji (Rinzai in Japanese) Sect of Chan is particularly noted for its emphasis on the practice of the *gong'an*. There is little or no evidence suggesting that *gong'an* practice was carried out in early Quanzhen circles—even though Wang Zhe certainly displayed a propensity for strange actions and enigmatic utterances.

5. *Chongyang quanzhen ji*, 1/17b.

6. See Heinrich Dumoulin, *Zen Buddhism: A History*, vol. 1 (New York: Macmillan, 1994, 1988), 179–209. Kubo Noritada also has observed that Wang Zhe's teachings bear some resemblance to those of the Linji Sect. See Kubo Noritada, *Chugoku*, 84, 111, 146.

7. *Chongyang quanzhen ji*, 1/17a

8. *Zhenxian zhizhi yulu* (DT1244/TT998), 1/19a. This text, compiled probably around 1300 by a certain Xuanquanzi, is an anthology of discourses (mostly of the "record of sayings" genre) by Ma Yu (1/1a–9b), Tan Chuduan (1/9b–10b), Liu Chuxuan (1/10b–12a), Qiu Chuji (1/12a–19a), Hao Datong (1/19a–22b), and Yin Zhiping (2/1a–16b).

9. A slightly expanded version of this discourse is found in *Chongyang jiaohua ji* (DT1145/TT795–796), 3/12b–13b. There this sentence reads, ". . . recognize your True Nature, and nurture your true energy."

10. The version in the *Chongyang jiaohua ji* here reads, ". . . clear and still."

11. *Chongyang quanzhen ji*, 10/20b.

12. Hachiya *Kindai*, 134.

13. *Danyang zhenren yulu* (DT1047/TT728), 4b.

14. *Daoyin* (lit. "leading and guiding") are light exercises and self-massages intended to open up the numerous channels of the body and enhance the flow of *qi* through them. Their origin dates back at least as far as the second century B.C.E., and they have always been among the principal longevity practices.

15. *Danyang zhenren yulu*, 8a.

16. The influence of Chan Buddhism is glaringly apparent in this statement.

17. *Chongyang lijiao shiwu lun* (DT1221/TT989), 3b.

18. Ibid., 3b–4a.

19. See Bhikkhu Nanamoli and Bhikkhu Bodhi, trans., *The Middle Length Discourses of the Buddha: A New Translation of the Majjhima Nikaya* (Boston: Wisdom, 1995), 38–41, 1100–1101. The sixth Chan Patriarch Huineng (638–713) taught the practice of the *Samadhi* (meditative absorption) of Oneness, where one employs the "straightforward mind" at all times, whether "walking, staying, sitting, or lying." This he describes as a state where the mind does not abide in things, thus allowing the "Tao" (apparently meaning the natural, unencumbered mind) to circulate freely. See Philip Yampolsky, trans., *The Platform Sutra of the Sixth Patriarch* (New York: Columbia University Press, 1967), 136–37.

20. *Danyang zhenren zhiyan* (DT1222/TT989), 1a.

21. *Zhenxian zhizhi yulu*, 1/10a–b.

22. Ibid., 1/11b.

23. Ibid., 1/15b.

24. Ibid., 1/20a.

25. Ibid., 2/1a.

26. *Qinghe zhenren beiyou yulu* (DT1298/TT1017), 1/5b–6a. This text, compiled by a disciple, Duan Zhijian, preserves various discourses uttered by Yin Zhiping in 1233 during a journey from Shandong to Beijing and parts of present-day Liaoning Province.

27. *Qinghe zhenren beiyou yulu*, 2/7b–8a.

28. In its original usage, the character *jing* denotes refined white rice. However, it has a wide variety of other uses. It commonly denotes the pure, subtle essence of a thing. When used in a physiological context, it refers abstractly to the body's vitality and its generative forces or, more concretely, to seminal fluid. In some contexts, it refers to the nutrients in foods. In other contexts, it refers to the spiritual component of a human or an animal, or to nature spirits that dwell in trees, rocks, and so on.

29. *Qinghe zhenren beiyou yulu*, 2/7a.

30. *Danyang zhenren yulu*, 9a.

31. "Da Ma shifu shisi wen" (Answers to Fourteen Questions by Master-Father Ma), in *Jin zhenren yulu*, 7a.

32. See chapter 1, note 43.

33. *Chongyang quanzhen ji*, 10/21a. A cognate passage is found in *Chongyang jiaohua ji*, 3/13a–b. The original passage quoted is found in *Jin zhenren yulu*, 3a.

34. *Danyang zhenren zhiyan*, 2a–b.

35. *Zhenxian zhizhi yulu*, 1/4a.

36. The translation of the phrase "to put yourself in accord with others" (*yi ji fang ren*) is tentative.

37. *Zhenxian zhizhi yulu*, 1/15b.

38. Interestingly, the Taoist Canon today contains two anonymous, undated scriptures that deal, respectively, with inner and outer daily sustenance (*Taishang Laojun neiriyong jing* [DT640/TT342] and *Taishang Laojun wairiyong jing* [DT641/TT342]). It appears highly likely that these texts bear a connection to the Quanzhen movement, but the nature of this connection is unclear. The Quanzhen masters perhaps drew some of their inspiration from these scriptures, if they were already extant. However, it is equally possible that the two scriptures were authored at a later date by Quanzhen adherents.

39. *Qinghe zhenren beiyou yulu*, 1/1b.

40. Ibid., 2/18b–19a.

41. "Da Ma shifu shisi wen," in *Jin zhenren yulu*, 7a. Again, it is not completely certain whether Wang Zhe is the speaker in this text.

42. *Chongyang quanzhen ji*, 10/20b. A cognate passage is found in *Chongyang jiaohua ji*, 3/12b–13a.

43. Evidence of this is found in remarks by Ma Yu, recorded in *Danyang zhenren yulu*, 10a. There Ma Yu warns that the reading of books should be kept to a minimum, since reading tends to disturb one's mind. However, he then says that it is all right to occasionally read the *Daode jing* with Heshanggong's commentary and the *Yinfu jing* with Jinlingzi's (Master Jinling, i.e., Tang Chun) commentary.

44. Tang Chun, *Huangdi yinfu jing zhu* (DT121/TT57), 1/1b.

45. *Chongyang zhenren jinguan yusuo jue* (DT1147/TT796), 4a.

46. The fact that the teachings of this obscure figure were considered highly authoritative by the Quanzhen masters is apparent in that they sometimes quote him. Also noteworthy in this regard is that the edition of his collected sayings (*Jin zhenren yulu*) preserved in the Taoist Canon has appended to it some discourses by Wang Zhe, records of conversations between Ma Yu and a teacher (presumably Wang Zhe), and some poems that perhaps were written by Wang Zhe.

47. The word translated here is *sidai*, which may refer to the Indo-Buddhist four elements of earth, water, fire, and wind. It also may refer to the arms and legs.

48. *Jin zhenren yulu*, 1b–2b.

49. *Chongyang lijiao shiwu lun*, 4b.

## Chapter 3

1. *Chongyang quanzhen ji*, 1/9a–b.

2. Ibid., 4/6a.

3. *Danyang zhenren yulu*, 4a.

4. Ibid., 7b.

5. Ibid., 10b-11a.

6. Penglai and Yingzhou, along with Fangzhang, make up the legendary Three Divine Islands—dwellings of immortals that were thought to exist somewhere to the east of the Shandong Peninsula. This legend was likely inspired by the mirages that are known to periodically appear off of the coast of this peninsula. It was taken quite seriously during the fourth through second centuries B.C.E., when several different kings and emperors ordered expeditions to try to find these islands and to bring back some potion or secret teaching that could confer immortality. While such expeditions soon ceased to occur, the Three Divine Islands have ever since been frequently alluded to in poetry (religious and otherwise) as metaphors for immortal life or for a free, blissful state of mind. While such seems to be the case with Ma Yu's poem quoted here, there is evidence that Qiu Chuji may have literally believed in the existence of a Penglai Island, which was a sort of temporary paradise for Taoist adepts of insufficient merit and deeds. In one source, he is quoted as having said, "If your merit is lacking and your deeds are few, you can only return (?) to Peng[lai] Island. [Then,] after 500 years, you will return to the world of humans to accumulate [more] merit. In heaven (?) it is difficult to accumulate merits and deeds, while in the world of humans, merits and deeds are easy to accumulate. When superior gentlemen acquire the Tao they transcend beyond the Three Realms (of *samsara*) and do not dwell on Peng Island" (*Zhenxian zhizhi yulu*, 1/15a).

7. *Jianwu ji* (DT1133/TT786), 1/2b.

8. Ibid., 2/21b.

9. *Jinlian zhengzong xianyuan xiangzhuan* (24b–25a) states: "The master (Ma Yu) returned to the Patriarchal Garden, locked himself in his hut, and stayed there. In the *wuxu* year, [Dading] 18 (1178), on the new moon (1st day) of the 8th month, he came out of his hut. On the first month of the next year, he traveled to Huating County. Li Dasheng invited the master and served him. [Starting from] the full moon (15th day) of the 2nd month [Ma Yu] lived with him in a hut at his home and came out after a hundred days. The master revived the withered apple tree outside the hut. In the spring of [Dading] 20 (1180), he arrived at Jingzhao (Xi'an). Zhao Penglai offered him his home as a hermitage. The master again resided in a hut for a hundred days, then came out" (see Goossaert, "La creation," 178–82).

10. See Goossaert, "La creation," 171–219.

11. *Wuwei qingjing changsheng zhenren zhizhen yulu* (DT1048/TT728), 3b.

12. Yan was the name for a region in northeast China that included present-day Beijing. Liu Cao served under the Liao dynasty, the Chinese name for the empire of the Khitan people that included parts of northern China. It existed from 937 to 1125.

13. *Danyang zhenren yulu*, 5b–6a.

14. *Chongyang quanzhen ji*, 1/1b. See Hachiya, *Kindai*, 94.

15. *Danyang zhenren yulu*, 13a. See Hachiya, *Kindai*, 232–33.

16. *Danyang zhenren yulu*, 12b.

17. Ibid., 13b.

18. *Dongxuan jinyu ji* (DT1140/TT789–790), 1/3a–b.

19. *Wuwei qingjing changsheng zhenren zhizhen yulu*, 6b–7a.

20. *Zhenxian zhizhi yulu*, 1/12a–13a.

21. Another passage in *Qinghe zhenren beiyou yulu* (3/7a) indicates that the method was called the "Breath Control Method of the the Immortality of the Valley Spirit" (*gushen busi tiaoxi zhi fa*).

22. *Qinghe zhenren beiyou yulu*, 2/9a–10b.

23. This probably had much to do with the fact that Ma Yu was twenty-five years older than Qiu Chuji, was highly educated, and came from a privileged background.

24. *Lishi zhenxian tidao tongjian xupian*, 1/9a.

25. Hachiya Kunio makes some interesting speculations on the symbolism of this act. Hachiya speculates that the four carp represent the four disciples. Mutton is the meat of a sheep (*yang*), which rhymes with *yang* (of the dual cosmic principles of *yin/yang*). A carp lives in the water and can be considered a *yin* creature. Thus the stew of mutton and carp symbolizes the *neidan* procedure in which one recovers the Real Nature through the reconciliation and fusion of its dual aspects of *yang* (spirit) and *yin* (*qi*). See Hachiya, *Kindai*, 139.

26. "Zhongnanshan shenxian Chongyangzi Wang zhenren quanzhen jiaozu bei," in *Daojia jinshi lüe*, p. 451.

27. *Jinlian zhengzong ji*, 4/5a.

28. *Jinlian zhengzong xianyuan xiangzhuan*, 32b.

29. *Jinlian zhengzong ji*, 5/2b.

30. Ibid., 5/7a–b.

31. Ibid., 5/10a.

32. *Jinlian zhengzong xianyuan xiangzhuan*, 28a. *Jinlian zhengzong ji* records this incident differently. There we are told that Tan Chuduan went to a Buddhist monastary to ask for some leftover food and then got punched by an angry Chan (Zen) master.

33. *Danyang zhenren yulu*, 11b–12a.

34. *Zhenxian zhizhi yulu*, 2/4b–5a.

35. There is presently a small active monastery at the sheer cliffs of Mt. Longmen near Longxian (northwestern Shaanxi Province), which I visited in the summer of 1998. The relic is a smooth, spherical rock—about two and a half feet in diameter—known as the Rock for Polishing the [Real] Nature (*moxingshi*). According to legend, Qiu Chuji used to repeatedly carry this rock up a steep hill, roll it down, and carry it up again. As a result, the rock wore down to its present shape.

36. "Person of purified body" (*jingshen ren*) is a term used to describe a castrated eunuch. Our passage seems to suggest that Qiu Chuji may have suffered excessive bleeding or acute shock after castrating himself. Another possible understanding, perhaps, is that he caught a bad cold or pneumonia after bathing in excessively cold conditions. In early Quanzhen literature, I have found no further evidence suggesting self-castration by Qiu Chuji or any other Quanzhen monk. However, Yao Tao-chung has brought to attention some interesting relevant information regarding a certain Yanjiu ("Yan [the old name for Beijing] on the nine[teenth]") festival that in pre-modern times took place on 1/19 (Qiu Chuji's birthday) every year in Beijing. On this day, large crowds of people would flock to worship at the Baiyun Guan (White Cloud monastery), the prominent Quanzhen monastery where Qiu Chuji is buried. The popular belief was that one could encounter an immortal (Qiu Chuji himself?) by worshipping there on that particular day. This festival also was alternatively referred to as "Yanqiu" ("castrated Qiu"), in memory of Qiu Yuanqing, a virtuous Ming period Quanzhen monk who castrated himself on 1/19 after reluctantly accepting a gift of two palace girls from the emperor. Yao Tao-chung further mentions that some people have confused this Qiu with the more famous Qiu Chuji. (See Yao, "Chüan-chen", 218.)

Our passage would seem to hint that Qiu Chuji indeed was a "castrated Qiu." It is perhaps somewhat worth noting that *Jinlian zhengzong xianyuan xiangzhuan*, which provides simple portrait drawings of each Quanzhen patriarch and master, shows us a picture of a beardless Qiu Chuji (32a). Sun Bu'er—who was, of course, a woman—is the only other master depicted without a beard. If Qiu Chuji was indeed beardless, was this caused by the hormonal effects of castration?

37. *Panshan xiyun Wang zhenren yulu* (DT1049/TT728), 15a–b.

38. *Qinghe zhenren beiyou yulu*, 3/10b.

39. Taoist rituals are commonly referred to as *zhai* ("retreats") or *jiao* ("libations").

40. *Zhenxian zhizhi yulu*, 2/11a–b.

41 *Qinghe zhenren beiyou yulu*, 3/11b–12a.

## Chapter 4

1. The physical body, made up of the four elements, earth, water, fire, and wind. This notion of four elements is of Indian Buddhist origin. The elements are deemed "provisional," in that they exist only temporarily and depend on certain causes and conditions for this fleeting existence.

2. *Chongyang quanzhen ji*, 2/12a.

3. A Buddhist term denoting the five constituents of the personality: (1) form = body; (2) feelings; (3) perceptions; (4) volitional impulses; and (5) consciousness. See Edward Conze, *Buddhist Scriptures* (London: Penguin, 1959), 248.

4. *Chongyang quanzhen ji*, 2/12b–13a.

5. The above verses by Wang Zhe describe his experiences and insights gained at Nanshi Village from the fall of 1161 to the fall of 1163. During this period, he lived and meditated inside of a burial mound that he had built for himself.

6. *Chongyang lijiao shiwu lun*, 5b–6a.

7. *Chongyang quanzhen ji*, 2/14b.

8. Ibid., 2/7b.

9. "Three lights" most likely refers to essence (*jing*), *qi*, and spirit (*shen*).

10. The meaning of "spring of four seasons" is unclear, but perhaps it means a prevailing state of fresh, youthful vitality.

11. *Chongyang quanzhen ji*, 1/6b–7a.

12. Ibid., 4/11a.

13. *Dongxuan jinyu ji*, 10/4a.

14. See Goossaert, "La Creation," 451; Hachiya, Kindai, 152.

15. The latter view is endorsed in Ren Jiyu, *Daozang tiyao*, 910–11.

16. As is pointed out in Ren Jiyu, *Daozang tiyao* (p. 175), the heading of this text states that it was preached by Qiu Chuji and refers to him as "Changchun Yandao Zhujiao Zhenren" (Changchun, the Realized Man Who Preaches the Tao and Leads the Religion). This title was bestowed upon him posthumously by the emperor in 1269. In 1310, the emperor bestowed all of the Quanzhen Seven Realized Ones (Wang Zhe's seven top disciples—Ma Yu, Tan Chuduan, Liu Chuxuan, Qiu Chuji, Wang Chuyi, Hao Datong, and Sun Bu-er) with the higher honorific title of Realized Lord (*zhenjun*).

17. *Wuming*—perhaps a mistranscription of *wuming*, which would mean "benighted" or "unenlightened."

18. The "ten evils," according to Buddhist doctrine, are: (1) killing; (2) stealing; (3) lechery; (4) lying; (5) eloquent deception; (6) slander; (7) double-talk; (8) greed; (9) wrath; and (10) ignorance. This, or something similar, is probably meant here.

19. *Chongyang zhenren jinguan yusuo jue*, 1a–b.

20. *Geng* is the seventh of the ten *gan* symbols ("stems"). It corresponds to the west, the season of fall, and the agent of metal. *You* is number ten among the twelve *zhi* symbols ("branches"), which also correponds to the west and refers to the two hours between 5–7 P.M. or to 6 P.M. *Jia* is the first of the ten *gan* symbols, which corresponds to wood, the east, and 8 P.M. *Mao* is the fourth of the *zhi*, which corresponds to wood, east, spring, and 6 A.M.

21. These are the beginnings of each of the four seasons, the summer and winter solstices, and the spring and fall equinoxes.

22. *Kan* is a trigram from the *Yi jing* (Book of Changes), which is made of one solid line in between two broken lines, thus representing the *yang* within the *yin*. *Li*, conversely, is made of one broken line in between two solid lines, thus representing the *yin* within the *yang*.

23. *Dadan zhizhi* tells us that "lead" is the "primal *yang* perfect breath" stored in the kidneys, and "mercury is the "essence of proper *yang*" stored in the heart.

24. In a physiological context, *jing* refers to the generative, nourishing principle or force thought to dwell primarily in bodily fluids—particulary in the semen in the male body.

25. *Chongyang zhenren jinguan yusuo jue*, 1b–2a.

26. Essentially, the passage seems to be saying that the cycle of the four seasons that takes place in the world over the span of a year takes place in the human body over the span of a single day. Apparently, the "spring equinox" at which the liver creates *jin* saliva is 6 A.M. The "summer solstice" at which the heart produces the blood is noon. The "fall equinox" at which the lungs produce *ye* saliva is 6 P.M. The "winter solstice" at which the kidneys produce semen is midnight.

27. In *Chongyang zhenren shou Danyang ershisi jue* (DT1149/TT796), Wang Zhe goes into detail correlating—rather randomly and incoherently—various parts of human beings to their counterparts in the universe. He says that the nine orifices of the human body correspond to the seven stars of the Big Dipper and the "Left Bulwark and Right Supporter" stars. The five viscera correspond to the five marchmounts (*wuyue*). The four limbs are correlated to the four seasons. Correlated to the four elements (Indo-Buddhistic) of earth, water, fire, and wind are the body, essence, mind, and breath (*qi*), respectively. The essence (*jing*), spirit (*shen*), and breath (*qi*) of a person are correlated to the sun, moon, and stars and with the symbols *ji*, *bing*, and *ding* of the earth. Also, the heart correlates to the sun, and the kidneys correlate to the moon (*Chongyang zhenren shou Danyang ershisi jue*, 3a–b).

28. Here the term *qi* is used in a more limited sense to denote the aspect of the vital principle that bestows the body with the capacity for motion and that in its external manifestation takes the form of the air or breath.

29. *Dangyang zhenren yulu*, 6a. The identity of "little Immortal Ren" is obscure.

30. *Danyang zhenren yulu*, 4a–b.

31. *Huangdi yinfu jing zhu* (DT122/TT57), 2a.

32. *Dadan zhizhi*, 1b–2a.

33. There also were thought to be central and upper Elixir Fields in the chest and the cranium, respectively. When the term *Elixir Field* appears with no specification as to its position, it generally refers to the Lower Elixir Field in the belly.

34. *Dadan zhizhi*, 1/2a–b.

35. *Huangdi yinfu jing zhu*, 6a–b.

36. *Chongyang zhenren jinguan yusuo jue*, 11a.

37. Books of this genre have been discovered at tombs from the Warring States, Qin, and Han periods. For a good study of the content of these books see Mu-chou Poo, *In Search of Personal Welfare: A View of Ancient Chinese Religion* (Albany: State University of New York Press, 1998), 69–101.

38. *Chongyang jiaohua ji*, 2/9a.

39. The latter (faith in oneself), it should be noted, is something that was strongly emphasized by the Chan master, Linji Yixuan (d. 866). See Dumoulin, *Zen Buddhism: A History*, vol. 1, 179–209.

40. See Wang Liyong, "Quanzhen di'erdai Danyang baoyi wuwei zhenren Ma zongshi daoxing bei," in *Daojia jinshi lüe*, p. 639; *Lishi zhenxian tidao tongjian xupian*, 1/15b. Both sources claim that Wang Zhe, by his clairvoyant powers, knew from afar that Ma Yu had drunk alcohol (the latter source states that he saw it in a dream).

41. This probably was a procedure in which Wang Zhe recited some chants, dissolved the ashes of a burnt paper talisman in water, and made Ma Yu drink the water. See *Lishi zhenxian tidao tongjian xupiani*, 1/15b, and *Jinlian zhengzong ji*, 3/5b. The latter source claims that the "talisman water" cured Ma Yu.

42. "Immortal" (*xian*) here is simply a respectful way of referring to a senior Taoist monk.

43. *Chongyang jiaohua ji* (2/3b) contains a poem that seems to have been written on this occasion. See discussion later in this chapter.

44. See Hachiya, *Kindai*, 229–32.

45. A "sweet heart" is a mind full of desires and wishes.

46. *Chongyang jiaohua ji*, 2/9b–10a.

47. See "Quanzhen di'erdai Danyang baoyi wuwei zhenren Ma zongshi daoxing bei," in *Daojia jinshi lüe*, p. 639; *Lishi zhenxian tidao tongjian*, 1/15b; Hachiya, *Kindai*, 232.

48. *Xuanfeng qinghui lu*, 1b.

49. Ibid., 5a–b.

50. *Chongyang zhenren jinguan yusuo jue*, 2b–3a.

51. The degree earned by passing the civil service examination, which qualifies one for administrative positions in the imperial bureaucracy.

52. The term *lou* ("leakage" or "outflowing") has its origins in Buddhist literature, where it denotes the three outflowings: (1) the craving for sensual pleasures; (2) the craving for existence; and (3) ignorance. A person without "outflowings," in the Buddhist sense, is thus an enlightened person, free of ignorance and corruptive desires.

53. The story also mentions that he cured his mother's hemorrhoids by feeding her the seeds of these jujubes.

54. After this point the narrative describes how family members and friends forced him to eat (whereupon he would regurgitate) or locked him up and monitored him to see if he in fact never did eat.

55. *Lishi zhenxian tidao tonjian*, 52/16b–18b.

56. Wanyan Shou (1172–1232). "Zhongnan shan shenxian Chongyang zhenren Quanzhen jiaozu bei," in *Daojia jinshi lüe*, p. 452.

57. See Eskildsen, *Asceticism*, 59, 67–68.

58. Ibid., 43–68.

59. *Chongyang zhenren jinguan yusuo jue*, 16b.

60. *Dongxuan jinyu ji*, 4/9a.

61. *Chongyang zhenren jinguan yusuo jue*, 16a.

62. *Chunyang dijun shenhua miaotong ji*, 7/11b–12a (story #106).

63. *Chongyang zhenren jinguan yusuo jue*, 10b.

64. Ibid., 13b–14a.

65. Ibid., 20b.

66. Ibid., 11a–b.

67. *Tixuan zhenren xianyi lu* (DT589/TT329), 1b–2a.

68. Ibid., 1a–b.

69. Ibid., 7b–8a.

70. Ibid., 11a–b.

71. It appears that he took up residence in a hole in the side of a hill that somebody had dug originally for the purpose of extracting clay to be used for ceramics. Another possible interpretation is that he began living in an abandoned mine shaft.

72. What this "muddy fluid" was, and how or why he swallowed it, is unclear. I know of one particular *neidan* manual where the term *fiery poison* frequently occurs and seems to refer to intense, feverish sensations in the body that are caused by breath-holding exercises. (see Eskildsen, "*Neidan* Master Chen Pu's Nine Stages of Transformation"). Of course, if such an interpretation is applied here, the meaning of the term rendered *muddy fluid* (*tujin*) needs to be reconsidered in a whole new light.

73. *Dongxuan jinyu ji*, 8/15b–16a.

74. The *zhen* has a long, black neck and a red beak, and it resembles the secretary falcon in its appearance. A deadly potion could be prepared by steeping its wings in liquor. The most detailed account of the incidents in question here is found in Yao Sui, "Yuyang tixuan guangdu zhenren Wang zongshi daoxing bei bing xu," in *Daojia jinshi lüe*, pp. 718–19. There we are told that Wang Chuyi, before departing to the house of his prospective assassin (who had invited him), told the disciples at his monastery to dig a pit and fill it with water. At the home of the conspirator, Wang Chuyi drank one cup of the tainted liquor, with no immediate ill effects. He then

requested a refill and gulped it down. Upon returning to his monastery, Wang Chuyi took off his clothes and jumped into the pond that his disciples had prepared. The water soon started to boil rapidly, and all of Wang Chuyi's hair fell out. However, he was otherwise completely unharmed. In 1187, Emperor Shizong summoned Wang Chuyi for an audience. On this occasion, the emperor inquired about the poisoning incident, but Wang Chuyi said that he held no grudge, and he refused to declare the identity of the unsuccessful assassin. The emperor then—under the advice of some slanderers—also gave Wang Chuyi a poisonous beverage to drink. Wang Chuyi again imbibed the poison and was unharmed. The emperor, now convinced that Wang Chuyi was a remarkable holy man, had the slanderers arrested. *Jinlian zhengzong ji* (5/3a) mentions only the incident at the palace and says that some Buddhist monks had bribed a high official to urge the emperor to poison Wang Chuyi. *Jinlian zhengzong xianyuan xiangzhuan* (37b) mentions only the first poisoning incident and does not record the emperor's misdeed.

75. *Chongyang zhenren jinguan yusuo jue*, 22a.

76. Ibid., 17b.

77. *Dadan zhizhi* 1/2b states: "I think the reason why ordinary people are unable to be intimate [with their Elixir Fields] is because they are controlled by their seven emotions and six desires and confusedly forget the place where [their breath is] originally supposed to go. [Therefore], the air that they exhale and inhale comes and goes, reaching only as far as the Sea of Breath. [The Sea of Breath is above the diaphragm. It is the Office of the Lungs.] Because they have never been able to make [their breath] reach the Office of Life in the Central Palace and come in contact with their primal *qi* and Real *qi*, their metal (lung *qi*, tiger) and wood (liver *qi*, dragon) remain separated. How then can they make the dragon and tiger copulate and produce [*qi*] that is pure and exquisite?"

78. *Dadan zhizhi*, 1/6b–7a.

79. Ibid., 9a–10a.

80. *Chongyang zhenren jinguan yusuo jue*, 10a.

81. *Huangting neijing yujing zhu* (DT400/TT189), 17b.

82. Ibid., 26b.

83. Ibid., 42b.

84. *Xuanfeng qinghui lu*, 8b–9a.

85. *Chunyang dijun shenhua miaotong ji*, 6/5a–6a.

86. *Danyang zhenren yulu*, 6a–b.

87. *Chongyang zhenren jinguan yusuo jue*, 6b.

88. The origins of these methods go back at least as far as the Han dynasty. A recent, detailed study of these methods is Douglas Wile, *Art of the Bedchamber: The Chinese Sexual Yoga Classics, including Women's Solo Meditation Texts* (Albany: State University of New York Press, 1992).

89. *Chongyang zhenren jinguan yusuo jue*, 7a–8a.

90. The term translated here as "frankincense" may actually refer to the woman's breasts. This seems possible, particularly in light of the information given in the next quoted passage (from "Chongzhen pian").

91. This probably means to concentrate the mind on a particular place (the breasts) and/or to hold the breath.

92. *Chongyang zhenren jinguan yusuo jue*, 8a.

93. "Chongzhen pian," in Zeng Zao, *Daoshu* (DT1008/TT641–648), 19th *juan*. Striking similarities between portions of this "Chongzhen pian" and another text known as *Jin zhenren yulu* hint strongly that Jin Daocheng was the same Realized Man Jin whose teachings influenced the Quanzhen masters.

94. Zhao Daoyi, *Lishi zhenxian tidao tongjian*, 52/2a–3b.

95. *Chongyang zhenren jinguan yusuo jue*, 8a.

96. It is unclear what tandem is designated here by "lead and mercury." Possible meanings would include sperm and blood, essence and breath, kidney *qi* and heart *qi*, and spirit [consciousness] and *qi* [vitality]).

97. *Dadan zhizhi*, 1/12a–b.

98. Ibid., 1/14a–b.

99. *Chongyang zhenren jinguan yusuo jue*, 11a–b.

100. Ibid., 12a.

101. Ibid., 22b.

102. *Chongyang lijiao shiwu lun*, 2a–b.

103. This probably involved drawing a paper talisman, burning it, and mixing its ashes into water.

104. *Chongyang jiaohua ji*, 2/3b.

105. *Chongyang quanzhen ji*, 7a–b.

106. From "Chongyang zushi xiuxian liaoxing bijue," in *Jin zhenren yulu*, 5b.

107. *Tixuan zhenren xianyi lu*, 11b–12a.

108. Ibid., 11a–b.

109. See *Lishi zhenxian tidao tongjian xupian*, 2/1b–2a; Wanyan Shou, "Changzhenzi Tan zhenren xianji beiming," in *Daojia jinshi lüe*, p. 454.

110. Here we have a rare instance in Quanzhen literature where mention is made of cosmic cycles and a cataclysmic flood. These were prominent themes in the Shangqing and Lingbao scriptures of the fourth and fifth centuries. See Eskildsen, *Asceticism*, 84–90, 105–106.

111. *Danyang zhenren yulu*, 15b–16a.

112. *Chongyang zhenren jinguan yusuo jue*, 2b–3a.

113. Ibid., 4b–5a.

114. Of course, to posit the existence of any sort of individual soul or spirit is out of line with Buddhist orthodoxy.

115. *Chunyang dijun shenhua miaotong ji*, 3/11a–12a (18th episode).

116. One would think that "Patriarch Wang" could only be Wang Zhe. But why would he be referred to as the "Twelfth Patriarch of the Western Mountain"? It would appear that Qiu Chuji (or whoever speaks in this text), whose teachings received considerable inspiration from the Northern Song Zhong-Lü text, *Xishan qunxian huizhen ji* (DT245/TT116), has inducted Wang Zhe into the ranks of the "10+ Realized Men of the Western Mountain" extolled in that work.

117. *Dadan zhizhi*, 8b. This discourse bears a strong resemblance to *Xishan qunxian huizhen ji*, 5/9a–b.

118. *Dadan zhizhi*, 2/8b–9a.

119. This is the stage where everything can be accomplished by acting spontaneously.

120. *Dadan zhizhi*, 2/9b.

## Chapter 5

1. This traditional three-day celebration took place in the spring, 105 days after the winter solstice. Cooking used to be forbidden during the festival, thus it used to be called the "Cold Food" festival.

2. *Qinghe zhenren beiyou yulu*, 2/15a–b.

3. Ibid., 2/15b.

4. Another conceivable interpretation might be that Yin Zhiping saw a vision of Wang Zhe, but could he have had a vision of a man whom he had presumably never met and had at best only heard of? Hagiographical sources mostly ignore the incident, with the exception of one source, which states: "At age seven, he met Grand Master Wang of Shaanxi and wished to follow him." The text quite apparently does not mean to say that this "Grand Master" was Wang Zhe, since Wang Zhe is referred to as "the Patriarch Master, Realized Man Chongyang" when he is alluded to later in the narrative. (See Yi Gou, "Xuanmen zhangjiao Qinghe miaodao guanghua zhenren Yin zongshi beiming bing xu," [1264], in *Daojia jinshi lüe*, pp. 567–70.) I also had considered the possibility that "Grand Master Wang" was Wang Zhe's disciple, Wang Chuyi (1142–1217), who in fact did bear the title of "Grand Master" ("Grand Master Who Embodies the Mysteries" [Tixuan Dashi], to be exact), which was given to him in 1197 by the Jurchen emperor. However, since Wang Chuyi hailed from Shandong and spent most of his life there, "from the west of the Pass" would not seem to be an apt description of him. Furthermore, he was in training at the Cloud Light Grotto (Yunguang Dong) on Mt. Cha (Wendeng county, in present-day Shandong) during the time of the incident. (See "Yuyang tixuan

guangdu zhenren Wang zongshi daoxing bei bing xu," [1307], in *Daojia jinshi lüe*, pp. 718–20.)

5. *Qinghe zhenren beiyou yulu*, 2/15b–16a.

6. *Qinghe zhenren beiyou yulu*, 2/16a–b. This episode also is translated (into French) and discussed in Goossaert, "La Creation," 384–85.

7. The idea here is that a perfected Taoist master can send his Radiant Spirit out of his body and appear before people in remote locations or even in their trance visions and dreams.

8. *Qinghe zhenren beiyou yulu*, 2/16b.

9. Ibid., 4/5a–b.

10. *Dongxuan jinyu ji*, 1/9a–b.

11. Ibid., 1/9b.

12. *Zhenxian zhizhi yulu*, 1/16b.

13. Wang Yuan (style name [zi], Fangping) was a legendary immortal of the second century, whose story is recorded in the *Shenxian zhuan*, the famous collection of immortality lore attributed to the early fourth-century alchemist, Ge Hong (see 2/6b–8a of the version included in Ding Fubao, comp., *Daozang jinghua lu* [Hangzhou: Zhejiang Guji Chubanshe, 1989, 1922]). Wang Yuan is said to have been an erudite scholar-official who abandoned the world to cultivate the Tao in the mountains. After describing how he shunned the summons of the Han Emperor Huan and worked various miracles, the narrative gives a lengthy description of how Wang Yuan arrived from the air, flanked by his immortal entourage, at the house of his disciple, Cai Jing. A sumptuous feast of the immortals then takes place, and the lovely and mysterious immortal maiden, Ma Gu, also arrives as a guest. When Cai Jing secretly harbors the desire to have his back scratched by the long fingernails of the lovely maiden, Wang Yuan reads his mind and beats him severely as a punishment for harboring such impure thoughts. See also Kubo Noritada, *Dôkyô no kamigami* (Tokyo: Hirakawa Shuppansha, 1986), 201–202.

14. *Yunguang ji* (DT1143/TT792), 4/3b. See also Hachiya, *Kindai*, 203.

15. Here he is most likely referring to the Three Pure Realms (Sanqing) of Jade Purity (Yuqing), Upper Purity (Shangqing), and Great Purity (Taiqing), the highest celestial realms in Taoist religious cosmology.

16. The passage in question reads as follows: "Danyang (Ma Yu) would constantly ask me why I drank nothing but cold water. I answered, "Ever since I got to meet the Perfected Man Chunyang (Lü Yan) at Ganhe, I have been drinking water" (*Chongyang fenli shihua ji* [DT1146/TT796], 2/6b).

17. For good discussions of this issue, see Kubo, *Chûgoku*, 87–103; Hachiya, *Kindai*, 29–36.

18. *Yunguang ji*, 4/1a.

19. The passage in question reads as follows: "Mr. Liu of Yaozhou dreamed of Haichan (Liu Cao) and studied how to train himself. Thus I presented him with this poem:

Hai-ch'an entered a dream to exhort Immortal Liu.
He sent you (Mr. Liu) to study what is marvelous and profound." (*Dongxuan jinyu ji*, 3/17a)

20. The passage in question reads as follows: "In the past at the hall in Shandong there was a guest who came to inquire [from Qiu Chuji]. He was originally a wealthy merchant of Xilu. He had encountered Perfected Man Zhengyang (Zhongli Quan) and had been conferred subtle lessons. That very day [of his encounter] he abandoned all his wealth. He calmly and naturally lost all his worldly desires. The Master-Father (Qiu Chuji) simply taught him to accumulate merit while being careful not to flaunt [his virtues] on the outside. When other people know [of your virtues] they inevitably heap their reverence upon you. After a long while there will be harm done [by this reverence paid to you], and it will be difficult for you to accomplish the Tao. Thus you should understand that even if you have met with a true transmission, you should accumulate even more merits and deeds in order to supplement your blessings. You shall then accomplish something" (*Qinghe zhenren beiyou yulu*, 3/8a).

21. *Qinghe zhenren beiyou yulu*, 2/14a.

22. *Zhenxian zhizhi yulu*, 1/14b.

23. Ibid., 1/15b–16a.

24. Interestingly enough, this is the same Xuanquanzi who compiled the *Zhenxian zhizhi yulu*, an anthology of *yulu* ["collected sayings"] of the Quanzhen masters.

25. *Dadan zhizhi*, 1/17b–18a.

26. The Three Corpses--also known as the Three Worms--are evil spirits that were believed to dwell in the three elixir fields (*dantian*) located in the head, chest, and lower abdomen. A detailed study on the development of this concept can be found in Kubo Noritada, *Kôshin shinkô no kenkyû* (Tokyo: Nihon Gakujutsu Shinkôkai, 1961). Also see Eskildsen, *Asceticism*, 46, 61.

27. A traditional Chinese view held that every body possessed three *hun* souls and seven *po* souls. The former are *yang* and ethereal in character, while the latter are *yin* and chthonic in character. Upon death and bodily decay, the *hun* disperse into the skies, and the *po* seep and dissipate into the soil. In Taoist texts, the *po* are sometimes—as in this case—seen as malicious beings that tempt and corrupt humans.

28. *Dadan zhizhi*, 2/4b.

29. The idea here seems to be that the devious devils disguise themselves as holy deities to distract the pious adept and lead him into a state of misguided pride and complacency.

30. In *Zhuzhen neidan jiyao*, 2/9–13a.

31. Since the text speaks of the seminal essence flowing backwards as one of the phenomena that occur, the author of the text probably does not have female practitioners in mind.

32. See note 26.

33. A similar cataloguing of special phenomena both auspicious and hazardous is carried out also in the *Zhong-Lü chuandao ji* (in a section entitled "Lun zhengyan" [On Signs of Proof]) and the "Lun liutong jue" ("Lesson on the Six Penetrations," in *Zhuzhen neidan jiyao*).

34. *Chongyang quanzhen ji*, 4/6a.

35. Ibid., 3/6b–7a.

36. Ibid., 2/14a. The meaning or identity of "Sir Ding" is unclear. It perhaps could be something related to the heart or mind, since *ding*, as one of the ten "stems," is said to correlate to the agent fire (as does the heart).

37. Ibid.

38. Ibid., 2/16a.

39. Wang Zhe's poetry occasionally alludes to the "Three Corpses and Nine Worms" as evil entities that can be exterminated through proper self-cultivation. A few examples would be as follows: "To my contentment the marvelous forms follow, completely eliminating the Three Corpses and Nine Worms" (*Chongyang quanzhen ji*, 12/20b); "Let your mind go freely in joyous serenity. You should make the Worms disappear and the Corpses leave" (*Chongyang quanzhen ji*, 13/19a).

40. The most vivid account of these eccentricities is found in "Zhongnan shan shenxian Chongyang zi zhenren Quanzhen jiaozu bei" (1275), in *Daojia jinshi lüe*, pp. 450–54.

41. *Chongyang quanzhen ji*, 3/7a.

42. *Qinghe zhenren beiyou yulu*, 3/11b.

43. Ibid., 2/14a–b.

44. *Zhenxian zhizhi yulu*, 2/5a–b.

45. If he was referring to the *jiazi* year of the sexegenary cycle (this how I have tentatively interpreted the passage), then he must have had the fourth year of the Taihe reign era (1204) in mind. However, hagiography reports that he passed away in the second lunar month of the previous year, so he perhaps meant to say figuratively here that a new sexegenary cycle was about to commence.

46. *Qinghe zhenren beiyou yulu*, 1/12b.

47. A slightly different version of this chapter has been published in the *Journal of Chinese Religions* 29 (2001): 139–60, under the title "Seeking 'Signs of Proof': Visions and Other Trance Phenomena in Early Quanzhen Taoism."

## Chapter 6

1. Here this means to die, with the understanding that the death of the physical body is a return to an alternate mode of existence that preceeded this life and that goes beyond it.

2. *Chongyang lijiao shiwu lun*, 5b.

3. Mahayana Buddhism teaches that the Buddha is in fact an eternal being that is the universal reality (Suchness, Emptiness) underlying all phenomena. The term *Dharma Body* (*dharmakaya*) is one used to speak of this eternal Buddha that is invisible and ineffable. The bodies of all of the Buddhas through the ages throughout the various worlds are said to be Transformation Bodies (*huashen*, *nirmanakaya*) or phantoms that are generated from the Dharma Body. The eternal Buddha also is said to manifest resplendent and marvelous Bodies of Communal Enjoyment (*baoshen*, *sambhogakaya*) for the benefit of faithful and worthy seekers of enlightenment. See Ch'en, *Buddhism in China*, 13–14.

4. *Dongxuan jinyu ji*, 8/22a.

5. *Zhenxian zhizhi yulu*, 1/21b.

6. Liu Zuqian, "Zhongnan shan Chongyang zushi xianji ji," in *Daojia jinshi lüe*, p. 461.

7. He relates how at night, while locked away inside of his meditation hut, Wang Zhe somehow projected his Spirit outside of the hut to speak to Ma Yu or to appear in his dreams. He also mentions how Wang Zhe clairvoyantly predicted the time of his death.

8. *Xuanfeng qinghui lu*, 1a–b.

9. *Panxi ji* (DT1150/TT797), 2/13a.

10. *Yunguang ji*, 3/18b.

11. A commonly used word that refers to the miraculous capacities that are born as a result of profound insight.

12. *Huangdi yinfu jing zhu*, 10a–b.

13. This last item, although not a miraculous attribute in the normally understood sense, is considered the most elusive and blessed attribute of the Buddhist saint. It is what distinguishes him or her from the non-Buddhist yogins with their magical powers.

14. We at least know that Xuanquanzi, the compiler of the anthology containing this essay, must have been an admirer or a follower of the Quanzhen School, since he also compiled *Zhenxian zhizhi yulu*—an anthology of *yulu* (collected sayings) of the Quanzhen masters.

15. See *Zhuzhen neidan jiyao*, 3/12a–14a. The Six Penetrations (*liutong*) enumerated there are: (1) Penetration of the Mind's Surroundings (*xinjingtong*)—the adept experiences his or her True Nature leaving the physical body; (2) Penetration of the

Spirit's Surroundings (*shenjingtong*)—the ability to see and know of things in places beyond the ordinary range of perception; (3) Penetration of the Heavenly Eye (*tianyantong*)—the adept sees landscapes of mountains and rivers within his or her own body; (4) Penetration of the Heavenly Ear (*tian'ertong*)—the adept in trance hears voices of gods and humans (which he or she must take care not to get distracted by); (5) Sudden Penetration of Signs from the Past (*suxinhutong*)—the ability to perceive the causes and effects (the workings of *karma* and reincarnation) of the Three Realms of *samsara*; (6) Penetration of the Minds of Others (*taxintong*)—the ability to manifest the "body outside the body" in multiple locations.

16. *Xianyue ji* (DT1132/TT785), 2/5b–6a.

17. Ibid., 5/11a.

18. For example, "Zhongnanshan shenxian Chongyangzi Wang zhenren quanzhen jiaozu bei" states, "In the fourth month of the *jizhou* year, the ninth year [of the Dading reign era] (1169), a certain Zhou Botong of Ninghai invited the Realized Man (Wang Zhe) to live in a hut. [The Realized Man] put up a sign that read 'Golden Lotus Hall.' At night there was spiritual light shining and radiating [from Golden Lotus Hall] as bright as day. People thought that it was on fire, but when they went close to it, they saw the Realized Man going about in [his] light's brilliance" (*Daojia jinshi lüe*, pp. 451–52).

19. An official who oversees the brewing of liquor that is to be consumed in the imperial palace.

20. *Tixuan zhenren xianyi lu*, 5a–6a.

21. "Zhongnanshan shenxian Chongyangzi Wang zhenren quanzhen jiaozu bei" states, "Sometimes [Wang Zhe] manifested two heads. While he was sitting in his hut, people would see him wandering amongst the shops" (*Daojia jinshi lüe*, p. 451).

22. *Jinlian zhengzong xianyuan xiangzhuan* (28a) states, "One day the master (Tan Chuduan) chained shut [the entrance to] his hut and went to Weizhou (in Henan). In the evening the Temple Director, Wen Liu, saw a fiery radiance inside the hut and saw the master sitting while holding fire. The Temple Director was amazed and sent a person to go to [Wei-]zhou and look for the master. The master was found sleeping in an inn by the northern entrance of the town and had not yet awakened. When [the person sent to look for him] returned to the hut, the fire and cinders had not yet burned out."

23. *Jinlian zhengzong xianyuan xiangzhuan* (30b) states, "In the second year of the Mingchang reign era (1191), the Commandant-escort (a high-ranking military official), Pu Sanchu, was in charge of Laizhou (in Shandong). He became deceived by a slanderous accusation and ordered Commandant of the Capitol Patrol, Luan Wujie, to pursue and arrest [Liu Chuxuan]. A short while after he was put in prison, the people in the marketplaces saw the master (Liu Chuxuan) conversing with friends of the Tao as usual at the south of the city walls. Zheng, the lackey, and Wang, the receptionist, also saw this and thought that the master had escaped. When they went and looked inside the prison, the master was in there, sound asleep. The two of them were bewildered, and they told of what they had seen to the Commandant[-escort]. The

Commandant[-escort] realized that the master was a person who has the Tao and immediately ordered his release."

24. *Jinlian zhengzong ji*, 5/9a–b.

25. "Zhongnan shan shenxian Chongyangzi Wang zhenren Quanzhen jiaozu bei," in *Daojia jinshi lüe*, p. 451.

26. A similar passage is found in *Jinlian zhengzong xianyuan xiangzhuan* (21b). There, however, it is claimed that Wang Zhe's bodily countenance—that which ordinary people encountered in normal, waking experience—was constantly changing. His left eye spun clockwise, his right eye spun counterclockwise, sometimes he appeared elderly, sometimes he appeared youthful, sometimes he was fat, and sometimes he was thin. Thus nobody could produce a portrait of him.

27. One night Ma Yu had a dream where he saw his mother, who proclaimed to him, "There is a guest named Lü Matong." The next day, Wang Zhe gave Ma Yu the name "Tong." Another night Ma Yu had a lengthier dream in which he finds himself in the company of Wang Zhe, an unidentified Taoist, and a certain Ma Jiuguanren. At Wang Zhe's behest, Ma Jiuguanren recited a poem that ended in the phrase, "Bake and obtain the white, refine and obtained the yellow. Thereby you will have obtained the method of long life and immortality." The next day, after waking, Ma Yu was bestowed (by Wang Zhe) the personal name "Yu" (the character for which combines the gold/metal radical with the character for "jade") and the sobriquet, Danyang ("elixir-*yang*"). Another night Ma Yu dreamed about going into the mountains with Wang Zhe. The following morning, Wang Zhe began to call him by the nickname "Mountain Fool" (*shantong*) (see "Zhongnan shan shenxian Chongyangzi Wang zhenren Quanzhen jiaozu bei," in *Daojia jinshi lüe*, p. 451).

28. *Jianwu ji*, 1/2a.

29. *Danyang zhenren yulu*, 13a.

30. *Jinlian zhengzong xianyuan xiangzhuan* (28a–b) states: "In the sixteenth year [of the Dading reign era] (1176), [Tan] went up to Luozhou (Luoyang). [Living] by the Baijia Rapids was a farmer with an illness that he had been treating for months without any good results. [One night,] he dreamed of a Taoist monk giving him some red-colored medicine that he then swallowed. When he woke up, the illness was cured. The next day he saw the master (Tan) and exclaimed, 'This is the master who gave me medicine in the dream!' He wanted to thank him, but the master paid no attention to him."

31. *Jinlian zhengzong ji*, 2/7a. The narrative later describes what happened when Ma Yu, Tan Chuduan, Liu Chuxuan, and Qiu Chuji were carrying Wang Zhe's body and coffin from Bianjing to Liujiang for reburial. It reads: "At every place they arrived, when they were about to pay for their lodging and food, the innkeeper would always say, 'A Taoist monk came by and has already paid for everything.' [The disciples] would then pursue [the Taoist monk] but were never able to find him. When they had the innkeeper describe his appearance, they would [always] realize that it was the Patriarch-Master's manifestation body" (2/7b).

32. *Jiao* is a word used to refer to a Taoist ritual administered by ordained priests and generally undertaken on a large scale for multiple days.

33. *Jinlian zhengzong ji*, 2/7b–8a.

34. Here the text provides annotation that reads: "My teacher, the Realized Man Chongyang, had ascended into the mists that day. In the evening, Sir Zang met him in the southern capital. He did not yet know that he had ascended into the mists and thought that he was living. Only later on did he know about it (Wang Zhe's death). [More incidents] such as this were to follow."

35. *Dongxuan jinyu ji*, 10/15b–16a. Ma Ya also mentions Wang Zhe's appearance atop the clouds in Wendeng in another poem, found in *Dongxuan jinyu ji*, 10/23a–b.

36. See Hachiya, *Kindai*, 251–52.

37. *Danyang shenguang can* (DT1141/TT791), 2b.

38. Ibid., 13a–b.

39. The poem reads: "Sir He the Master Uncle, after ascending to the mists, was strange, marvelous, and truly unusual. He healed the friend of the Tao Sir Zhang of Lintong, who was facing certain death. Divine immortals do not seek rewards from people. They only wish that people of virtue will turn their heads, repent, and become enlightened. Who would have known that you (Sir Zhang) would come from afar to Difei (the Zhongnan mountains), [only to] burn incense and hastily leave? [Hereby] I write a short poem to persuade you. Even though death may cause you to depart, you should quickly wave your sleeves. Subdue your mind and cultivate yourself outside objects, and make the tiger and dragon copulate. One morning your deeds and merit will be full, and the nine-cycle elixir will be completed. With your spiritual light radiating, you mount a phoenix and return to say thanks to the Master for rescuing you" (*Danyang shenguang can*, 13b–14a).

40. *Qizhen nianpu*, 12a–b.

41. *Lishi zhenxian tidao tongjian xupian*, 1/21b–22a; *Jinlian zhengzong ji*, 3/11a–b, "Quanzhen di'erdai Danyang baoyi wuwei zhenren Ma zongshi daoxing bei," in *Daojia jinshi lüe*, p. 639.

42. *Jinlian zhengzong ji* mentions as many as four such incidents.

43. *Lishi zhenxian tidao tongjian xupian*, 1/22b. The same incident also is recorded in *Jinlian zhengzong ji*, 3/12b, and *Qizhen nianpu*, 12b.

44. *Yunguang ji*, 2/4b.

45. *Jinlian zhengzong ji*, 3/10b.

46. See *Qizhen nianpu*, 6a–7a.

47. *Jinlian zhengzong ji*, 2/4b.

48. The three topknots represent the three *ji* 吉 that make up the character for Wang Zhe's personal name.

49. See *Jinlian zhengzong ji*, 2/4b, and Li Daoqian, *Zhongnan shan zuting xianzhen neizhuan* (DT949/TT604), 1/6a. The latter account does not mention Ma's possessing an identical painting.

50. *Chongyang quanzhen ji*, 2/7a.

51. See Kubo, *Chûgokû*, 132–33.

52. *Qizhen nianpu*, 9a.

53. *Chongyang quanzhen ji*, 2/8a.

54. Ma Yu proposed that they drink together. When Shi Chuhou took out some money to try to purchase some wine, Ma Yu demanded that he go begging in the streets to acquire money to puchase wine. Shi Chuhou complied, after which Ma Yu alone drank the wine.

55. See "Zhongnan shan shenxian Chongyangzi Wang zhenren Quanzhen jiaozu bei," in *Daojiao jinshi lüe*, p. 451; *Lishi zhenxian tidao tongjian xupian*, 1/4a; *Jinlian zhengzong xianyuan xiangzhuan*, 24a. *Jinlian zhengzong ji* (3/4a–b) gives a significantly different version of the incident. There we are told that Ma Yu had a dream of two cranes alighting in his garden, whereupon he built a Taoist monastery and had a certain Taoist Lu preside there.

56. *Jinlian zhengzong ji*, 5/4a.

57. *Qizhen nianpu*, 14a.

58. Ibid., 16b.

59. "Yuyang tixuan guangdu zhenren Wang zongshi daoxing bei bing xu," in *Daojia jinshi lüe*, p. 719.

60. *Tixuan zhenren xianyi lu*, 10a–11a.

61. *Yunguang ji*, 2/34b.

62. Ibid., 2/27a–b.

63. Ibid., 3/16a–b.

64. *Panxi ji*, 4/3b.

65. "Zhongnan shan shenxian Chongyangzi Wang zhenren Quanzhen jiaozu bei," in *Daojia jinshi lüe*, p. 452.

66. *Panxi ji*, 3/3a.

67. Ibid., 3/3a–b.

68. *Jinlian zhengzong ji*, 3/5b.

69. This probably refers to water into which the ashes of a burnt paper talisman are mixed.

70. *Jinlian zhengzong ji*, 3/10a.

71. Ibid., 3/7b.

72. Ibid., 3/8a–9b.

73. Ibid., 5/3b–4a.

74. *Tixuan zhenren xianyi lu*, 11a–b.

75. *Dongxuan jinyu ji*, 1/22a–b.

76. Ibid.

77. *Dongxuan jinyu ji*, 1/23a–b.

78. *Panxi ji*, 4/1a–2a.

79. *Jinlian zhengzong ji*, 3/8a. A similar incident pertaining to Liu Chuxuan is recorded in *Qizhen nianpu*, 12b.

80. *Dongxuan jinyu ji*, 4/1a–b.

## Chapter 7

1. "Zhongnan shan shenxian Chongyangzi Wang zhenren Quanzhen jiaozu bei," in *Daojia jinshi lüe*, p. 452.

2. *Lishi zhenxian tidao tongjian xupian*, 1/10a. According to *Jinlian zhengzong ji*, Wang Zhe said, "In the past, the Master-Realized One in the woolen garment secretly told me, 'When the Nine Cycles are accomplished, enter the Southern Capital (Bianjing). Acquire some friends, and go to Penglai.' I am now going to keep this promise" (2/7b).

3. *Qizhen nianpu*, 9a.

4. The tentative translation is based on Hachiya's interpretation, according to which the sun and moon, respectively, refer to the primal spirit (consciousness) and primal *qi* (vitality) that the Taoist practitioner nurtures and harmonizes in order to recover the Real Nature/Radiant Spirit. See Hachiya, *Kindai*, 54–55.

5. *Qizhen nianpu*, 6b; *Lishi zhenxian tidao tongjian xupian*, 1/10a; *Chongyang quanzhen ji*, 9/16b.

6. "Zhongnan shan shenxian Chongyangzi Wang zhenren Quanzhen jiaozu bei," in *Daojia jinshi lüe*, p. 452.

7. *Lishi zhenxian tidao tongjian xupian*, 1/10a; *Jinlian zhenzong xianyuan xiangzhuan*, 22a.

8. *Lishi zhenxian tidao tongjian xupian*, 1/10a.

9. *Lishi zhenxian tidao tongjian xupian*, 1/10a–b; *Jinlian zhengzong ji*, 2/7b; *Chongyang Quanzhen ji*, 1a–b.

10. According to one source, Wang Zhe's initial death and revival occurred late in the twelfth month of the Dading 9, and his second, final death took place some days later, on 1/4/Dading 10. See "Zhongnan shan shenxian Chongyangzi Wang zhenren Quanzhen jiaozu bei," in *Daojia jinshi lüe*, p. 452.

11. "Zhongnan shan Chongyang zushi xianji ji," in *Daojia jinshi lüe*, p. 461.

12. There we are told that the four top disciples discovered that this was the case when they were in the process of transferring their master's coffin from Bianjing to Liujiang for reburial at the site at his old hermitage. See *Jinlian zhengzong ji*, 2/7b.

13. The Jasper Pond (Yaochi) is a pond located atop the legendary western mountain of immortality Mt. Kunlun, the dwelling of the Queen Mother of the West (Xiwangmu).

14. The Three Realms (*sanjie*, a concept borrowed from Buddhism) are the Realm of Desires (*yujie*), the Realm of Forms (*sejie*), and the Realm of No Forms (*wusejie*). The Realm of Desires, where ordinary mortals dwell, is the most wretched realm that also includes the hells and the lower heavens. The latter two realms encompass heavenly realms that are pure and sublime above our imagination, yet still are within the range where the laws of karma and rebirth hold sway.

15. *Lishi zhenxian tidao tongjian houji*, 6/18b.

16. Ibid., 6/18a–b.

17. See *Jinlian zhengzong ji*, 3/10a, 5/10b–11a; *Jinlian zhengzong xianyuan xiangzhuan*, 42b.

18. The *Zhuangzi* (ch. 18) relates that when Zhuang Zhou's wife died, his friend, Hui Shi (the logician), went to console him, only to find him "lolling on the floor with his legs sprawled out, beating a basin and singing." (see Victor Mair, trans., *Wandering on the Way: Early Taoist Tales and Parables of the* Chuang-tzu [Honolulu: University of Hawaii Press, 1998], 168.)

19. *Lishi zhenxian tidao tongjian xupian*, 1/21b; "Quanzhen di'erdai Danyang baoyi wuwei zhenren Ma zongshi daoxing bei," in *Daojia jinshi lüe*, p. 640. The poem in its entirety can be found in *Dongxuan jinyu ji*, 6/8b–9a.

20. *Lishi zhenxian tidao tongjian xubian*, 1/21b–22a; *Jinlian zhengzong ji*, 3/11a–b, "Quanzhen di'erdai Danyang baoyi wuwei zhenren Ma zongshi daoxing bei," in *Daojia jinshi lüe*, p. 640.

21. *Lishi zhenxian tidao tongjian xubian*, 1/21b–22a; *Jinlian zhengzong ji*, 3/11a–b, "Quanzhen di'erdai Danyang baoyi wuwei zhenren Ma zongshi daoxing bei," in *Daojia jinshi lüe*, p. 640.

22. *Jinlian zhengzong xianyuan xiangzhuan*, 26a.

23. Zhang Ziyi, "Danyang zhenren Ma gong dengzhen ji," in *Daojia jinshi lüe*, p. 433.

24. *Jinlian zhengzong ji*, 3/12b. This incident also is recorded in *Lishi zhenxian tidao tongjian xupian*, 1/22b–23a.

25. One is compelled here to think of Western parallels. What comes to mind here is the biblical account relating how the authorities suspected that Jesus' followers might steal his body from his tomb (Matthew 27: 62–66). What also comes to mind is Dostoevsky's *The Brothers Karamazov* ("The Breath of Corruption," pp. 305–15 [New york: Barnes and Noble Books, 1995]), where the rapid decay of Father Zossima's body causes embarrassment and disillusionment among his faithful.

26. "Changchun zhenren benxing bei," in *Daojia jinshi lüe*, p. 457. Similar accounts are given in *Lishi zhenxian tidao tongjian xupian*, 2/21a–22a; *Jinlian zhengzong ji*, 4/12a; Li Zhichang, *Changchun zhenren xiyou ji* (DT1417/TT1056). The latter two sources claim that the amazing burial incident took place *three* years after his death.

27. "Changchun zhenren benxing bei," in *Daojia jinshi lüe*, p. 457; *Changchun zhenren xiyou ji*.

28. Most likely this was a Taoist shrine dedicated to and named after the immortal Lü Yan.

29. *Lishi zhenxian tidao tongjian shubian* (2/4b–5a).

30. "Changzhenzi Tan zhenren xianji beiming," in *Daojia jinshi lüe*, p. 455.

31. This is the monastery built on the site where Wang Zhe, He Dejin, and Li Lingyang had lived alongside each other in grass huts. The monastery, known currently as the Chongyang Gong, still stands there today and is once again active.

32. *Zhongnan shan zuting xianzhen neizhuan*, 1/3b–4a; *Jinlian zhengzong ji*, 2/13a–b.

33. Wang E., "Xiyun zhenren Wang zunshi daoxing bei," in *Daojia jinshi lüe*, p. 563.

34. Although Li Lingyang's age at his death is not known, his date of birth was likely close to Wang Zhe's. If so, this means that he would have been in his mid to late seventies when he died.

35. See Padmanabh S. Jaini, *The Jaina Path of Purification* (Berkeley: University of California Press, 1979), 228–33.

36. See George J. Tanabe Jr., "The Founding of Mt. Kôya and Kûkai's Eternal Meditation," in *Religions of Japan in Practice*, ed. George J. Tanabe Jr. (Princeton: Princeton University Press, 1999), 354–59.

37. See Uryû Naka and Shibuya Nobuhiro, *Nihon shûkyô no subete* (Tokyo: Nihon Bungeisha, 1996), 142–43.

38. Needham, *Science and Civilization in China*, vol. 5, no. 2, 299–301. Over fifty cases of self-mummification are recorded in Chinese Buddhist literature, almost all of whom were Buddhists. Some were very famous figures such as the Tiantai master, Zhiyi (d. 597 or 598), the Indian Esoteric master, Subhakarasimha (d. 735), and the sixth Chan Patriarch, Huineng (638–713). Huineng's mummy is reportedly still kept intact at the Caoxi Nanhua Si Temple in Jiujiang, Guangdong Province. The earliest known mummified Taoist is Shan Daokai, who hailed from Dunhuang (Gansu Province) and died in Guangzhou (Guangdong Province) in 359.

Holmes Welch has reported on some modern cases of Buddhist self-mummification (or attempts at it) in Taiwan and Hong Kong. See *The Practice of Chinese Buddhism* (Cambridge: Harvard University Press, 1967), 342–45.

39. See Hachiya, *Kindai*, 322. In claiming that Ma Yu was extremely gaunt in physique, Hachiya cites the same poem that I quoted in chapter 4.

40. *Lishi zhenxian tidao tongjian houji*, 6/3a–6b.

41. *Lishi zhenxian tidao tongjian*, 48/18b–20b.

42. Needham, *Science and Civilization in China*, vol. 5, no. 2, 299–301.

43. *Zhenxian zhizhi yulu*, 1/13a.

44. See Edward Conze, *Buddhism: Its Essence and Development* (New Delhi: Munshiram Manoharlal Press, 1999), 105–14; Nanamoli and Bodhi, "Introduction," *The Middle Length Discourses of the Buddha: A New Translation of the Majjhima Nikaya*, 38–41.

45. *Panshan xiyun Wang zhenren yulu*, 37a–b.

46. This phrase appears in *Jin zhenren yulu*, 1a.

47. *Panshan xiyun Wang zhenren yulu*, 10b–11a.

48. Ibid., 11b–12b.

## Chapter 8

1. *Dongxuan jinyu ji*, 3/12a.

2. Ibid., 1/1b.

3. *Jinlian zhengzong ji*, 1/8b.

4. *Wuwei qingjing changsheng zhenren zhizhen yulu*, 25a.

5. On the mythology of the Lingbao movement, see Eskildsen, *Asceticism*, 105–21.

6. One *li* during the period in question was equal to 552.96 meters.

7. *Jinlian zhengzong ji*, 4/13a–14a.

8. *Panxi ji*, 1/9a–b.

9. Ibid., 3/10a.

10. Ibid., 2/6b.

11. *Dongxuan jinyu ji*, 7/17a–b. Evidence of this type of activity also is found in Wang Chuyi's *Yunguang ji* (4/6a–b). There we find a poem that bears the heading "Directing my disciples to go to Wendeng to administer to the needs of the poor." The poem is addressed to three men, Peng, Li, and Liu. The charitable project (referred to as a *shepinhui* or "gathering for administering to the needs of the poor") to which he dispatched his disciples appears to have taken place in the winter and to have primarily involved cooking grain to feed to the poor. Wang Chuyi exhorts the men to bravely face the wind and snow and not to shirk the labor of hauling firewood and water.

12. For some examples of stories of this sort dating back to the early centuries of the Common Era, see Eskildsen, *Asceticism*, 19–20, 84.

13. *Chunyang dijun shenhua miaotong ji*, 3/5b–6b.

14. From "Chongyang zushi xiuxian liaoxing bijue," in *Jin zhenren yulu*, 5b–6a.

15. Chen Shike, "Changchun zhenren benxing bei," in *Daojia jinshi lüe*, p. 458.

16. *Chongyang quanzhen ji*, 3/3b.

17. This term (of Buddhist origin) refers to rebirth in purgatory, rebirth as an animal, and rebirth as a hungry ghost.

18. *Panxi ji*, 6/10b.

19. *Chongyang quanzhen ji*, 3/16a.

20. *Dongxuan jinyu ji*, 1/16b.

21. *Chongyang quanzhen ji*, 10/14b.

22. *Shuiyun ji* (DT1151/TT798), 1/18b–19a.

23. *Dongxuan jinyu ji*, 8/16a–b.

24. A transliteration of the Buddhist Sanskrit term *sabha*, which refers to the wretched realm of reincarnation and suffering that we inhabit.

25. *Yunguang ji*, 1/3a–b.

26. Ibid., 1/1b–2a.

## Chapter 9

1. The money referred to here is most likely the mock currency made of paper that is burned and offered to the gods in Taoist or popular rituals. This practice continues up to the present day.

2. Also known as Mt. Luofeng, this mountain is said to be the location of a subterranean realm of the dead that contains six hells. An actual mountain by this name is located in Sichuan Province.

3. The "pacing of the void" is a standard procedure in Taoist rituals in which the priests circumambulate the altar while chanting verses addressed to the gods and immortals.

4. There is a river by this name that runs through Hebei Province; this perhaps is what is being referred to here.

5. *Panxi ji*, 3/12a–b.

6. The term *jiao* (the character for which contains the liquor radical) has been used since ancient times to denote various types of rituals that involve offering and/or drinking alcoholic beverages. In the Taoist religion, it denotes a large-scale ritual officiated by ordained Taoist priests, and it lasts multiple days.

7. *Chongyang quanzhen ji*, 12/9b–10a.

8. It is unclear whether the inner demons are to be conquered strictly through one's personal training regimen outside of the ritual arena, or whether the ritual method here contains preliminary procedures for capturing the "corpses and worms."

9. *Chongyang quanzhen ji*, 11/3a.

10. The meaning of this verse is unclear. "Medicine spoon" is frequently used in external and internal alchemy when speaking of some potion so powerful that just a spoonful works wonders. In internal alchemy, this potion is sometimes none other than the saliva that wells up in the mouth and brings on a cooling, refreshing, and nourishing effect.

11. *Chongyang quanzhen ji*, 6/4a–b. These two poems are "hidden head" (*zangtou*) poems, meaning that they have been written with the first character of each verse deleted. The reader (or listener) has to figure out what the missing character is but also is provided with a hint—the missing character is one formed out of a portion of the character (or is the same character) used at the end of the previous verse. The Ching Chung Taoist Church of Hong Kong has published an edition of *Chongyang quanzhen ji* in which the missing characters in "hidden head" poems are filled in and indicated in parentheses. I have based my translation on this edition. This edition also includes *Chongyang jiaohua ji*, *Chongyang fenli shihua ji*, *Chongyang zhenren jinguan yusuo jue*, *Ma Ziran jindan koujue*, and *Chongyang zhenren shou Danyang ershisi jue*.

12. *Chongyang quanzhen ji*, 3/15b–16a.

13. Apparently Ma Yu here is comparing his master's profound wisdom to that of the venerable commentary to the *Yi jing* (Book of Changes).

14. Fufeng is the place in Shaanxi from which Ma Yu's ancestors had originally hailed. See *Lishi zhenxian tidao tongjian*, 1/12a.

15. *Chongyang jiaohua ji*, 1/5b–6a. These poems are "hidden head" (*zangtou*) poems.

16. Hachiya surmises that this refers to a certain Dong Defu, who was magistrate of either Xianyang or Zhongnan. See Hachiya, *Kindai*, 63.

17. *Chongyang quanzhen ji*, 2/7a–b.

18. See Hachiya, *Kindai*, 63.

19. *Dongxuan jinyu ji*, 1/12b.

20. Ibid., 4/12b.

21. *Jiachi* (Jap., *kaji*) is a term commonly used to refer to the special ritual procedures (chants [mantras ], hand gestures [mudras], and visualizations) employed by Tantric Buddhist monks and priests.

22. This appears to be the same Mr. Ma who burned thousands of debt statements for grain that he had lent to the poor, after witnessing the mirages brought on by the arrival of Ma Yu. His home was in Huang County in Shandong.

23. *Dongxuan jinyu ji*, 3/20a.

24. This is another word commonly used to denote Taoist rituals. It originally referred to the ritual purification and abstention observed since ancient times on occasions of certain state, popular, and ancestral rituals. See Eskildsen, *Asceticism*, 112–21.

25. *Dongxuan jinyu ji*, 6/4a–b.

26. *Qizhen nianpu*, 11b. See also Hachiya, *Kindai*, 290.

27. *Qizhen nianpu*, 12a. See also Hachiya, *Kindai*, 307.

28. *Dongxuan jinyu ji*, 8/3b.

29. Ibid., 7/16b.

30. *Xianyue ji*, 2/4a.

31. Ibid., 3/8a–b.

32. Ibid., 3/2b.

33. Ibid., 3/3b.

34. Ibid., 4/7a.

35. *Panxi ji*, 1/13a.

36. Ibid., 6/12b–13a.

37. This seems to refer to a governmental or clerical administrator of some importance.

38. *Yunguang ji*, 2/16a.

39. Ibid., 2/28a.

40. Ibid.

41. This most likely refers to the active members of the congregations, including the older leading members as well as the younger novice members.

42. *Danyang zhenren yulu*, 14a–b.

43. One does wonder why these people were so surprised to hear about the austere lifestyle of Ma Yu and his disciples. One would think that they would have known about this characteristic of the Quanzhen clergy if they were indeed members of a congregation started by Wang Zhe. Perhaps during the decade or so following Wang Zhe's death, the five congregations had been left without much clerical supervision.

44. Liu Chuxuan, *Huangdi yinfu jing zhu*, 9b–10a.

45. In this context, this probably means to abstain from sexual activity.

46. *Xianyue ji*, 3/1b.

47. Ibid., 3/15a.

48. Ibid., 4/17b.

49. *Panxi ji*, 3/9a–b.

50. Ibid., 6/11a.

51. *Dongxuan jinyu ji*, 7/13b.

52. Ibid., 2/1a.

53. *Xianyue ji*, 3/4b.

54. This presumably refers to the six forms of existence in *samsara* (borrowed, of course, from Buddhism): (1) god; (2) Titanic being (*asura*); (3) human; (4) hungry ghost; (5) beast; (6) denizen of purgatory.

55. *Xianyue ji*, 3/6b–7a.

56. See Davis, *Society and the Supernatural in Suny China*, 21–66.

57. See "Shangqing beiji tianxin zhengfa", in *Taishang zhuguo jiumin zongzhen biyao* (DT1215/TT986-987), 1/3a.

58. This famous text was studied and drawn upon for inspiration by a Taoist religious sect, the Taiping Dao, or Way of Great Peace. Led by faith healer Zhang Jue, this sect orchestrated the famous Yellow Turban Revolt in 184. Although suppressed within a year, this revolt was instrumental in the destabilization and ultimate collapse of the Han dynasty. See Isabelle Robinet, *Taoism: Growth of a Religion* (Stanford: Stanford University Press, 1997), 53–55. Taoists in subsequent periods have disowned and denounced Zhang Jue and the Yellow Turban Revolt but have nevertheless held the *Taiping jing* and Gan Ji in high esteem.

59. Zhang Daoling was the semilegendary founder of the Tianshi Dao or Heavenly Masters School of Taoism. Along with the Way of Great Peace, the Heavenly Masters School is one of the two earliest organized Taoist religious movements known to modern scholars. Although it never staged a revolt against the Han dynasty, the Heavenly Masters School—led by Zhang Daoling's grandson, Zhang Lu—ruled over an autonomous religious and political state in western China (parts of present-day Sichuan and Shaanxi) for roughly thirty years up until 215. (See Robinet, *Taoism*, 53–77.) The Heavenly Masters School continues to exist today, headed by a Zhang family lineage that claims direct, unbroken descent from Zhang Daoling. Known also as the Zhengyi or Orthodox Unity School, it nominally includes within its fold ordained, householding Taoist priests of various smaller factions and lineages.

60. Wang Zuan was a Taoist of Mt. Maji in Jintan, in present-day Jiangsu Province. During the final years of the Western Jin period (265–316), during a severe epidemic, Wang Zuan is said to have prayed and presented memorials to Heaven. The Most High Lord of the Tao then allegedly appeared to him and presented him with a lengthy text, the *Taishang dongyuan shenzhou jing*. (See Ren Jiyu, *Daozang tiyao*, 1189.) *Taishang dongyuan shenzhou jing* is preserved in the Taoist Canon (DT334/TT170-173), and a full-length monograph in French has been devoted to it. (See Christine Mollier, *Une apocalypse taoïste du Ve siecle* [Paris: Institut des Hautes Etudes Chinoises, 1990].)

61. These alleged revelations took place in 415 and 423. Kou Qianzhi (d. 448), declaring himself the new Heavenly Master, set out to institute the Xin Tianshi Dao, or New Heavenly Masters School, and to purge the Heavenly Masters School of Taoism of practices that he considered corrupt (e.g., sexual rites, hereditary priestly succession, mandatory taxation of members). Emperor Taiwudi of the Turkic Northern Wei dynasty, who then ruled northern China, adopted Kou Qianzhi's new Taoism as the national religion and proceeded to brutally persecute Buddhism in 446. (See Robinet, *Taoism*, 74–77; Ch'en, *Buddhism in China*, 147–51.)

62. *Xuanfeng qinghui lu*, 4a.

63. See Ren Jiyu, *Zhongguo daojiao shi*, 474.

64. This admiration for Lin Lingsu has previously been noted by Kubo Noritada. See Kubo, *Chûgoku*, 158.

65. *Xuanfeng qinghui lu*, 6a.

## Chapter 10

1. See *Daojiao yishu*, 1/3a-8a. This text, in a section bearing the heading "Dharma Body," quotes passages from various medieval Taoist scriptures referring to various bodies in which the Tao manifests itself in order to benefit and guide sentient beings. On the Buddhist theories of the Three Bodies, see ch. 6, note 3.

2. See Ren Jiyu, *Zhongguo daojiao shi*, 646–72 (this portion of the book is written by Chen Bing). On the rise of the Longmen faction under the Qing, also see Monica Esposito, "Longmen Taoism in Qing China: Doctrinal Ideal and Local Reality," *Journal of Chinese Religions* 29 (2001): 191–232; Livia Kohn, ed., "Daoism in the Qing (1644–1911)," *Daoism Handbook* (Leiden: E. J. Brill, 2000), 623–57.

3. To my knowledge, there are only a few places in China today where one can view old, impressive specimens of Taoist architecture, painting, or sculpture. Mt. Wudang (Hubei Province) features a building on its summit that dates back to the Yuan period, and its main sanctuaries and beautiful statues also are centuries old. The Xuanmiao Guan temple in Suzhou houses gigantic bronze statues of the Three Pure Ones (*sanqing*, the supreme Taoist trinity of Yuanshi Tianzun, Taishang Daojun, and Taishang Laojun) that date back to the Song period. The Yongle Gong monastery (Ruicheng, Shanxi Province) is famous for its Yuan-period frescoes depicting supreme Taoist deities and the legendary exploits of Lü Yan and Wang Zhe (the images once housed in its buildings were destroyed).

On the cruelties suffered by Taoist clergy during the Cultural Revolution, see Li Yangzheng, ed., *Dangdai daojiao* (Beijing: Dongfang Chubanshe, 2000), 67–70.

4. Householding Taoist priests of various lineages and factions nominally belong to this school, which claims provenance from the Heavenly Masters School of the second century. See ch. 9, note 58.

5. By "priest," I refer to the non-monastic, householding clergy of the loosely organized Zhengyi School.

6. The sources for this discussion of Taoism in modern times are Qing Xitai, *Zhongguo daojiao shi*, vol. 4, 479–518 (written by Tang Dachao and Bo Dengji); Li Yangzheng, *Dangdai daojiao*, 38–146.

7. These first three men are cited for having helped establish the Han dynasty and for propagating the "non-active governance of Huang-Lao."

8. This famous hero of the *Sanguo yanyi* (Romance of the Three Kingdoms) is lauded for ably overseeing the governance of the Three Kingdoms Shu state.

9. Wei Zheng, who served as prime minister of Taizong, who is widely regarded as the greatest of the Tang emperors.

10. Sun Simiao was the famous physician who flourished in the early Tang period. He is frequently referred to as the "King of Medicines" (Yao Wang).

11. Liu Bowen served as an advisor to Taizu (Zhu Yuanzhang), the founding emperor of the Ming dynasty.

12. Monasteries, Taoist and Buddhist, are today expected to support themselves on money earned through various side ventures, such as the operation of tourist hostels, restaurants, and medical clinics, or the production of commodities, such as wine or handicrafts. Rural monasteries that are not tourist destinations support themselves by cultivating their own agricultural fields. Prior to the land reforms of the Communist government, it was common for monasteries to have large landholdings, the rent income from which constituted their primary source of revenue. In light of this fact, one needs to question whether and to what degree mendicancy continued to be considered mandatory after the early years of the Quanzhen movement. Once the movement gained large landholdings, begging would have made sense only as a means of fostering humility and would have been largely unnecessary as a means of sustenance.

13. See Li Yangzheng, *Dangdai daojiao*, 187–98.

# Bibliography

## Secondary Sources in English and French

Baldrian-Hussein, Farzeen. "Lü Tung-pin in Northern Sung Literature." *Cahiers d'Extreme Asie* 5 (1989–1990): 133–69.

———. *Procedes secrets du joyaux magique: Traite d'alchimie taoiste du Xie siecle.* Paris: Les deux oceans, 1984.

Bokenkamp, Stephen R. *Early Daoist Scriptures.* With a contribution by Peter Nickerson. Berkeley: University of California Press, 1997.

Boltz, Judith. *A Survey of Taoist Literature: Tenth to Seventeenth Centuries.* Berkeley: Institute for East Asian Studies, 1987.

Ch'en, Kenneth. *Buddhism in China: A Historical Survey.* Princeton: Princeton University Press, 1964.

Cleary, Thomas. *Immortal Sisters: Secret Teachings of Taoist Women.* Boston: Shambhala, 1989.

Conze, Edward. *Buddhism: Its Essence and Development.* New Delhi: Munshiram Manoharlal Press, 1999. (First published in 1951 [Oxford: Bruno Casirer].)

———. *Buddhist Scriptures.* London: Penguin, 1959.

Davis, Edward L. *Society and the Supernatural in Song China.* Honolulu: University of Hawaii Press, 2001.

Dostoevsky, Fyodor (1821–1881). *The Brothers Karamazov.* New York: Barnes and Noble Books, 1995.

Dumoulin, Heinrich. *Zen Buddhism: A History.* Vol. 1. Translated from German by James W. Heisig and Paul Knitter. New York: Macmillan, 1994, 1988.

Eskildsen, Stephen. "Asceticism in Ch'üan-chen Taoism." *B.C. Asian Review* 3–4 (1990): 153–91.

———. *Asceticism in Early Taoist Religion.* Albany: State University of New York Press, 1998.

———. "The Beliefs and Practices of Early Ch'üan-chen Taoism." Master's thesis, University of British Columbia, 1989.

———. "Early Quanzhen Daoist Views on the Causes of Disease and Death." *B.C. Asian Review* 6 (1992): 53–70.

———. "*Neidan* Master Chen Pu's Nine Stages of Transformation." *Monumenta Serica* 49 (2001): 1–31.

———. "Seeking 'Signs of Proof': Visions and Other Trance Phenomena in Early Quanzhen Taoism." *Journal of Chinese Religions* 29 (2001): 139–60.

———. "Severe Asceticism in Early Daoist Religion." Ph.D. diss., University of British Columbia, 1994.

Esposito, Monica. "Daoism in the Qing (1644–1911)." In *Daoism Handbook*, edited by Livia Kohn, 623–57. Leiden: E. J. Brill, 2000.

———. "Longmen Taoism in Qing China: Doctrinal Ideal and Local Reality." *Journal of Chinese Religions* 29 (2001): 191–232.

Fairbank, John King. *China: A New History.* Cambridge: Belknap Press of Harvard University Press, 1992.

Goossaert, Vincent. "Entre quatre murs: Un ermite taoïste du XIIe siècle et la question de la modernite." *Toung Pao* 85 (1999): 391–418.

———. "The Invention of an Order: Collective Identity in Thirteenth-Century Quanzhen Taoism." *Journal of Chinese Religions* 29 (2001): 111–38.

———. "La creation du taoïsme moderne: L'ordre Quanzhen." Ph.D diss., Ecole Pratique des Hautes Etudes, Section des Sciences Religieuses, 1997.

———. "Poemes taoïstes des cinq veilles." *Etudes chinoises* 19: 1–2 (spring–autumn 2000): 249–70.

Jaini, Padmanabh S. *The Jaina Path of Purification.* Berkeley: University of California Press, 1979.

Jordan, David, and Daniel Overmyer. *The Flying Phoenix: Aspects of Chinese Sectarianism in Taiwan.* Princeton: Princeton University Press, 1986.

Katz, Paul R. *Images of the Immortal: The Cult of Lü Dongbin at the Palace of Eternal Joy.* Honolulu: University of Hawaii Press, 1999.

Kohn, Livia, ed. *Daoism Handbook.* Leiden: E. J. Brill, 2000.

———. ed. *The Taoist Experience: An Anthology.* Albany: State University of New York Press, 1993.

Mair, Victor, trans. *Wandering on the Way: Early Taoist Tales and Parables of the* Chuang-tzu. Honolulu: University of Hawaii Press, 1998.

Marsone, Pierre. "The Accounts of the Foundation of the Quanzhen Movement: A Hagiographic Treatment of History." *Journal of Chinese Religions* 29 (2001): 95–110.

Mollier, Christine. *Une apocalypse taoïste du Ve siecle.* Paris: Institut des Hautes Etudes Chinoises, 1990.

Nanamoli, Bhikkhu, and Bhikkhu Bodhi, trans. *The Middle Length Discourses of the Buddha: A New Translation of the Majjhima Nikaya.* Boston: Wisdom, 1995.

Needham, Joseph. *Science and Civilization in China.* Vol. 5, no 2. Cambridge: Cambridge University Press, 1974.

———. *Science and Civilization in China.* Vol. 5, no. 4. Cambridge: Cambridge University Press, 1981.

———. *Science and Civilization in China.* Vol. 5, no. 5. Cambridge: Cambridge University Press, 1983.

Poo, Mu-chou (Pu Muzhou 蒲慕州). *In Search of Personal Welfare: A View of Ancient Chinese Religion.* Albany: State University of New York Press, 1998.

Reiter, Florian C. "The Ch'üan-chen Patriarch T'an Ch'u-tuan and the Chinese Talismanic Tradition." *Zeitschrift des deutschen morgenländischen Gesselschaft* 146, part 1 (1996): 139–55.

———. "Ch'ung-yang Sets Forth His Teachings in Fifteen Discourses." *Monumenta Serica* 36 (1984–1985): 33–54.

———. "How Wang Ch'ung-yang, the Founder of Ch'üan-chen Taoism, Achieved Enlightenment." *Oriens* 34 (1994): 497–508.

———. "The Soothsayer, Hao Ta-t'ung (1140–1212), and His Encounter with Ch'üan-chen Taoism." *Oriens Extremus.* No. 28, Part 2 (1981): 198–205.

Robinet, Isabelle. *Introduction à l'alchimie intérieure taoïste: De l'unite et de la multiplicite.* Paris: Le Cerf, 1995.

———. *Taoism: Growth of a Religion.* Translated from French by Phyllis Brooks. Stanford: Stanford University Press, 1997.

Tanabe, George J. Jr. "The Founding of Mt. Kôya and Kûkai's Eternal Meditation." In *Religions of Japan in Practice*, edited by George J. Tanabe Jr., 354–59. Princeton: Princeton University Press, 1999.

Tsui, Bartholomew. *Taoist Tradition and Change: The Story of the Complete Perfection Sect in Hong Kong.* Hong Kong: Hong Kong Christian Study Center on Chinese Religion and Culture, 1991.

Waley, Arthur, trans. *Travels of an Alchemist: The Journey of the Taoist Ch'ang-ch'un from China to the Hindukush at the Summons of Chingiz Khan.* London: George Routeledge and Sons, 1931.

Welch, Holmes. *The Practice of Chinese Buddhism.* Cambridge: Harvard University Press, 1967.

Wile, Douglas. *Art of the Bedchamber: The Chinese Sexual Yoga Classics, including Women's Solo Meditation Texts.* Albany: State University of New York Press, 1992.

Wong, Eva. *Seven Taoist Masters: A Folk Novel of China.* Boston: Shambhala, 1990.

Yampolsky, Philip, trans. *The Platform Sutra of the Sixth Patriarch.* New York: Columbia University Press, 1967.

Yao Tao-chung. 姚道中. "Ch'üan-chen: A New Taoist Sect in North China during the Twelfth and Thirteenth Centuries." Ph.D. diss., University of Arizona, 1980.

———. "Quanzhen: Complete Perfection." In *Daoism Handbook*, edited by Livia Kohn, 567–93. Leiden: E. J. Brill, 2000.

Yoshioka Yoshitoyo. "Taoist Monastic Life." In *Facets of Taoism: Essays in Chinese Religion*, edited by Holmes Welch and Anna Seidel, 229–52. New Haven: Yale University Press, 1977.

## Secondary Sources in Chinese

Chen Bing. 陳兵. "Lüelun quanzhen dao de sanjiao he'i sixiang." 略論全真道的三教合一思想. *Shijie zongjiao yanjiu* 世界宗教研究, 1984-1, 7–21.

Chen Guofu. 陳國符. *Daozang yuanliu kao.* 道藏源流考. Beijing: Zhonghua shuju, 1963.

Chen Junmin. 陳俊民. "Quanzhen daojio sixiang yuanliu kaolüe." 全真道思想源流考略. *Zhongguo zhexue* 中國哲學. 1984-1, 140–68.

Chen Minggui. 陳銘珪. (1824–1881). *Changchun daojiao yuanliu.* 長春道教源流. Taipei: Guangwen Shuju, 1975.

Chen Yuan. 陳垣. *Nansong chu hebei xindaojiao kao.* 南宋初河北新道教考. Beijing: Furen Daxue 1941.

Hu Qide. 胡其德. Wang Chongyang chuang Quanzhen jiao de beijing fenxi." 王重陽創全真教的背景分析. *Taiwan zongjiao xuehui tongxun* 臺灣宗教學會通訊 8 (May 2001): 26–33.

Li Yangzheng 李養正, ed. *Dangdai daojiao.* 當代道教. Beijing: Dongfang Chubanshe, 2000.

Min Zhiting. 閔智亭. *Daojiao yifan.* 道教儀範. Beijing: Zhongguo Daojiao Xueyuan, 1990.

Qing Xitai, ed. 卿希泰. *Zhongguo daojiao shi.* 中國道教史. 4 volumes. Chengdu: Sichuan Renmin Chubanshe, 1996.

Ren Jiyu, ed. 任繼愈. *Daozang tiyao.* 道藏提要. Beijing: Zhongguo Shehui Kexue Chubanshe, 1991.

———, ed. *Zhongguo daojiao shi.* 中國道教史. Shanghai: Shanghai Renmin Chubanshe, 1990.

Wang Shiwei. 王士偉. *Louguan dao yuanliu kao.* 樓觀道源流考. Xi'an: Shaanxi Renmin Chubanshe, 1993.

Yao Congwu. 姚從吾. Jin-Yuan quanzhen jiao de minzu sixiang yu jiushi sixiang." 金元全真教的民族思想與救世思想. *Dongbei shi Luncong* 東北史論叢. 2 (1959): 175–204. Taipei: Zhengzhong Shuju, 1959.

Zhang Guangbao. 張廣保. *Jin-Yuan Quanzhen dao neidan xinxing xue.* 金元全真道內丹心性學. Beijing: Sanlian Shudian, 1995.

Zheng Suchun. 鄭素春. "Jin-Yuan zhi ji Quanzhen daoshi de shengsi guan." 金元之際全真道士的生死觀. *Taiwan zongjiao xuehui tongxun* 8 (May 2001): 34–45.

———. *Quanzhen jiao yu da menggu dishi.* 全真教與大蒙古帝室. Taipei: Taiwan Xuesheng Shuju, 1987.

## Secondary Sources in Japanese

Hachiya, Kunio. 蜂屋邦夫. "Chôyô-shinjin kinkangyokusaketsu ni tsuite." 重陽真人金闕玉鎖訣について. Tôyô Bunka Kenkyûjo Kiyô. 東洋文化研究所紀要 58 (1972): 75–163.

———. *Kindai dôkyô no kenkyû: Ô Chôyô to Ba Tan-yô.* 金代道教の研究：王重陽と馬丹陽. Tôkyô Daigaku Tôyô Bunka Kenkyûjo Hôkoku. Tokyo: Kyûko Shoin, 1992.

Kubo Noritada. 窪德忠. *Chûgoku no shûkyô kaikaku: Zenshin Kyô no seiritsu.* 中國の宗教改革：全真教の成立. Kyoto: Hôzôkan, 1967.

———. *Dôkyô no kamigami.* 道教の神々. Tokyo: Hirakawa Shuppansha, 1986.

———. *Kôshin shinkô no kenkyû* 庚申信仰の研究. Tokyo: Nihon Gakujutsu Shinkôkai, 1961.

———. "Zenshinkyô no seiritsu." 全真教の成立. *Tôyô Bunka Kenkyûjo Kiyô* 東洋文化研究所紀要. 42 (1966): 1–60.

Uryû Naka 瓜生中 and Shibuya Nobuhiro 渋谷申博. *Nihon shûkyô no subete* 日本宗教のすべて. Tokyo: Nihon Bungeisha, 1996.

## Primary Sources from the Taoist Canon (Daozang 道藏)

Anonymous. *Huangdi yinfu jing.* 黄帝陰符經. DT31/TT27. (seventh c. or earlier).

———. *Huangting neijing yujing.* 黄庭內景玉經. DT330/TT167. (ca. fourth c.).

———. *Taishang dongyuan shenzhou jing.* 太上洞淵神咒經. DT334/TT170–173 (ca. fifth c.).

———. *Taishang Laojun neiriyong jing.* 太上老君內日用經. DT640/TT342. (twelfth or thirteenth c.).

———. *Taishang Laojun shuo chang qingjing miaojing.* 太上老君說常清靜妙經. DT615/TT341. (ca. seventh or eighth c.).

———. *Taishang Laojun wairiyong jing.* 太上老君外日用經. DT641/TT342. (twelfth or thirteenth c.).

———. *Taishang xuanling beidou benming yansheng zhenjing*. 太上玄靈北斗本命延生真經. DT617/TT341. (ca. tenth c.).

———. *Tixuan zhenren xianyi lu*. 體玄真人顯異錄. DT589/TT329. (thirteenth c.).

———. *Xiuzhen shishu*. 修真十書. DT262TT122–131. (late thirteenth c.).

Cheng Xuanying. 成玄英. *Nanhua zhenjing zhushu*. 南華真經註疏. DT739/TT519. (seventh c.).

Fu Dongzhen. 傅洞真. *Taishang xuanling beidon benming yansheng zhenjing zhu*. 太上玄靈北斗本命延生真經註. DT746/TT529 (ca. eleventh c.).

Hao Datong (1140–1212). 郝大通. *Taigu ji*. 太古集. DT1152/TT798. (1178).

He Zhiyuan 何志淵, comp. *Chunyang zhenren huncheng ji*. 純陽真人渾成集. DT1045/TT727. (1251).

Heshanggong. 河上公. *Daode zhenjing zhu*. 道德真經註. DT677/TT363. (ca. second–fifth c.).

Ji Zhizhen (1193–1268). 姬志真. *Yunshan ji*. 雲山集. DT1131/TT783–784. (ca. 1250).

Jin Zhenren. 晉真人. *Jin zhenren yulu*. 晉真人語錄. DT1046/TT728. (twelfth century).

Li Daoqian (1219–1296) 李道謙, comp. *Ganshui xianyuan lu*. 甘水仙源錄. DT967/TT611. (1288).

———. *Qizhen nianpu*. 七真年譜. DT174/TT76. (1271).

———. *Zhongnan shan zuting xianzhen neizhuan*. 終南山祖庭仙真內傳. DT949/TT604.

Li Rong. 李榮. *Daode zhenjing zhu*. 道德真經註. DT717/TT430. (seventh c.).

Li Zhichang (1193–1256). 李志常. *Changchun zhenren xiyou ji*. 長春真人西遊記. DT1417/TT1056. (1228).

Liu Chuxuan (1147–1203). 劉處玄. *Huangdi yinfu jing zhu*. 黃帝陰符經註. DT122/TT57. (ca. 1200).

———. *Huangting neijing yujing zhu*. 黃庭內景玉經注. DT400/TT189. (ca. 1200).

———. *Wuwei qingjing changsheng zhenren zhizhen yulu*. 無為清靜長生真人至真語錄. DT1048/TT728. (1202).

———. *Xianyue ji*. 仙樂集. DT1132/TT785. (ca. 1203).

Liu Zhixuan 劉志玄 and Xie Xichan. 謝西蟾. *Jinlian zhengzong xianyuan xiangchuan*. 金蓮正宗仙源像傳. DT173/TT76. (1326).

Ma Yu (1123–1184). 馬鈺. *Danyang shenguang can*. 丹陽神光燦. DT1141/TT791 (ca. 1175).

———. *Danyang zhenren yulu*. 丹陽真人語錄. DT1047/TT728. (ca. 1183).

———. *Danyang zhenren zhiyan*. 丹陽真人直言. DT1222/TT989. (ca. 1175).

———. *Dongxuan jinyu ji*. 洞玄金玉集. DT1140/TT789–790. (compiled late thirteenth c.).

———. *Jianwu ji*. 漸悟集. DT1133/TT786. (ca. 1180).

Meng Anpai. 孟安排. *Daojiao yishu*. 道教義樞. DT1120/TT762. (late seventh c.).

Miao Shanshi. 苗善時. *Chunyang dijun shenhua miaotong ji*. 純陽帝君神化妙通紀. DT304/TT159. (1310).

Qin Zhi'an (1188–1244). 秦志安. *Jinlian zhengzong ji*. 金蓮正宗記. DT172/TT75–76. (1241).

Qiu Chuji (1143–1227). 丘處機. *Panxi ji*. 磻溪集. DT1150/TT797. (1208).

———. (attributed). *Dadan zhizhi*. 大丹直指. DT243/TT115. (compiled late thirteenth c.).

Shi Jianwu 施肩吾. (attributed). *Xishan qunxian huizhen ji*. 西山群仙會真記. DT245/TT116. (ca. 1100).

Tan Chuduan (1123–1185). 譚處端. *Shuiyun ji*. 水雲集. DT1151/TT798. (1187).

Tang Chun. 唐淳 (a.k.a. Jinlingzi 金陵子). *Huangdi yinfu jing zhu*. 黃帝陰符經註. DT121/TT57. (ca. eleventh c.).

Tao Hongjing (456–536). 陶弘景. *Zhen'gao*. 真誥. DT1007/TT637–640. (ca. 500).

Wang Chuyi (1142–1217). 王處一. *Yunguang ji*. 雲光集. DT1143/TT792. (ca. 1217).

Wang Xuanlan. 王玄覽. *Xuanzhu lu*. 玄珠錄. DT1039/TT725. (seventh c.).

Wang Zhe (1113–1170). 王嚞. *Chongyang fenli shihua ji*. 重陽分梨十化集. DT1146/TT796. (compiled 1183).

———. *Chongyang jiaohua ji*. 重陽教化集. DT1145/TT795–796. (compiled 1183).

———. *Chongyang lijiao shiwu lun*. 重陽立教十五論. DT1221/TT989. (ca. 1165).

———. *Chongyang quanzhen ji*. 重陽全真集. DT1144/TT793–795. (compiled ca. 1188).

———. (attributed). *Chongyang zhenren jinguan yusuo jue*. 重陽真人金關玉鎖訣. DT1147/TT796. (ca. 1170).

———. *Chongyang zhenren shou Danyang ershisi jue*. 重陽真人授丹陽二十四訣. DT1149/TT796. (ca. 1170).

Xu Daoling. 徐道齡. *Taishang xuanling beidou benming yansheng zhenjing zhu*. 太上玄靈北斗本命延生真經註. DT744/TT527–528. (1334).

Wang Zhijin (1178–1263). 王志謹. *Panshan xiyun Wang zhenren yulu*. 盤山棲雲王真人語錄. DT1049/TT728. (1247).

Xuanquanzi. 玄全子. *Zhenxian zhizhi yulu*. 真仙直指語錄. DT1244/TT998. (ca. 1300).

———. *Zhuzhen neidan jiyao.* 諸真內丹集要. DT1246/TT999. (ca. 1300).

Xuanyuan Zhenren 玄元真人. *Taishang xuanling beidon benming yansheng zhenjing zhujie.* 太上玄靈北斗本命延生真經註解. DT745/TT528. (ca. 1300).

Yelu Chucai (1190–1244), ed. 耶律楚材. *Xuanfeng qinghui lu.* 玄風慶會錄. DT175/TT76. (1232).

Yin Zhiping (1169–1251). 尹志平. *Baoguang ji.* 葆光集. DT1137/TT787. (ca. 1250).

———. *Qinghe zhenren beiyou yulu.* 清和真人北遊語錄. DT1298/TT1017. (1237).

Yuan Miaozong 元妙宗, comp. *Taishang zhuguo jiumin zongzhen biyao.* 太上助國救民總真秘要. DT1215/TT986–987. (1116).

Zeng Zao 曾慥, comp. *Daoshu.* 道樞. DT1008/TT641–648. (1136).

Zhao Daoyi. 趙道一. *Lishi zhenxian tidao tongjian.* 歷世真仙體道通鑑. DT295/TT139–148. (late thirteenth c.).

———. *Lishi zhenxian tidao tongjian houji.* 後集. DT297/TT150. (late thirteenth c.).

———. *Lishi zhenxian tidao tongjian xupian.* 續篇. DT296/TT149. (late thirteenth c.).

Zhongli Quan (attributed). 鍾離權. *Bichuan zhengyang zhenren lingbao bifa.* 秘傳正陽真人靈寶畢法. DT1181/TT874. (ca. 1100).

Zhu Xiangxian. 朱象先. *Zhongnan shan shuojing tai lidai zhenxian beiji.* 終南山說經臺歷代真仙碑記. DT950/TT605. (ca. 1279).

## Other Primary Sources

Anonymous. *Qizhen zhuan.* 七真傳. (ca. seventeenth c.).

Chen Shike. 陳時可. "Changchun zhenren benxing bei." 長春真人本行碑. In *Daojia jinshi lüe*, edited by Chen Yuan, Chen Zhichao, and Zeng Qingying, 456–58. (1228).

Chen Yuan 陳垣, Chen Zhichao 陳智超, and Zeng Qingying 曾慶瑛, comp. *Daojia jinshi lüe.* 道家金石略. Beijing: Wenwu Chubanshe, 1988.

Daoyuan. 道原. *Jingde chuandeng lu.* 景德傳燈錄. In *Taishô zôkyô.* 大正藏經. (Buddhist Canon), no. 2076, vol. 51 (1004–1007).

Ding Fubao. 丁福保. comp., *Daozang jinghua lu.* 道藏精華錄. Hangzhou: Zhejiang Guji Chubanshe, 1989, 1922.

Ge Hong. 葛洪. (283–364). *Shenxian zhuan.* 神仙傳. In *Daozang jinghua lu,* 道藏精華錄, Vol. 2, edited by Ding Fubao 丁福保 in 1922. Hangzhou: Zhejiang Guji Chubanshe, 1989.

Ji Zhizhen (1193–1268). 姬志真. "Changchun zhenren chengdao bei." 長春真人成道碑. In *Daojia jinshi lüe*, 587–88.

———. "Chongyang zushi kaidao bei." 重陽祖師開道碑. In *Daojia jinshi lüe*, 586–87.

Jia Yu. 賈餓. "Dayuan Qinghe dazongshi Yin zhenren daoxing bei." 大元清和大宗師尹真人道行碑. In *Daojia jinshi lüe*, 680–81. (1295).

Li Daoqian (1219–1296). 李道謙. "Quanzhen diwudai zongshi Changchun yandao zhujiao zhenren neizhuan." 全真第五代宗師長春演道主教真人內傳. In *Daojia jinshi lüe*, 634–37. (1281).

Li Zhiquan (1191–1261). 李志全. "Qinghe yandao xuande zhenren xianji zhi bei." 清和演道玄德真人仙跡之碑. In *Daojia jinshi lüe*, 538–41. (1314).

Liu Zuqian. 劉祖謙. "Zhongnan shan Chongyang zushi xianji ji." 終南山重陽祖師仙跡記. In *Daojia jinshi lüe*, 460–62. (1232).

Qin Zhi'an (1188–1244). 秦志安. "Changsheng zhenren Liu zongshi daoxing bei." 長生真人劉宗師道行碑. In *Daojia jinshi lüe*, 469–70. (between 1224 and 1244).

Shen Qingyai, 沈青崖, Wu Tingxi 吳廷錫, et al. *Shaanxi tongzhi Xu tongzhi.* 陝西通志續通志. Taipei: Huawen Shuju, 1933.

Song Lian. 宋濂. (1310–1381). *Yuan shi.* 元史. Beijing: Zhonghua Shuju, 1976.

Wang E. (1190–1273). 王鶚. "Xiyun zhenren Wang zunshi daoxing bei." 棲雲真人王尊師道行碑. In *Daojia jinshi lüe*, 562–64. (1264).

Wang Liyong (ca. 1231–1307). 王利用. "Quanzhen di'erdai Danyang baoyi wuwei zhenren Ma zongshi daoxing bei." 全真第二代丹陽抱一無為真人馬宗師道行碑. In *Daojia jinshi lüe*, 638–41. (1283).

Wang Yun (1227–1304). 王惲. Dayuan gu Qinghe miaodao guanghua zhenren xuanmen zhangjiao dazongshi Yin gong daoxing beiming bing xu." 大元故清和妙道廣化真人玄門掌教大宗師尹公道行碑銘并序. In *Daojia jinshi lüe*, 689–90. (1297).

Wanyan Shou 完顏璹 (1172–1232). "Changzhenzi Tan zhenren xianji beiming." 長真子譚真人仙跡碑銘. In *Daojia jinshi lüe*, 454–55.

———. "Zhongnan shan shenxian Chongyangzi Wang zhenren Quanzhen jiaozu bei." 終南山神仙重陽真人全真教祖碑. In *Daojia jinshi lüe*, 450–54. (1275).

Xiang Mai. 祥邁. *Zhiyuan bianwei lu.* 至元辯偽錄. *Taishô zôkyô*, Vol. 48, no. 2116 (late thirteenth c.).

Xu Yan (d. 1301). 徐琰. "Guangning tongxuan Taigu zhenren Hao zongshi daoxing bei." 廣寧通玄太古真人郝宗師道行碑. In *Daojia jinshi lüe*, 672–74. (1286).

Yao Sui (1238–1313). 姚燧. "Yuyang tixuan guangdu zhenren Wang zongshi daoxing bei bing xu." 玉陽體玄廣度真人王宗師道行碑并序. In *Daojia jinshi lüe*, 718–20. (1307).

Yi Gou. 弋彀. "Xuanmen zhangjiao Qinghe miaodao guanghe zhenren Yin zongshi beiming bing xu." 玄門掌教清和妙道廣化真人尹宗師碑銘并序. In *Daojia jinshi lüe*, 567–70. (1264).

Yu Yingmao. 俞應卯. "Huxian Qinduzhen chongxiu Zhidao guan bei." 鄠縣秦渡鎮重修志道觀碑. In *Daojia jinshi lüe*, 478–79. (between 1232 and 1289).

Zhang Xiaochun (d. 1144). 張孝純. "Gaoshang chushi xiuzhen ji." 高尚處士修真記. In *Daojia jinshi lüe*, 1007–1009. (1144).

Zhang Zhongshou (b. 1252). 張仲壽. "Danyang zhenren guizang ji." 丹陽真人歸葬記. In *Daojia jinshi lüe*, 740–41. (1313).

Zhang Ziyi. 張子翼. "Danyang zhenren Ma gong dengzhen ji." 丹陽真人馬公登真記. In *Daojia jinshi lüe*, 433–34. (1185).

# Glossary

*an* 庵
*anle* 安樂
Baijia 白家
Baiyun Guan 白雲觀
*bajie* 八節
*bange* 伴哥
*baoshen* 報身
*Beidou jing* 北斗經
Beimang (Mt.) 北邙
*benchu* 本初
*benlai* 本來
Bianjing 汴京
*bing* 丙
Binzhou 濱州
*Biyan lu* 碧巖錄
*budongxin* 不動心
*bulou* 不漏
*buxu* 步虛
Cai Jing 蔡經
Cangzhou 滄州
Cao Can 曹參
Cao Zhen 曹瑱
Caoxi Nanhua Si 曹溪南華寺
Cha (Mt.) 楂
Chan (Zen) 禪
Chang'an 長安
Changchun 長春
Changchun Yandao Zhujiao Zhenren 長春演道主教真人
*Changchun zhenren xiyou ji* 長春真人西遊記
Changsheng 長生
Changsheng Dadijun 長生大帝君
Changyang 昌陽
Changyi (county) 昌邑
Changzhen 長真
Chaoyuan 朝元
Chaoyuan Guan 朝元觀
Chen Luqing 陳旅清
Chen Ping 陳平
Chen Xiyi 陳希夷
Cheng Xuanying 成玄英
Cheng'an 承安
Chi Fashi 遲法師
Chongyang 重陽
Chongyang Gong 重陽宮
*Chongyang jiaohua ji* 重陽教化集
*Chongyang lijiao shiwu lun* 重陽立教十五論
*Chongyang quanzhen ji* 重陽全真集
*Chongyang zhenren jinguan yusuo jue* 重陽真人金關玉鎖訣
Chongzhen 崇真
"Chongzhen pian" 承安
*chou* 丑
*chujia* 出家
Chunyang 純陽
*Chunyang dijun shenhua miaotong ji* 純陽帝君神化妙通紀
*chushen rumeng* 出神入夢
Cizhou 磁州
Da'an 大安
*Dadan zhizhi* 大丹直指
Dadao 大道

Dading 大定
*dantian* 丹田
Danyang 丹陽
*Danyang zhenren yulu* 丹陽真人語錄
Danzao (Mt.) 丹灶
*Daode jing* 道德經
*daoguan* 道觀
*daohao* 道號
*Daojiao yifan* 道教儀範
*daoli* 道力
*daoshi* 道士
*Daoshu* 道樞
*daoyin* 導引
*daoyou* 道友
Daoyuan 道原
*daozhe* 道者
Dawei (village) 大魏
Dazhu Huihai 大珠慧海
*dazuo* 打坐
Dengzhou 登州
Di (Sir) 翟
Difei 地肺
*ding* 丁
Ding (Sir) 丁
*dingwei* 丁未
*dingyou* 丁酉
Dong Defu 董德夫
Dong Qingqi 董清奇
Dongbin 洞賓
Donghua Dijun 東華帝君
Dongmou 東牟
*Dongxuan jinyu ji* 洞玄金玉集
Dongzhou 董州
Dunhuang 敦煌
Erzu 二祖
Fan Mingshu 范明叔
Fangping 方平
Fangzhang 方丈
*fangzhongshu* 房中術
*fashen* 法身
"Feng ru song" 風入松
Feng Xiangu 風仙姑
Fengdu (Mt.) 酆都
*fu* (sixth month) 伏
*fu* (talisman) 符
Fufeng 扶風
*Fuji* 扶乩
*fashui* 法水
Fushan 福山
*fushui* 符水
Gan Ji 干吉
Ganhe 甘河
Gansu 甘肅
*gaogong* 高功
Gaoshang 高尚
*geng* 庚
*gengwu* 庚午
*gengzi* 庚子
*gong* 功
*gong'an* 公案
*gongxing* 功行
Guan (Realized Woman) 關
Guangdong 廣東
Guangning 廣寧
Guangzhou 廣州
*guizhen* 歸真
Guo Heng 郭亨
*gushen busi tiaoxi zhi fa* 谷神不死調息之法
Gushuizhuang 沽水莊
Hachiya Kunio 蜂屋邦夫
Haichan 海蟾
Haifeng 害風
*haitang* 海棠
Han 漢
Hao Datong 郝大通
Hao Sheng 郝昇
He Dejin 和德瑾
Hebei 河北
Henan 河南
Heng (Mt.) 衡
Hengyang 衡陽
Heshanggong 河上公
Hu Qide 胡其德
Hua (Mt.) 華
*huandu* 環堵
Huang (district) 黃
*huanglu* 黃籙
*Huangting neijing jing* 黃庭內景經
Huangtong 皇統

*huanqiang* 環牆
*huashen* 化身
Huating 華亭
Huayang Guan 華陽觀
Huayin 華陰
*hui* 會
Hui Shih 惠施
Huineng 慧能
Huizong 徽宗
*hun* 魂
Hunan 湖南
*jia* 甲
*jia* (provisional) 假
*jiachi* 加持
*jian* 箋
*jiao* (ritual) 醮
*jiao* (teaching) 教
*jiawu* 甲午
*jiazi* 甲子
*jichou* 己丑
*jie* (*kalpa*) 劫
*jin* 津
Jin (Jurchen dynasty) 金
Jin (dynasty, 265–419 C.E.) 晉
Jin Daocheng 晉道成
*Jin zhenren yulu* 晉真人語錄
"Jindan zhengyan" 金丹證驗
*jing* 精
*Jingang jing* 金剛經
*jinggong* 靜功
*jingshen* 精神
Jingzhao 京兆
Jinlian Hui 金蓮會
*Jinlian zhengzong ji* 金蓮正宗記
Jinlingzi 金陵子
*jinshi* 進士
Jintan 金壇
*jisi* 己巳
*jiu daojiao* 舊道教
Jiujiang 九江
Jizhou 薊州
*juan* 卷
Junyi (bridge) 濬儀
Kaifeng 開封
*kan* 坎
Kôbô Daishi 弘法大師
Kou Qianzhi 寇謙之
Kôya (Mt.) 高野
Kubo Noritada 窪德忠
Kûkai 空海
*kun* 坤
Kunlun (Mt.) 崑崙
Kunming (pond) 昆明
Kunyu (Mt.) 崑崳
*la* 臘
Lai Lingyu 來靈玉
Lai Yanzhong 來彥中
Laizhou 萊州
Lan Fang 藍方
Laozi 老子
*Laozi bashiyihua tu* 老子八十一化圖
*Laozi huahu jing* 老子化胡經
*leifa* 雷法
Leng Qi 冷七
*li* (measurement) 里
*li* (trigram) 離
Li Dasheng 李大乘
Li Guan 李觀
*Li ji* 禮記
Li Lingyang 李靈陽
Li Rong 李榮
*li yu fen li* 栗芋分梨
*li yu fen li* 立遇分離
Li Zhichang 李志常
Liao 遼
*Liezi* 列子
Lin 璘
Lin Lingsu 林靈素
Lingbao 靈寶
*Lingbao bifa* 靈寶畢法
Linji Yixuan 臨濟義玄
Linqiong 臨邛
Lintong 臨潼
Liquan 醴泉
*Lishi zhenxian tidao tongjian xubian* 歷世真仙體道通鑑續編
Liu Biangong 劉卞功
Liu Bowen 劉伯溫
Liu Cao 劉操
Liu Chuxuan 劉處玄

Liu Daojian 劉道堅
Liu Deren 劉德仁
Liu Tongwei 劉通微
Liu Zhenyi 劉真一
Liu Zhi 劉植
Liu Zuqian 劉祖謙
Liujiang 劉蔣
*liutong* 六通
Longmen 龍門
Longquan 龍泉
Longxian 隴縣
Longzhou 隴州
*lou* 漏
Lou Daoming 婁道明
Louguan 樓觀
*lu* 籙
Lu Daoren 陸道人
Lü Matong 呂馬通
Lü Yan 呂巖
Luan (Village) 灤
Luan Wujie 欒武節
Luan Zhou 欒周
"Lun baguanjie" 論八關節
"Lun liutong jue" 論六通訣
Luofeng (Mt.) 羅酆
Luofu (Mt.) 羅浮
Luojing 洛京
Luoyang 洛陽
*luqi* (donkey contract) 驢契
*luren* 路人
*ma* 馬
Ma Congyi 馬從義
Ma Gu 麻姑
Ma Jiuguanren 馬九官人
Ma Yu 馬鈺
Maji (Mt.) 馬跡
"Manting fang" 滿庭芳
*mao* 卯
Mao (Mt.) 茅
Miao Shanshi 苗善時
Min Zhiting 閔智亭
Ming (dynasty) 明
*ming* (Life) 命
*ming* (personal name) 名
Mingchang 明昌
Mouping 牟平
*moxingshi* 摩性石
Nanchang 南昌
Nanshi 南時
*nanzong* 南宗
*neidan* 內丹
*neiriyong* 內日用
Nimang Ku 尼厖窟
Ninghai 寧海
Niuxian (Mt.) 牛仙
Niwan 泥丸
*pangmen xiaofa* 旁門小法
*Panshan xiyun Wang zhenren yulu* 盤山棲雲王真人語錄
Panxi 磻溪
*Panxi ji* 磻溪集
Penglai 蓬萊
Pingdeng Hui 平等會
*po* 魄
Pu Canchu 僕散出
*qi* 氣
*qian* 乾
Qiang (Mr.) 強
Qibao Hui 七寶會
*qin* (harp) 琴
Qin 秦
Qin Zhi'an 秦志安
Qindu 秦渡
Qing 清
Qinghe 清和
Qingjing 清靜
*qingjing* (clear and pure) 清淨
*qingjing* (pure and still) 清靜
*Qingjing jing* 清靜經
*qingjing wuwei xiaoyao zizai buran buzhao* 清淨無為逍遙自在不染不著
*qingpin* 清貧
Qingsong Guan 青松觀
Qiu Chuji 丘處機
Qiu Yuanqing 丘元清
Qiyang 岐陽
*Qizhen* 七真
*Qizhen zhuan* 七真傳
Quanzhen 全真
Quanzhen An 全真庵

Ren ("little Immortal") 任
Ren Farong 任法融
Ren Fashi 仁法師
Renzong 仁宗
*rishu* 日書
*riyong* 日用
*roushen* 肉身
"Rui zhegu" 瑞鷓鴣
*ruxiang* 乳香
*sandongzhou* 三冬粥
Sanguang Hui 三光會
*sanjiao* 三教
*sanjie* 三界
Sanqing 三清
Sanyangzi 傘陽子
*sanzhen* 三真
*se* (harp) 瑟
*sejie* 色界
Shaanxi 陝西
Shan Daokai 單道開
Shangqing Gong 上清宮
Shantong 山侗
*shen* 神
*shen'gong* 神功
*sheng* (lute) 笙
*shenguang* 神光
*shengxian* 聖賢
*shenjingtong* 神境通
*shenren* 神人
*shentong* 神通
*shenzutong* 神足通
*shepinhui* 設貧會
Shi (girl's family) 石
Shi Chuhou 史處厚
Shi Jianwu 施肩吾
*shi'e* 十惡
*shijie* 尸解
Shingon (Zhenyan) 真言
*shiseng* 師僧
*shitong* 師童
*shizhen* 師真
Shizong 世宗
Shu 蜀
*si* 巳
Sichuan 四川
*sida* 四大
*sijia* 四假
*sokushin butsu* 即身佛
Song (Mt.) 嵩
Song Defang 宋德方
*sui* 歲
*sumingtong* 宿命通
Sun Bu'er 孫不二
Sun Simiao 孫思邈
*suopo* 娑婆
*suxintong* 宿信通
Taiping Dao 太平道
Taiping Gong 太平宮
*Taiping jing* 太平經
Taishang 太上
Taishang Daojun 太上道君
*Taishang dongyuan shenzhou jing* 太上洞淵神咒經
Taishang Laojun 太上老君
Taiwudi 太武帝
Taiyi 太一
*Taiyi hunyuan zhen falu* 太一混元真法籙
*Taiyi sanyuan falu* 太一三元法籙
Tan Chuduan 譚處端
Tang Chun 唐淳
Tao Hongjing 陶弘景
*taxintong* 他心通
Tiande 天德
*tian'ertong* 天耳通
Tianran 恬然
Tianshi Dao 天師道
Tiantai 天台
*Tianxin zhengfa* 天心正法
*tianyantong* 天眼通
Tixuan Dashi 體玄大師
*Tixuan zhenren xianyi lu* 體玄真人顯異錄
*tong* 通
Tong 通
*tuan* 彖
*tujin* 土津
*waidan* 外丹
*wairiyong* 外日用
Wang Changyue 王常月

Wang Chuyi 王處一
Wang Quan 王筌
Wang Xuanfu 王玄甫
Wang Xuanlan 王玄覽
Wang Yasi 王押司
Wang Yuan 王遠
Wang Zhe 王嚞
Wang Zhijin 王志謹
Wang Zhong 王忠
Wang Zuan 王纂
Wei 魏
Wei Zheng 魏徵
Weizhou 濰州
Weizhou 衛州
Wen Liu 溫六
Wendeng 文登
Wenzhou 溫州
Wozhou 沃州
*wu* 午
Wudang (Mt.) 武當
*wulou* 無漏
*wuloutong* 無漏通
*wuming* (benighted) 無明
*wuming* (nameless) 無名
*wusejie* 無色界
*wuwei* 無為
*wuxu* 戊戌
*wuyue*五嶽
Wuzhen pian 悟真篇
Wuzong 武宗
Xi'an 西安
*xian* 仙
*xianhe* 仙鶴
Xianyang 咸陽
Xiao Baozhen 蕭抱珍
Xiao Daoxi 蕭道熙
*Xiao jing* 孝經
Xiao Sanniang 蕭三娘
*xiaojiao'er* 小角兒
*xiaoxi* 消息
*xin daojiao* 新道教
*Xin jing* 心經
Xin Tianshi Dao 新天師道
*xing* (deeds) 行
*xing* (nature) 性
*xing gang* 性剛
*xinjingtong* 心境通
*Xishan qunxian huizhen ji* 西山群仙會真記
*xiuxing* 修行
Xiuzhen Guan 修真觀
Xiwangmu 西王母
Xixia 西夏
Xiyun 棲雲
Xu Benshan 徐本善
Xu Shaozu 徐紹祖
*Xuandu baozang* 玄都寶藏
*Xuanfeng qinghui lu* 玄風慶會錄
Xuanjing 玄靖
Xuanquanzi 玄全子
Xuanting Gongzhu 玄庭宮主
Xuanyuan 軒轅
*xukong* 虛空
Yan Chuchang 嚴處常
Yan Hui 顏回
*yang* 陽
*yangqi quanshen* 養氣全神
*yangshen* 陽神
*yangzhushen* 陽主神
Yanjiu 燕九
Yanqiu 閹邱
Yanshan 鹽山
Yanxia Dong 煙霞洞
Yaochi 瑤池
*yaokong* 窰埪
*ye* 液
Ye (county) 掖
"Yeyou gong" 夜遊宮
*yi* 乙
*yi ji fang ren* 以己方人
*Yi jing* 易經
*yin* 陰
Yin Xi 尹喜
Yin Zhiping 尹志平
*Yinfu jing* 陰符經
*yingyan* 應驗
Yingzhou 瀛州
*yiren* 異人
*yiwei* 乙未
*you* 酉

Youxian Guan 遊仙觀
Yu Zhiyi 于知一
Yuan (Mongol dynasty) 元
Yuan (Vinaya Master) 源
Yuanshi Tianzun 元始天尊
Yuanwu Keqin 圜悟克勤
Yuchan 玉蟾
Yudi 玉帝
Yuhua Hui 玉花會
Yuhuang 玉皇
*yujie* 欲界
*yulu* 語錄
Yunfang 雲房
Yunguang Dong 雲光洞
*Yunguang ji* 雲光集
Yutian 玉田
Yuyang 玉陽
Zang (Old Man) 臧
*zangtou* 藏頭
*zhai* 齋
Zhang (Mr.) 張
Zhang Boduan 張伯端
Zhang Daoling 張道陵
Zhang Gong 張拱
Zhang Jue 張角
Zhang Liang 張良
Zhang Lu 張魯
Zhan'gu 戰姑
Zhao He 趙何
Zhao Penglai 趙蓬萊
Zhao Xiangu 趙仙姑
Zhejiang 浙江
*zhen* (bird) 鴆
*zhen* (real) 真
Zheng (the lackey) 鄭
*Zhen'gao* 真誥
Zhenghe 政和
Zhenglong 正隆
*zhen'gong* 真功
*Zhengtong daozang* 正統道藏
*zhengyan* 證驗
Zhengyang 正陽
Zhengyi 正一
*zhenjun* 真君
*zhenqi* 真氣
*zhenshen* 真身
*zhenxing* (Real Nature) 真性
*zhenxing* (true deeds) 真行
*zhi* 志
Zhi Erweng 遲二翁
Zhiyang 芝陽
Zhiyi 智顗
*Zhong-Lü chuandao ji* 鍾呂傳道集
*Zhongguo daojiao* 中國道教
Zhongguo Daojiao Xiehui
中國道教協會
Zhongli Quan 鍾離權
Zhongnan (Mt., county) 終南
Zhongtong 中統
Zhou Botong 周伯通
Zhou Deqing 周德清
*zhouhou fei jinjing* (". . . crystals . . .")
肘後飛金晶
*zhouhou fei jinjing* (". . . essence . . .")
肘後飛金精
*zhoutian huohou* 周天火候
Zhu Bu 鞠斌
Zhuang Zhou 莊周
*Zhuangzi* 莊子
Zhuge Liang 諸葛亮
*Zhuzhen neidan jiyao* 諸真內丹集要
*zi* 字
Zou (Mr.) 鄒
*zu* 祖
*zuo* 作
Zuting 祖庭.

# Index

*Note:* In the references to endnote material, the numbers in parentheses indicate the page of the main text on which the number of the note is printed.

Made in the USA
Lexington, KY
24 May 2017